Advertising and Consumer Citizenship

In so
plays
prov
highl
imag
racial
this s
politi
Th
medi

Anne
for C

Transformations: Thinking Through Feminism

Edited by: Maureen McNeil, *Institute of Women's Studies, Lancaster University*, Lynne Pearce, *Department of English, Lancaster University*, Beverley Skeggs, *Department of Sociology, Manchester University.*

Other books in the series include:

Advertising and Consumer Citizenship

Gender, images and rights

Anne M. Cronin

London and New York

First published 2000
by Routledge
11 New Fetter Lane, London EC4P 4EE

Simultaneously published in the USA and Canada
by Routledge
29 West 35th Street, New York, NY 10001

Routledge is an imprint of the Taylor & Francis Group

© 2000 Anne M. Cronin

Typeset in Times New Roman by Taylor & Francis Books Ltd
Printed and bound in Great Britain by Biddles Ltd, Guildford and
King's Lynn

British Library Cataloguing in Publication Data
A catalogue record for this book is available from the British Library

Library of Congress Cataloging in Publication Data
Cronin, Anne M.
Advertising and consumer citizenship : gender, images, and rights /
Anne M. Cronin.
p. cm. – (Transformations)
Includes bibliographical references and index.
1. Advertising–Psychological aspects. 2. Consumer behavior. 3. Sex
role in
advertising. I. Title. II. Series.
HF5822 .C76 2000
659.1'042–dc21

00-030518

ISBN 0-415-22323-7 (hbk)
ISBN 0-415-22324-5 (pbk)

Contents

Plates

Series editors' preface

There has been a long-standing acknowledgement that advertising is a profoundly gendered domain within both popular culture and the academy in the Western world. There has also been a strong, steady stream of critical research, mainly but not exclusively feminist, which has highlighted and explored the linking of women with the realm of consumption. Western conceptions of citizenship have also come under feminist scrutiny, as scholars have shown that apparent gender neutrality associated with citizenship masks gender specificity and precipitates consequent inequalities. The Transformations series now welcomes Anne Cronin's *Advertising and Consumer Citizenship* which cuts across these three domains to examine theoretically and concretely how Western European advertising works in the creation of gendered selfhood and citizenship.

This book demonstrates that, far from being outmoded or irrelevant, gender questions continue to be crucial in the study of contemporary culture and capitalism. In this study, this involves asking where and how gender emerges as a significant organising principle in the contemporary advertising world. Posing such questions carries Anne Cronin in fascinating trajectories, as she interrogates the gendering of the self constructed through advertising address, the differences between the modes of male-targeted and female-targeted advertising and the 'masculinist productivist' orientation of some critical analyses of this crucial sphere. *Advertising and Consumer Citizenship* exemplifies the kind of detailed, theoretically informed studies which are required to understand the complex production and reproduction of gendered selves today.

This volume is also indicative of our commitment to produce a series which will offer critical feminist perspectives on transformations in many realms. This volume provides an analysis of the evolving forms of contemporary capitalism – as manifested in advertising, together with a critical feminist perspective on the transformations of scholarly understanding of this field. Cronin's study evokes a wariness about the promise of transformation embedded in the modes of both recent advertising itself and recent scholarship about it. In both realms ideas of 'interpretative flexibility' and 'gender fluidity' are to the fore, implying that conventions have been shaken, binarisms suspended and restrictions lifted. Cronin warns that, nevertheless, advertising continues to be a profoundly gendered domain. This is a salutary warning for the Transformations series and its readers: promises and conceptualisations of transformations are not necessarily the harbingers of change; they need themselves to be interrogated.

Maureen McNeil
Lynne Pearce
Beverley Skeggs

Acknowledgements

I would like to thank the many people who have helped me develop the ideas for this book. Celia Lury and Bev Skeggs were a continual source of inspiration and encouragement (and also coffee and cakes). Sara Ahmed and Mike Featherstone have given me very useful comments and have helped frame my ideas into the form of a book. My thanks also to Maureen McNeil, Lynne Pearce (and Bev again), who edited this book series. I would also like to thank the members of Lancaster University's Institute for Women's Studies who have provided inspiration and help and a lot of laughs. My particular thanks to Jean Carroll, Kath Cross, Breda Gray, Janet Hartley, Rose Jack, Jane Kilby, Cathie Holt, Yu Ying Lee, Ruth McElroy, Sue Penna, Fran Stafford, and Heather Wilkinson. Thanks to Becky Passmore for hunting down an image for me. Thanks also to my mum, Noreen.

I would also like to thank the following companies for granting permission to reproduce their advertisements: Scottish Courage Ltd, Parfums Christian Dior, Fendi, Guerlain, Lancôme, Philip Morris Ltd.

Chapter 4 has been published previously in a slightly different form: (1997) 'Temporalities of the visual and spaces of knowledge: branding "the third dimension" in advertising', *Space and Culture – the Journal* 1, 1: 85–104. I would like to thank *Space and Culture – the Journal* for permitting me to reproduce the article here.

Introduction

In studies of consumerism it has become almost a truism to claim that the purchase, use and display of goods in some way expresses social identities. Such acts of consumption are imagined as symbolic work in the reflexive project of the self, communicating to others messages of identity, belonging and distinction. The parallel claim that advertising is the prime mediator of these meanings has also gained axiomatic status. This conceptual framework has set up a familiar problematic; we apply individual agency by using the meanings in advertising as symbolic resources in the processes of the construction and communication of our identities. Simultaneously, advertising manipulates us and bends our individual agency to its own commercial ends.

This conceptual framework has recently attracted considerable critical attention (e.g. Campbell 1997, 1999; Falk and Campbell 1997). Indeed, I would argue that the model assumes a preconstituted, core subject – however amenable to modification – which takes on the consumerist project of the self. What if the meanings in advertising are not purely directed towards the expression or communication of identities? Rather than expressing individual agency in the interpretation and 'use' of advertising, what if agency were produced only in the very act of interpreting? How should we then consider advertising images and their role in the construction and communication of identities?

These are some of the questions which have inspired this book and have opened up new connections between the cultural and the political, the visual and the material, advertising and belonging, consumerism and the rights of citizenship. Of course, innovation and the production of the new are intrinsic to consumerism and tend to structure the conceptual field of the study of consumerism. It is often suggested that in the West we live in a culture of innovation in which ideas, identities, pleasures, goods and images have a short shelf-life. Planned obsolescence presides over cultural life – advertising pushes relentlessly onward, making the new appear outdated in no time. This 'no time' of consumer culture is constructed as a 'perpetual year zero' in which consumer culture is relentlessly refigured as new (Slater 1997: 10). The advertising industry appears to manufacture or recycle the new – innovation and consumerism merge conceptually and appear to form a co-extensive terrain of novelty, possession and capitalist exchange. In this dynamic, consumerism and advertising are often posited as emblematic of cultural change. Yet the research I outline in this book points to complex and contradictory relations between time, innovation and advertising. Alongside its status as epitome of cultural change, consumer culture has also been figured (and denigrated) as a feminine domain inscribed with inertia and passivity (Bowlby 1985, 1993; Felski 1995; Radner 1995). In late nineteenth-century Europe, consumerism was consistently figured as a woman, embodying the 'feminine' characteristics of capriciousness and hedonism (Bowlby 1985, 1993). The 'consuming woman' became a 'dense site of cultural imaginings of the modern' (Felski 1995: 65), a recurrent trope for understanding cultural change.

In many contemporary accounts, the consumerist desire for the new has been conceptualised as a gendered structuring of longing, will and self-control (Bowlby 1993). Indeed, women are often imagined to be particularly susceptible to seduction by advertising images (Nava 1997). Yet many studies do not adequately address the centrality of gender's discursive role in consumption; they symbolise consumerism as feminine whilst simultane-ously reinscribing a masculine productivist bias within their conceptual framework (Slater 1997). In effect, whilst gender is constantly invoked to represent consumerism, gender as an organising principle remains under-theorised within mainstream studies of consumption. In many accounts, gender functions to underwrite consumerism's imagined status as a privi-leged site for the study of cultural change. For instance, consumption practices function as an imagined litmus test for women's increased partici-pation in the public sphere. However, the study of advertising outlined in this book indicates that cultural innovation and gender operate in complex ways; gendered cultural shifts cannot be read off from consumer culture in an unproblematic way. In the results of my study, I found innovation to be strongly associated with male-targeted advertisements, producing particular forms of textual address aimed at male consumers. So, whilst gender is a central organising principle of consumer culture, innovation and adver-tising, the relationship between gender and consumerism is neither transparent nor immutable. This book explores these paradoxes of time, gender and advertising in the visual realm of consumer culture and expands this conceptual framework to consider consumer-citizenship and European belonging.

In academic circles, innovation and obsolescence also organise the field – the 'sell-by' date of ideas is often as short as the novelty factor in consumer goods. Don Slater (1997) remarks on the tendency to rediscover consumer culture as a site of study every few decades and repackage it as a new academic product. This promotional remarketing of ideas is perhaps unsur-prising in the context of the shifting markets for academic texts and the pressures to publish. In this climate, studies of advertising appear to offer the ideal site for tracking 'the new' across a range of cultural, political and economic realms. This summons up rather unflattering images of academics running to catch up with innovations in advertising in order to brand them with conceptual innovations of their own.[1] In this study, I focus on forms of cultural change in the West whilst attempting to avoid the pitfall of fetishising the new as the ever-receding horizon of academic progress. In a highly influential argument about cultural change, Mike Featherstone (1991) has argued that we are witnessing a general 'aestheticisation' of everyday life. The cultural takes on a new, intensified significance in which forms of self-reflexivity are brought to the fore. Indeed, it has been argued that we now live in 'a culture of the image' in which hedonism and aestheticism replace the classical duality of the moral and the political (Maffesoli 1997). This culture of the image is a culture of heterogeneity, plurality and fracture which emphasises the role of the imagination. However, this emphasis on the 'new' significance of the aesthetic and increased self-reflexivity risks over-shadowing other persistent structuring themes. Such an emphasis may tend to overestimate the destabilising and emancipating effects on identities and blur the focus on the enduring nature of inequalities (McNay 1999).

It is this dynamic relation of the cultural and aesthetic to the political which has inspired this study and which has encouraged my focus on the articulation between advertising and citizenship. This may seem an uneasy juxtaposition, yet it is one which promises to expand the conceptual horizon of studies of advertising and consumerism. Kevin Robins (1994) argues that such studies have tended to focus too narrowly, largely confining their analysis to meaning, identity, distinction and pleasure. Robins suggests that more energy should be devoted to an analysis of the 'consumer-citizen', a concept which combines the aesthetic and the political. Debates about the consumer-citizen have until recently been played out in theories of the mediated public sphere rather than in consumption studies. For example, access to media images has been seen as crucial to imagining and contesting national identities, which in turn comes to be framed as a citizenship right (Murdoch 1992). Yet the nature of the relation between images, rights and contested belongings remains under-theorised and it is this challenge which has inspired this book.

In this book I explore the concept of the consumer-citizen with an emphasis on visuality, gender, cultural difference and advertising. How might an intensification of the role of the cultural and the aesthetic within society articulate with the political discourses of citizenship? How do images 'mediate' identities and the differential rights accorded to identities? How can citizenship rights be accessed and deployed by individuals? What forms of individual freedom are we talking about here? Don Slater (1997) remarks on how freedom has come to be defined as 'consumer sovereignty', which resonates deeply within contemporary Western culture; 'it provides one of the few tangible and mundane experiences of freedom which feels personally significant to modern subjects. How emotionally charged within everyday life is the right to vote?' (*ibid.*: 27). This book explores the relationship between citizenship and the everyday world of consuming goods and images and examines the relation between citizenship rights and consumer rights. It has frequently been noted that individual freedoms and rights in Western societies have been framed as consumer choices and consumer rights (e.g. Bauman 1998; Lee 1993; Wernick 1991). Within European nation-states, individuals' access to citizenship rights has increasingly been framed through discourses of consumerism. For instance, the *Citizen's Charter* (1991) in Britain redefined the citizen's role and rights as those of taxpayer and of consumer of goods, public services and images (Gabriel and Lang 1995; Miller 1993). The political rhetoric of 'active citizenship' (in buying into private pension schemes, buying own council houses, etc.) has framed the individual as an 'enterprising consumer' (Heelas and Morris 1992).

These themes of contractual relations between state and individual, over-laid with the individual's status as consumer of services, have been developed in Gidden's (1998) *The Third Way* which has proved influential on Tony Blair's Labour government in Britain. Yet this 'individual' who is granted such rights and freedoms cannot be assumed to be a universal citizen, unproblematically neutral to a range of 'differences' of sex, 'race', ethnicity, class, age and dis/ability. A broad range of feminist analysis has argued that the category of 'the individual' which underpins discourses of citizenship rights (and consumer rights) is structured as male, Western, white, heterosexual, classed and able-bodied (Cornell 1993; Diprose 1994; Fraser 1989; 1997; Pateman 1998; Yeatman 1994). If such exclusions operate in the discourses and practices of citizenship, in what ways might the articulation of consumerism alter these terms of exclusion? Indeed, it has been argued that consumerism paradoxically offers women the opportunity to act in consuming goods and images whilst framing these actions in terms which deny any specificity of female identity (Radner 1995). What, then, are the terms of the female 'consumer-citizen'? And how does gender articulate with 'race', ethnicity and cultural difference within this framework of consumer-citizenship?

The relation between definitions of culture and rights of belonging has a long pedigree. Citizenship within Europe has historically involved a cultur-ally mediated and complex relation between definitions of nationality and the attribution of citizenship rights (Soysal 1996). In effect, diffuse and contested ideas of cultural belonging and ethnicity have been highly influen-tial in decisions about the conferral or denial of citizenship status and rights (*ibid.*). Furthermore, these debates about national citizenship and rights are occurring in the context of 'a new Europe' and new forms of interaction between nations. Flexible flows of goods, people, finance and images are replacing conventional bilateral exchanges between Western nation-states (Appadurai 1990). Indeed, the significance of national boundaries within Europe is being altered in the face of growing transnational co-operation and debate in organisations like the UN, NATO and the EU (Soysal 1994).

For example, the Maastricht Treaty, which was ratified in 1993, provides a multilevel structure of citizenship and in effect opens up questions of belonging and entitlement in new ways (*ibid.*).

This fluidity across traditional borders brings into question the very nature of those boundaries and spatialises them in new ways (Featherstone 1990). This is a 'rendering problematic of the boundary' in which new, instantaneous encounters with cultural 'others' can occur through new media networks (Morley and Robins 1995: 75). New media technologies, such as satellite and digital advances, transpose a 'new and abstract electronic space across earlier physical and social geographies' producing a '"placeless" geography of image and simulation' (Robins 1991: 28, 29). This aestheticisation of everyday life and the intensification of the influence and range of media networks provides a potential new context for the contestation of national and transnational identities. What might a consideration of consumerism bring to these debates about belonging and citizenship rights?

Indeed, interest in consumer-citizenship has been gathering pace, with work such as that of Gabriel and Lang (1995) broadening studies of the consumer to areas such as education, citizenship, and environmental activism. This is a timely focus on consumer acts which are interpreted through a broad range of emergent discourses. Yet less attention has been granted to the relation between advertising and citizenship. Studies have tended emphasise how advertising is a ubiquitous and powerful contemporary set of discourses which mediate the practices of consumption (Leiss *et al.* 1990). In an account which is typical of much of the literature on advertising, Leiss *et al.* argue that the decline of the moral authority of established social institutions such as religion has left a gap in society which has been filled by advertising, 'the discourse through and about objects' (*ibid.*: 1). Advertising is seen as appropriating symbols for its own commercial ends, reconfiguring the very terms of communication between people;

> its unsurpassed communicative powers recycle cultural models and references back through the networks of social interactions. This venture is unified by the discourse through and about objects, which bonds together images of persons, products and well-being.
>
> (*ibid.*: 5)

In many accounts, then, advertising is seen as a highly significant player in the field of culture, working to shift the very terms of social relations for its own self-promotional ends. Individuals are imagined to construct their identities in an ongoing practice or project. Within this project, advertising is thought to play a key role as mediator of meanings. Yet the specific relationship between the interpretation of visual advertising and consumerism is not fully developed in the literature. To bridge this gap, I will focus on the role of the imagination in processes of vision. Arjun Appadurai (1997) suggests that the imagination has long held a crucial role in society, but recent cultural shifts have altered its significance in the everyday world. The imagination is no longer primarily confined to the 'special expressive space of the arts', nor is it restricted to exceptional, charismatic individuals. Now it plays an *explicit* role in the 'quotidian mental work of ordinary people' (Appadurai 1997: 5). For Appadurai (1990), the imagination is not a matter of individual psychology but, rather, a social practice. It comes to the fore in a world of expanded media networks and advancing media technologies which 'seem to impel (and sometimes compel) the work of the imagination' (Appadurai 1997: 4). Colin Campbell's (1989) work on the romantic ethic and the imagination has linked the imagination to consumerism and provides an important starting point for my analysis. My concern in this book is to explore what this expanded role of the imagination may mean for the relationship between consumerism, advertising and citizenship. Yet, rather than considering the imagination as a staging ground for action, as in Appadurai's (1997) approach, I consider the ways in which processes of imagination are *in themselves* action. Focusing on the visual in advertising, I examine the shifting relations between political and cultural representation: that is, between representation in the sense of the political status of the citizen and sovereign subject, and representation in the sense of images.

This book is essentially about 'mediation' – the ways in which the visual mediates (or *is*) action, the ways in which advertising mediates consumerism, and the ways in which consumerism mediates identities. To tackle this range of areas and approaches I have employed what Linda Alcoff (1997: 9) calls 'a conscious eclecticism' in my theoretical repertoire, which I hope opens up productive questions about the relations between cultural phenomena and disciplinary and conceptual boundaries.

In Chapter 1, I outline the conceptual framework of the book by focusing on the construction of the category of 'the individual' which underpins many theories of the consumer. The structurally sexed, classed and racialised nature of the ostensibly neutral, universal 'individual' goes some way to explain the uneven and paradoxical way in which gender has been theorised in consumerism. Women have been imagined as the epitome of consumer ideals, the prototypical consumer, the active subject who is newly empowered in the public realm of consumer culture. Yet women have also been imagined as passive victims, cultural dupes, pseudo-subjects who are the epitome of the alienation and objectification inherent in consumer capitalism (Bowlby 1985, 1993; Felski 1995; Nava 1997; Radner 1995). In this chapter, I explore feminist work which argues that the discursive constitution of the category of 'the individual' occurs through an imagined dialogue with *his* others in order to demarcate *his* boundaries of selfhood. This dialogue, I argue, is mediated by an imagined transparency of knowledge of self and 'other'. I show, however, that 'the individual' has historically developed as an exclusive category based on rationality and the assumed capacity to possess 'property in his person' (Pateman 1988). This has excluded groups such as women, racialised others, children, the working classes and 'the insane', who have historically been framed as lacking in rationality and seen as property rather than owners. The contractual relations which structure society (such as the marriage, the employment and the citizenship contracts) require that excluded groups participate in certain contracts. Yet, paradoxically, they posit that these groups do not have the capacities required in order to initiate that participation.

I relate these paradoxes to contemporary politics of identity. Here, 'individuality' operates through contradictory frameworks of both identity and difference held together by a discourse of individual potential. I track how this 'individuality' relates to Stolcke's (1995) formulation of 'cultural fundamentalism' which operates on a national and transnational level. Here, a politics of national identity functions through the idea that all (national) cultures are equally different and differently equal. Yet are there nations which operate under subordinated terms? Through the concept of 'consumer-citizenship', I link ideas of national belonging and citizenship to consumerism and focus on choice as a prime mechanism in the production of these identities. Using the concept of performativity, I explore the contradictions in contractual relations, citizenship and choice, focusing particularly on time and identities on an individual and national level.

In Chapter 2, I draw on and develop these notions of the performative construction of selfhood and 'individuality' in relation to advertising. Through a discussion of the British advertising industry's trade paper *Campaign*, I analyse how the advertising industries operate in targeting particular gendered, racialised and classed markets. Yet neatly segmented markets do not exist as social facts to be discovered and manipulated by advertising agencies. In targeting groups of consumers, advertising campaigns actively *generate* them as categories and create subject positions which are refracted through gender, 'race', class and ethnicity. I argue that the reflexive processes of knowledge-circulation between advertising agencies, clients and magazines selling advertising space articulate with specific masculinist working practices and masculine inflected ethos of 'creativity' and 'individuality'. I conclude by considering how this masculinist ethos (based on 'creativity', innovation and a particular form of 'individuality') is re-produced in advertising campaigns through exclusionary forms of visual address.

In Chapter 3, I discuss the methods and the findings of my study of British and French print advertisements sampled between 1987 and 1995. Here I outline why I selected print advertising in French and British popular magazines as the site of my analysis. I also discuss my choice of three French and three British popular (colour) magazines, including a glossy women's magazine, a popular culture/'youth' magazine, and a current affairs/business magazine – I focus on *Elle*, *Première* and *L'Expansion*, selecting the nearest British equivalents as *Elle*, *Q*, and *The Economist*.

I outline my pilot study and my development of successive coding frameworks for my textual analysis. I go on to discuss the findings of this analysis which revealed sharply drawn contrasts between the forms of textual address in advertisements targeted at male viewers and those targeted at female viewers. In my study, reflexivity, innovation and a rapid turnover in campaigns are typical characteristics of male-targeted advertisements. In contrast, female-targeted advertisements predominantly use a 'literal' or non-reflexive form of address and have a far slower cycle of innovation. This male gendering of innovation in advertising targeting is perhaps ironic, as consumer culture has consistently been figured as a feminine domain, and consumer culture itself is often presented as the epitome of cultural change. In this chapter, I develop a theoretical analysis of the operation of reflexivity and innovation in visual address to explore these contradictions. In my findings, I show how reflexivity functions relationally to a 'literal' form of address. I argue that irony is a key form of reflexivity and I maintain that irony can function as a useful site of study for the temporality of performativity – it is explicit in its address and holds together different levels of meaning (and different temporalities) in tension. I use an analysis of two typical advertisements in my study to chart the different gendered, classed and racialised forms of textual address. In this analysis, I explore the nature of media 'non-space' which can potentially disembed conventional combinations of signifiers and allow for a rearticulation of meaning.

In Chapter 4, I extend this discussion of textual address to explore the processes of interpretation and vision. How do advertising images mediate meanings? What is their relation to the viewer? I draw on the ideas of discursive transparency and knowledge, which I initially developed in Chapter 1, and explore how the constitution of selfhood can occur in *visual performativity*. I explore how this performative articulates with signifiers of social difference and with shifting frameworks of visibility and invisibility. To expand this notion, I investigate the 'moment' of visual interpretation. This draws on the future, the present and the past, referencing the historical constitution of 'the individual' through colonial, class and sexual subordination. I argue that an ironic visual address allows (for some) an interpretative flexibility which provides a privileged position from which to contest cultural belonging and rights. It is this 'moment' of interpretation and self-constitution, I argue, that advertising attempts to brand in its own commercial terms.

Chapter 5 extends this analysis to explore the exclusion of women from the category of 'the individual' and its implications for women's relation to images. I use the concept of narrative to explore the complex relation between women viewers and images of women (de Lauretis 1989). In connection with narrative and the temporalities of interpretation, I analyse metaphor as a medium for a certain flexibility of interpretation available to women. This flexibility belies the conventionally 'unreflexive' appearance of the literal address of some female-targeted adverts. Yet, I argue, women are

denied access to ways of connecting interpretative practices to the generation or re-production of social privilege. Furthermore, the terms of the
interpretative flexibility are limited to white, middle-class women through
discursive frameworks of European cultural heritage.

In Chapter 6, I link together the themes that have run throughout my
analysis – citizenship rights and obligations in 'a New Europe', the performative constitution of selfhood and its temporality, knowledge and
interpretation, the visual and discourses of consumerist choice. I explore the
disruptions in the temporal narratives of the self produced through the
visual. I argue that these shifts in the relation between images, meanings and
identities provide the conditions of possibility for what I call 'retroactive
intentionality'. This is a discursive structuring of intent, vision and action
which redefines rights and responsibilities. Mediated by advertising, citizenship obligations become disengaged from a responsibility to the histories of
subordination implicated in the constitution of 'the individual'. In effect, the
terms in which privileged groups have access to images as a site of identity
production have altered such that the terms of 'agency', rights and obligations must be addressed in new ways.

This is a shift in the terms of the conventional political affiliation of
national citizenship within Europe. It draws on the imagined historical
constitution of 'European' identities in a new, flexible manner. In the
context of a 'New Europe', the 'cultural' modes of the visual and processes
of interpretation articulate in new ways with the 'political' of citizenship in
emergent discourses of consumer-citizenship.

1 The individual, the citizen and the consumer

Il y a nulle parité entre les deux sexes quant à la conséquence du sex. Le mâle n'est mâle qu'en certains instants, la femelle est femelle toute sa vie ou du moins toute sa jeunesse; tout rapelle sans cesse à son sexe.

Jean-Jacques Rousseau 1782[1]

[There is no parity between the two sexes due to the nature of sexual difference. The male is only male at certain moments, the female is female all her life or at least all her youth; her sex is continually invoked.][2]

In this chapter, I explore the links between the political culture of citizenship and the consumer culture of advertising. The chapter's focus is an investigation of the category of 'the individual' which bridges two of my central concerns. Firstly, historically embedded discourses of 'the individual' are primary defining forces of the nature and the rights of both the citizen and the consumer. Secondly, feminists have engaged in a range of theoretical critiques which have demonstrated that the ostensibly neutral, universal category of the individual veils a sexed, racialised and classed particularism. In effect, the rights of the individual are based on a white, male, classed, heterosexual model which excludes subordinate groups. Exploring the structurally sexed, classed and racialised nature of the ostensibly neutral, universal 'individual' goes some way to explain the uneven and paradoxical way in which gender has been theorised in consumerism. Thus, focusing on the individual as a socio-political taxonomy enables me to explore how gender is a central, structuring principle of citizenship and consumerism. It also provides a way into thinking through the assumptions about 'the subject' of consumer culture. Many studies posit a preformed subject who engages with discourses of consumerism, 'applying' individual agency in acts of consumption. Examining the discursive construction of this subject allows a more nuanced analysis of agency, mediation and power.

My focus on discourse aims to explore social identities as 'complexes of meaning, networks of interpretation' (Fraser 1997: 152). Nancy Fraser usefully summarises what a theory of discourse can contribute to feminism,

First, it can help us understand how people's social identities are fash-ioned and altered over time. Second, it can help us how, under conditions of inequality, social groups in the sense of collective agents are formed and unformed. Third, a conception of discourse can illumi-nate how the cultural hegemony of dominant groups in society is secured and contested. Fourth and finally, it can shed light on the prospects for emancipatory social change and political practice.

(Fraser 1997: 152)

I carry over these concerns with identity, agency and contested cultural legit-imacy into the following sections and later chapters. In the first section of this chapter I examine feminist work on the exclusive nature of 'the indi-vidual' focusing on how women and other groups have an ambiguous relationship to this category. In certain respects women are included within the category, yet in others they are excluded from it. This borderline status also becomes a central concern of later sections, which examine women's relation to citizenship rights in the West. However, this ambiguity is not arbitrary but rather functions as the force which holds together 'the indi-vidual' as a discursive category. In the following section, I propose that the concept of performativity can be employed to explore these contradictions. A performative understanding of identity and discourse does not assume a pre-formed, core subject who expresses individual agency through acts, as in the purchase, use and display of consumer goods or services. Performativity focuses on how categories of selfhood do not pre-exist discourse; through discourse they are continually created and recreated in ways which both produce and challenge forms of exclusion. I go on to link this political and discursive arena of 'the individual' to that of the cultural by exploring contemporary discourses of identity politics. These draw on notions of authenticity and individual potential and promote rights of 'self-expression' which are often played out on the terrain of culture. By exploring contem-porary discourses of cultural difference, I argue that these politics of identity and difference function on the level of both the individual and the nation. In the final section I draw together the concerns of this chapter by exploring how the current intensified focus on the cultural as a terrain of political contestation has transformed the relation between discourses of citizenship and cultural belonging. Central to these new forms of cultural belonging and exclusion are transformations in sexed, racialised and classed identities.

The individual

It has often been claimed that historical shifts in the West have produced more fluid social structures, in which status is not fixed in rigid hierarchies determined by birth. The advent of the shift from 'status to contract' altered the terms of social stratification and increased mobility – for some (Pateman

1988). The erosion of narrowly defined access to social status highlighted the role of consumption in Western societies in displaying social distinction (Slater 1997). The individual display of status through consumption threatened established hierarchies in which each person's place was preordained and immutable: any person could now display the indices of status through clothing or food consumption. The old order responded by introducing forms of symbolic consumption-regulation: only certain groups were entitled to wear particular clothes or eat particular animals. In time, modern structures of market exchange dismantled this system of symbolic regulation and established a contract-based system enabling greater individual social mobility (*ibid.*). As I examine in this chapter, contract has gained a renewed prominence in Britain with the 1991 *Citizen's Charter* and the influence of Gidden's (1998) *The Third Way* on the Blairite British government of the late 1990s.

Yet is this social mobility equally available to all? With the aim of examining social inequalities, certain analysts have focused their attention on the category of 'the individual' which underpins contract. In dissecting this category, they have made visible how certain social groups are excluded from 'being individuals' and are therefore not accorded full social, political or cultural rights, such as rights of citizenship. In examining notions of equality and difference in citizenship, feminists have explored how the social contract forms a major structuring principle of contemporary Western societies. In a range of studies, feminists have revealed a fundamental contradiction at the heart of social relations: women and other subordinated groups are positioned by the social contract as both individuals and non-individuals, both inside and outside society. In what follows I outline the significance for women of this ambiguous status, in which they are said to both participate in civil relations, yet are negated as full individuals.

Carole Pateman's (1988) work examines the concept of 'contract' as a 'political story' or 'conjectural history'. The concept of contract was developed by political theorists, in particular Locke, as an attempt to construct a narrative about the legitimation of political right in civil society. Contract is a constructed fiction in so far as it represents only *one* way of explaining social relations; yet it is very real in the effects it produces when deployed in structuring society. Pateman argues that the political fiction of contract theory actively forms the basis of the contemporary ideal of free civil relations. This ideal is embodied in social institutions such as marriage, employment and citizenship, taking the form of contracts which are based ostensibly on free and equal exchange. However, alongside its generally unrecognised counterparts of the racialised 'slave' and the 'sexual' contracts, the original social contract is founded on exclusion rather than equality. Indeed, the original contract which forms the blueprint and legitimation for subsequent contractual relations only *appears* to be neutral, egalitarian and universal. In fact it is based on a white, male, classed, heterosexual, Western model of disembodied rationality. This excludes and disenfranchises women, racialised groups, children, 'the insane' and the disabled (Diprose 1994; Pateman 1988, 1989; Yeatman 1994). The model of society produced is one of a fraternal, rather than the earlier paternal, patriarchy of property owner- ship and dominion over 'the household'. In contemporary fraternal patriarchy, men are guaranteed ordered sexual access to women as objects of exchange through the marriage contract (Pateman 1988). According to Pateman, this produces a model of structural heterosexuality founded on certain notions of the 'complementarity' of the sexes, and structures the classed subordination and exchange of women.

Other feminists have expressed reservations about Pateman's work on contract. Nancy Fraser (1997) is broadly sympathetic to Pateman's approach, but cautions against imagining contract as the only or the most powerful form of social relation. Fraser argues for a more nuanced critique which does not propose such a seamless fit between capitalist power and patriarchal power. Contemporary discourses of gender, sex, 'race' and others are more fragmented and highly contested than Pateman suggests (Fraser 1997). Indeed, in later chapters I explore the terms of this fragmen- tation and contestation of meanings in relation to advertising and the images it produces.

Fraser (1997) does, however, support Pateman's analysis of ownership rights and 'possessive individualism' which reveals structural gender exclu- sions. Pateman (1988) argues that women and racialised groups are 'structured out' of the category of 'the individual' through the concept of ownership rights. 'The individual' is defined through *his* capacity to own property in *his* person (Pateman 1988). In effect, the individual is defined as owning himself as an item of property: he is a self-possessive individual. He is seen to have the capacity to stand outside himself, to separate 'himself' from 'his body', and then to have a proprietal relation to himself as bodily property (*ibid.*). For example, according to contract theory the labour power expended in work is detachable from the body of the individual. Therefore, what is said to be sold or exchanged in an employment contract is an indi- vidual's capacity to perform labour, rather than the individual *himself.* The exchange of 'the man himself' would count as slavery and run counter to the principle of freedom expressed by contract theory (*ibid.*). Indeed, the consti- tution of the category of the individual is also based on the slave contract and the construction of ideas of the European 'self' and the 'savage other' developed through European colonial encounters and violent domination of indigenous populations of Africa, India and the Americas. As I discuss in more detail in later chapters, 'the colonial other' formed the necessary foil to the European notion of 'the individual' as rational, 'civilised', Christian and democratic. In effect, this construction of self and other justified the violent oppression of what came to be seen as sub-human 'others' (McClintock 1995; Parekh 1995; Pratt 1992).

At this point I would like to turn to the ambiguous social positioning of women according to the terms of contract theory. How is it that women both participate in and are excluded from society in multiple ways? Pateman (1988) argues that an examination of the terms of the marriage contract and other contracts, such as employment and citizenship, exposes a contradiction. In contract, women and other overlapping subordinated groups are posited simultaneously as 'non-individuals' and 'individuals'. They hold the position of 'non-individuals' as they are considered to be naturally excluded from the rationality of the purportedly 'disembodied' (yet, in fact, male) model of 'natural right' which was necessary to participate in contract. For Pateman (1988), it is this tension in the discursive status of women and others which forms the constitutive force needed to hold together the political fiction of the category of 'the individual': women and others are *required* to participate in contract *as individuals*, yet at the same time they are discursively *excluded* from the category of 'individual'. They participate as 'individuals' in the civil, public sphere through their enactment of employment, marriage and citizenship contracts. However, they do not hold the capacities of 'self-possessiveness' required for 'free' exchange in contract and the constitution of their status as 'individuals'. In this paradoxical way they form the constitutive elements of the realm outside the civil, for 'women are property, but also persons; women are held both to possess and to lack the capacities required for contract – and contract demands that their womanhood be both denied and affirmed' (Pateman 1988: 60). As exemplified in the Rousseau quotation at the head of this chapter, women cannot but inhabit the category of 'Woman', and yet even this ambiguous and subordinated status is restricted to certain women at certain times of their lives.[3] Rousseau indicates that this access is circumscribed by youth in what I take to be a reference to marriageability and reproductive status. In this sense, (classed) heterosexual marriage and reproduction form women's only access to a limited form of 'individual' status through relations with men. Yet this limited status is one which simultaneously denies women a coherent, unified selfhood and restricts even this access to certain groups of women. Indeed, I would argue that it is this gendered ambiguous and denigrated status which is reflected in many studies of consumerism and advertising. Women are imagined to be active, consuming subjects, yet also cultural dupes and passive ciphers for consumerist ideology (Bowlby 1985, 1993; Felski 1995; Nava 1997; Radner 1995). How should we think about the category 'woman' when her only characteristics appear to be ambiguity and contradiction?

This ambiguity of the positioning of women and racialised groups in relation to the category of 'the individual' can be usefully considered in terms of Teresa de Lauretis' (1989) approach to theory as process. She argues for a subject of feminist analysis whose definition should be *in progress*, so that the analytical category 'woman' used in research, and by extension 'race', should be a working construct which is 'a way of conceptualising, of understanding, of accounting for certain *processes*, not women' (de Lauretis 1989: 10). This approach enables de Lauretis to explore the contradictory, disjointed and mobile nature of the discursive production of sexual, racial and class difference. At the same time, this approach attempts to avoid the reification and naturalisation of certain formulations of 'women' and 'race'. In the work of both Pateman and de Lauretis, 'women' can be seen as inhabiting a discursive position that is both impossible and yet necessary. De Lauretis points to,

> the discrepancy, the tension, and the constant slippage between Woman as representation, as the object and the very condition of representation, and, on the other hand, women as historical beings, subjects of 'real relations', are motivated and sustained by a logical contradiction in our culture and an irreconcilable one: women are both inside and outside gender, at once within and without representation.
>
> (de Lauretis 1989: 10)

In addition to women's decentred positioning in relation to gender, women are positioned as neither individuals nor non-individuals, neither citizens nor non-citizens. In Pateman's (1988) analysis, the categories of 'women' and subordinate others are both inside and outside civil society. They are the very groups necessary to constitute the social system of contractual relations: they form 'the other' for 'the individual' and enable *him* to come into existence. Yet they are outside the social system because they are denied the full status of individual themselves. Women are positioned within the discursive space of the individual in that they are required to perform the contractual relations such as marriage or citizenship that regulate society. In this capacity, women require the status of individual to participate. Yet they are simultaneously outside the discursive space of the individual through the logical contradiction that they *cannot* hold the status of individual required for participation.

Furthermore, this ambiguity of status should not be considered to be static. Pateman (1988) argues that these contractual relations must be constantly repeated in order to reproduce the social system. The rights of 'the individual', defined through contract as ownership of the self as resource of labour power and the free and equal exchange of that power and property, must be *actively expressed* and reiterated through continuous engagement in contracts (*ibid.*). This is not an act of free will which produces the self through an expression of agency. There must be a *compulsory reiteration* of the category 'individual' through the repetition of contracts if the (exclusive) status and rights of 'the individual' are to be maintained (*ibid.*). Pateman states that this requires at least two individuals to mutually recognise each other's status *as* individuals for the contract to be enacted and validated. This exchange of recognition in turn reinforces the legitimacy of the system of contractual relations. Therefore, it is in this mutually informing process of exchange of recognition that an individual expresses, enacts and materialises *his* civil rights of freedom and possession.

Yet we have seen from de Lauretis' (1989) approach that women and other subordinate groups are positioned ambiguously in discourses of the individual, thus complicating the processes of mutual recognition. Women are framed as both inside and outside the discursive space of the individual. In terms of temporality, they are positioned as having achieved individual status already and yet, contradictorily, they can never attain individual status. In the following section I address these contradictions of mutual recognition through theories of performativity which explore the paradoxes of time, identity and difference.

Performativity and the individual

Pateman's (1988) analysis of contract opens up a wide field of questions for feminists by pointing to the structural nature of sexual and racial exclusions in social relations. My focus in this section will be on the way in which such exclusions are re-produced through time. How do historically embedded discourses impact on the contemporary? I would like to begin by exploring the force of 'the political story' or 'conjectural history' of the nature of the individual. What is the status of the knowledge produced by this narrative of the historical constitution of 'the individual'?

Judith Butler (1990) suggests that the force of narratives of historical origin may reside in their capacity to naturalise social relations:

> The fabrication of those origins tends to describe a state of affairs before the law that follows a necessary and unilinear narrative that culminates in, and thereby justifies, the constitution of the law. The story of origins is thus a strategic tactic within a narrative that, by telling a single, authoritative account about an irrecoverable past, makes the constitution of the law appear a historical inevitability.
>
> (Butler 1990: 36)

But a single statement of a historical narrative of origins cannot be sufficient to secure discursive privilege once and for all. In order to re-produce the ideals of civil society through the political narrative of the constitution of the individual, Pateman (1988) emphasizes the necessity of continually producing replicas of the original contract. Individuals must engage in a repetition of social contracts, comprising the exchange of recognition of status, in order to maintain their civil status as rights-bearers. Ironically, women and other subordinate groups can only ever attain the status of mere replicas of 'the individual'. In de Lauretis' (1989) terms, they are constrained to be the condition of discursive representation, yet they can be neither fully inside nor outside those discourses.

Rosalyn Diprose (1994) extends Pateman's (1988) discussion of contract by focusing on the related concepts of self-presence and identity. Diprose explores the work of the political theorist Locke who has greatly influenced the terms of contemporary social relations. According to Diprose, Locke posits not only the fundamental detachment between the body and labour power, such that the individual possesses his body, but also stresses the temporal and spatial unity of the individual. This formula is crucial to understanding the contractarian model of identity and difference as intrinsically spatial and temporal in nature.

Diprose (1994) states that the Lockean model defines the individual as an entity which maintains the same consciousness over time and through corporeal changes, for example illness or pregnancy, thus giving primacy to the mind or consciousness over the body. Furthermore, the individual is defined as having identical self-presence in which, 'an entity is identical with itself if it has the same origin in time and space' (Diprose 1994: 9). So the individuation necessary for the processes of mutual recognition to occur requires a temporally bounded entity. Simultaneously, the individual is spatially bounded through the distinction between self and not-self which is produced in that same process of recognition. Here arises the constitutive contradiction of contract, identical self-presence and exchange: in these political fictions, the individual is said to have a self-contained identity *prior* to contract or relations with others (Diprose 1994). Pateman's (1988) analysis of the contradictory production of women's and subordinate groups' status in contract echoes this tension. For the processes of contractual exchange to occur, an individual must recognise another *as an individual*. The characteristics that this requires are rationality and the possession of property in the person, or self-possessiveness, thereby excluding women and subordinated others. This implies a prediscursive, coherent, spatially and temporally unified self (which has already-established rights of possession and exchange) awaiting the moment of recognition by another individual. However, it is only in the process of exchange that each participating self is constituted *as an individual*; it is at this moment that the rights of the individual *produce* the individual. The necessary recognition of the status of 'individual', and the productive moment of exchange, stand in neither a temporal nor a causal prior relation to the other. The status of 'the individual' does not exist before the moments of contractual exchange of recognition. Yet the capacity of an individual to confer recognition on another is required for the process of exchange to begin. These elements form a 'necessary contradiction': they engender the conditions of possibility one for the other. Seen in this light, the ambiguous status of women and subordinated groups form part of the generative potential for 'the individual' to come into being, or to be discursively represented.

This system can be said to operate performatively in that it is a 'reiterative and citational practice by which discourse produces the effects it names' (Butler 1993: 2). Discourse can be seen as performing an action, for example, in the active constitution of individuals in contract, and confers a 'binding power' on that action (*ibid.*: 225). The acts of constitution cannot be said to derive from a prediscursive subject who expresses her/his will through those acts. Judith Butler (1993) argues that one can only claim an identity, or say 'I', through being named or called in a process of recognition which forms that very 'I',

> Indeed, I can only say 'I' to the extent that I have first been addressed, and that address has mobilized my place in speech; paradoxically, the discursive condition of social recognition *precedes and conditions* the formation of the subject: recognition is not conferred on a subject, but forms that subject.
>
> (Butler 1993: 225–6)

Diprose (1994) explores these contradictory moments of recognition and exchange through a discussion of Hegel's concept of self-presence. Whilst Diprose states that Hegel was opposed to contract, his stress on the inter-subjective nature of social relations may be useful in examining the processes of mutual recognition in contractual relations. The dialectics of self-presence operate with a conception of, and work to produce, a subject who is divided both spatially and temporally. In parallel with Lockean principles, the individual is unified and present 'now', in distinction from the past and the future – that is, 'self-present identity is divided between what is present and what is not' (Diprose 1994: 40). Spatially, the individual is divided by a boundary between itself and the outside composed of others (*ibid.*). This boundary is the delimitation necessary to generate an 'inside' to the individual. This is an interior space of consciousness and materiality, defining its self-presence in opposition to what it is not. Contrary to Locke, Hegel emphasizes that the individual is not self-present or self-identical in any straightforward way, as *his* identity relies on difference from the other, and hence on a mutual relationship (*ibid.*).

Diprose (1994) argues, along with Pateman (1988), that this relationship with others is based on 'mutual' recognition which requires the establishment of a structure of transparency and equivalences to facilitate the exchange. This exchange is seen in terms of a discursive dialogue between individuals in which transparency functions as the potential for access to knowledge of the other. The equivalences required for the transparency of mutual recognition in this dialogue are achieved through the abstraction, or 'disappearance', of the particularities of the body of the individual (Diprose 1994). The product of this abstraction is the norm of the universal, white, heterosexual, Western, middle-class, male body, generated through the partial exclusion in contract (or constitutive contradiction) of the particular, 'different', female, racialised, 'other' bodies. This is only a partial exclusion, because sameness, transparency and equivalences are required for the processes of mutual recognition: there is a need for similarity or a common ground in order to recognise the other. This requirement of sameness and transparency plays in tension against a need for the difference of 'the other' in order to generate boundaries of the self through that very dialogue.

However, Diprose (1994) argues that the difference produced through this framework of equivalences is, in fact, derived from self-identity. It cannot encompass a difference which is radical and alien to its logic, as it is dependant upon the exclusion of such difference. This imagined 'dialogical egalitarianism' (Crapanzano 1991: 437) promotes an ideal of equal participation in dialogue and self-constitution, but in fact dissimulates the hierarchical nature of its structure. This recalls de Lauretis' (1989) concept of women's and others' ambiguous and contradictory status, moving between the inside and outside of discourse. At the same time, women's ambiguous status comprises the productive tension which forms the basis of discursive representation,

> Insofar as the thesis of a social unity assumes an individual identity which is transparent to itself and to the Other (the unity of identity and difference) it assumes differences which are really variations of the same. In assuming that the other's difference is transparent to and contained within that identity which is the ethos of the community, the value of this ethos is maintained by the exclusion of others.
>
> (Diprose 1994: 49)

Diprose (1994) continues by highlighting Hegel's stress on the significance of action in the constitution of the individual in intersubjective relations. Action is crucial to the formation of the individual 'not because the will comes before the signifier but because, through action, the self is both constituted and expressed', and also because the self becomes transparent to the other through action (*ibid.*: 51). Referring back to Pateman's (1988) argument in earlier sections, action in the form of the repetitive engagement in contracts of mutual recognition, is compulsory. In the West the democratic ideal of 'freedom' is articulated as the right to engage in contract: contract is the moment at which the individual expresses and enacts *his* rights, and so is constituted. This is a necessary contradiction as the process requires preconstituted individuals to initiate the process of mutual recognition, and yet it is only at that moment of recognition that those individuals become constituted.

Diprose's (1994) primary concern here is the assumed mutual transparency of the relation between self and other in this model. Differences become flattened or merely variations of the same, in which 'differences are partial signs of, and are expressed within, the communal ethos' (*ibid.*: 51). In effect, this produces a concept of community which expresses and enacts the rights of the universal, abstracted individual who is white, Western, heterosexual, middle-class and male. In a move to establish equivalency and transparency, it also brackets out the 'particularities' of others who operate to represent the boundaries of 'the individual'. Despite their central role in processes of representation, these 'others' can never themselves gain access to representation except through the system of 'differences'. However, this system can only offer them variations of the same, or the potential of being mere replicas of 'the individual' excluded from full selfhood.

What I have outlined so far has raised issues around the constitution of self–other relations. I have focused on the negotiation of spatial distance or difference between the self and the other, showing how space functions to construct the individual. And I have also highlighted the importance of the temporal unity or self-presence of the individual in this construction. Through the knowledge-producing processes of equivalency, transparency and dialogue, women and subordinated groups operate as the constitutive outside or generative potential of the individual. I will go on to argue that the concept of 'potential' is crucial for gaining an understanding of how this model of the constitution of the individual relates to concepts of authenticity, self-actualisation and difference which are central to certain discourses of consumerism.

Authenticity, individuality and the politics of difference

The discussion of contract in previous sections has mapped out the centrality of the concepts of exchange, difference and the possession of the body in the political category of the individual. These concepts have become a significant part of powerful discourses which define autonomy and free social relations in capitalist societies,

> since exchange relations become the prototypical expression of efforts to extend individual propertied jurisdictions without invading the dominion of other individuals, the sphere of the market becomes identified as the central arena for the expression of individual freedom.
>
> (Yeatman 1994: 66)

Anna Yeatman (1994) here indicates that the 'dominion' and autonomy of the individual are held sacred in contemporary Western societies. Yet, at the same time, those subjects who have been accorded the status of 'individual' are guaranteed access to relations of exchange/dialogue with 'others' in the society. This emphasis on guaranteed access to 'others' in forms of recognition and exchange can be seen in terms of an identification and discursive valuing of the rights to express and fulfil 'individual potential'.

Charles Taylor (1994) traces the historical emergence of a particular form of Western selfhood tied to the concepts of potential, recognition, authenticity and self-actualisation. He maps the shift from the philosophical concept of 'honour' to that of 'dignity' which, he argues, emerged in late eighteenth-century Europe. 'Honour' was an exclusive form of distinction based on European hierarchies of nobility or exceptional achievement. Its fundamental premise was the definition of 'honour' as an elite characteristic reserved for the few (*ibid.*). This concept gradually came to be displaced by that of human 'dignity' which was seen as a characteristic shared by all.

Taylor argues that from the late eighteenth century, philosophers began to reject the notion of morality as divine reward or punishment, and came to believe that humans were endowed with an inner moral sense. Rather than contact with God, people were seen to have contact with an inner voice guiding their morality (*ibid.*). Taylor sees this conceptual shift as intrinsically tied to emergent ideas of 'an *individualized* identity' (*ibid.*: 77) in which individual contact with 'the inner self' came to define 'authentic' identity.

Alongside what Foucault (1988) identifies as 'technologies of the self', this framework of individualised identity provided the conditions for thinking of the self as having inner depths (Taylor 1994: 77). The self is encouraged to embark on processes of self-monitoring through the production of 'authentic self-knowledge' of the self's interiority. We are directed towards engaging reflexively with the self as a project to be worked upon. Taylor argues that contact with this inner self takes on a moral accent or form of duty to oneself. Added to this morally inscribed interrogation of interiority is the idea that each person has a unique, original inner essence which is considered as individualised potential (Taylor 1994). The realisation of this potential as a form of self-actualisation becomes a duty in the imperative to live one's life 'authentically', that is, in touch with one's inner, true, self.

> Being true to myself means being true to my own originality, which is something only I can articulate and discover. In articulating it, I am also defining myself. I am realizing a potentiality that is properly my own.
>
> (Taylor 1994: 78)

Yet I want to argue that this project of the self should not be seen as the expression of an innate, inner core of selfhood – the consumption and display of certain goods is not the outward sign of an inner essence. Nor should this project of the self be imagined as the expression and application of individual agency. As with the constitution of 'the individual', this articulation of potentiality can be seen as a performative process. Each person is posited as *innately* original and unique, and yet cannot be named as such until that person articulates their inner essence or potential. However, the particular form that this originality will take, that which defines the very 'individuality' of the person, can only be articulated by that same person. Yet they are authorised and enabled to begin to search for it by the very qualities of unique selfhood for which they are searching. Indeed, this potential and individuality will only be realised, materialised or recognisable as such in the moment of contact, articulation and definition.

Taylor (1994) goes on to argue that such processes of self-actualisation are dialogical in nature in that they are reliant on contact and dialogue with others. An individual cannot hold the status of unitary and authentic identity without gaining recognition of this identity through dialogue, or exchange, with others. Moreover, these attempts at gaining recognition are not guaranteed to succeed (*ibid.*). Taylor (*ibid.*: 82) discusses the significance of recognition in relation to two contemporary discourses of identity which he calls 'the politics of universalism' and 'the politics of difference'. This emphasis on both the individual formation of selfhood and the group formation of identity is crucial to later arguments I outline about cultural difference.

For Taylor, the politics of universalism is based on an ideal of an equality of rights for each individual. This is founded on a view that all individuals are equal, as they share 'universal human potential' which is of intrinsic value (*ibid.*: 84). The politics of difference initially appears to be in opposition to such stance, for in this model there is an imperative to recognise each individual for their unique identity – for their difference from others, rather than for their equality with others (*ibid.*). Disregard, assimilation or denigration of differences, then, is an affront to the principles of uniqueness and authenticity (*ibid.*). Taylor argues that a concept of universal equivalence or equality in fact underlies the politics of difference, because it posits that we are all *equally distinct* or unique. It demands that 'we give due acknowledgment only to what is universally present – everyone has an identity – through recognizing what is peculiar to each. The universal demand powers an acknowledgment of specificity' (*ibid.*: 82). So in this way, the politics of universalism and the politics of difference are seen to gravitate around the interrelated principles of sameness/identity and difference.

Taylor (1994) does not here address specific issues of sexual and racial difference. Indeed, Linda Nicholson (1996) has argued that Taylor's failure to incorporate these elements highlights flaws in his theory of the politics of recognition. Nicholson argues that Taylor fails to appreciate how the shifting politics of emancipation – instanced in the 1960s feminist movements and African American movements, or contemporary lesbian and gay movements – involve a complex of recognition claims which cannot be reduced to Taylor's rather generalised approach. Such movements demand more than simple recognition as in Taylor's account. Rather, they demand a sweeping change in the very practices of the conferral of recognition (Nicholson 1996). In the context of my discussion, Taylor's generalised theory needs to address the structurally inegalitarian nature of discursive practices discussed earlier in relation to Diprose's (1994) and Yeatman's (1994) analyses. These map out how the constitution of 'the individual' as a political category both requires and negates women and subordinated others in the imperative to delimit the boundaries of *his* selfhood. They are required for the processes of mutual recognition, yet do not hold the status necessary for that recognition. In de Lauretis' (1987) terms, women and subordinated others are constituted in a movement between the inside and outside of discursive representation. They cannot occupy the position of identical self-presence because their 'difference' is the structural requirement of that presence and identity. This raises questions of the discursive 'potential', the inner depths, the originality and the authenticity of women and subordinated others. In later chapters I address these issues through asking the following questions: If these subordinated groups are discursively produced as merely variations of the same (Diprose 1994), in what terms may they be potentially unique? In what ways may they realise that potential and engage in processes of self-actualisation? What processes occur in the establishment of equivalences and transparency in the identification and expression of potential?

In the following section, I relate the above issues of identity, difference and potential to my concerns around belonging and citizenship. Indeed, Appadurai (1997) suggests that these identity politics exist on the level of the nation-state in what he calls 'culturalism'. I explore how these discourses of uniqueness and potential relate to national and transnational communities and cultural difference.

Cultural difference and identity

In this section I am going to explore the ways in which European historical formulations of the category of 'the individual' are imbricated with the discursive production of the Western nation-state. This relation has been seen by Benedict Anderson (1991) as a form of mapping in which national communities plotted their histories as boundary-defined geographies. This created an image of the supposed antiquity, and hence legitimacy, of bounded territorial units by producing a 'political-biographical narrative of the realm' (*ibid.*: 175) in a form parallel to the biography of an individual. Kathleen Kirby (1996) ties this emphasis on the mapping of the boundaries of both the individual and the colonial European nation-state to eighteenth- and nineteenth-century discourses of capitalist ownership and possessiveness. The individualised self-possessiveness, in Pateman's (1988) terms, was crucial for the production of the 'unitary' status of both the individual and the colonial nation-state. This cartography etched out the boundaries of these entities and stressed their impermeability. Cartography, then, functioned as a technology of knowledge and of possession which was central to the violent colonial remapping of European nations' sovereignty and rights of possession; 'map-making became the servant of colonial plunder, for the knowledge constituted by the map both preceded and legitimized the conquest of territory' (McClintock 1995: 27). Indeed, the superiority of the European, male, classed 'individual' over women and lower classes legitimised colonial expansion and expropriation through a naturalisation of certain modes of 'rational', 'civilised' characteristics. This subsequently transformed the sovereignty of the male, classed 'individual' in terms of *European* superiority of 'civilisation', democracy, culture and capitalism over colonised 'others' (Parekh 1995; Pratt 1992). Mapping the category of 'the individual' and the historical mapping of the nation-state generated the interiority and the transparency of those spatialised and temporalised identities,

The space that mapping propagates is an immutable space organized by invariable boundaries, an a-temporal, objective, transparent space. Not coincidentally, the same physical qualities characterize the kinds of subjectivity that we would name, variously, Cartesian monadism, Enlightenment individualism or autonomous egoism. But the relationship is not only metaphoric – one of comparability; it is also metonymic – one of contiguity. The similarity of mapped space and the mapping subject stems from the way the boundary between them is patterned as a constant barricade enforcing the difference between the two sites, preventing admixture and the diffusion of either entity.

(Kirby 1996: 47)

The formulations of identity and difference explored by Taylor (1994), then, should not be seen as restricted to an individual level of self-actualisation, but rather can be seen in relation to concepts of national and cultural difference, as Appadurai (1997) suggests. In parallel to Taylor's emphasis on individuality and authenticity, Verena Stolcke's (1995) analysis of European discourses of cultural difference and national identity examines the relations of authenticity, culture and difference. As I discuss in greater depth in later chapters, Stolcke argues that much of the contemporary European debate over immigration, citizenship, definitions of nationhood and Europe displaces older discourses of 'racism' and mobilises new discourses of 'cultural fundamentalism' (*ibid.*: 7). She defines modern Western 'racism' as a discourse which attributes a range of negative characteristics to particular groups based on the category 'race' which may be 'phenotypical' or a complex construction of diverse elements. These negative characteristics are construed as innate, biological and therefore immutable, producing a hierarchy of distinct groups (*ibid.*). In this discourse, recognition between the 'white, European self' and the 'racialised other' is thus unimaginable, due to the imagined inherent inequalities of 'race'. This underlines the impossibility of the establishment of a system or currency of equivalences. However, Stolcke goes on to argue, racism as a means of sealing the boundaries of the nation-state has begun to lose its discursive weight as more evidence emerges of the scientific invalidity of the concept of distinct biological 'races'.

Stolcke argues that there is now a move towards 'cultural fundamentalism', which shifts the accent of identity onto *cultural* difference.[4] 'Culture' is here defined as, 'a compact, bounded, localized, and historically rooted set of traditions and values transmitted through the generations' (*ibid.*: 4).

Cultural fundamentalism, by contrast [to 'racism'], assumes a set of symmetric counterconcepts, that of the foreigner, the stranger, the alien as opposed to the national, the citizen. Humans by their nature are bearers of culture. But humanity is composed of a multiplicity of distinct cultures which are incommensurable, their relations between their respective members being inherently conflictive because it is human nature to be xenophobic. An alleged human universal – people's natural propensity to reject strangers – accounts for cultural particu-larism.

(Stolcke 1995: 7)

Here Stolcke's argument highlights how the concept of 'culture' becomes reified and functions as the container of the specificity of a particular group. Parallels may be drawn between Taylor's (1994) formulation of the linkages between the politics of difference and the politics of universalism in which the characteristic of specificity or difference functions as the universal measure or system of equivalence. In cultural essentialism a reified concept of 'culture' comes to define all 'cultural' groups. Yet, contradictorily, the very specificity of their nature posits them as incommensurable and indeed 'naturally' hostile to one another.

Culture becomes a way of redefining ethnicity as contained within national borders and as ostensibly divorced from 'race'. In Anderson's (1991) terms, the mapping of the nation-state's cultural 'origins' in local traditions and values lend it discursive 'authenticity'. This in turn confers an authority of established, bounded identity. In this discourse, culture can be viewed as a form of collective 'potential' which is innate in each cultural/ethnic group. It follows, then, that the identification and expression of this collective potential is framed as a fundamental right and duty to the authenticity and originality of that culture. As I discuss in later chapters, the expression of this bounded, national/cultural potential and specificity takes many forms. It is instanced in the tightening of immigration controls and the withholding of full citizenship rights for some, glossing over the rights of 'minority cultures'/'ethnic minorities'.

Stolcke (1995) insists that the conceptual movement from racism to cultural essentialism should not be seen merely as a new form of racism, but rather as a qualitatively different comparative discourse. Unlike 'racism', Stolcke argues, cultural essentialism maps out distinct cultures spatially rather than inherently hierarchically, and assumes cultural homogeneity within their boundaries. The effect can be seen as a kind of geographical mosaic of a multiplicity of distinct cultures. Benedict Anderson (1991) discusses an earlier form of this spatial plotting in relation to developments in cartography in the late nineteenth and early twentieth centuries. This plot-ting produced world maps using different colours for each country and colony, generating a jigsaw-like appearance of national relations. The map, he argues, became a kind of logo in which each 'jigsaw' piece became a sign imagined as detachable from its geographical context of place names and longitude and latitude. This mapping gains a new significance in the context of the emergence of cultural essentialism: nations as conceptual markers of belonging have become signs of difference which are potentially discursively interchangeable in their now-detachable form. In relation to Diprose's (1994) analysis of the establishment of equivalences or interchangeability for the process of mutual recognition, the contemporary concept of 'culture' functions as the universal, the standard, or the measure. This universal generates a means of comparison or currency of equivalence and posits the transparency of cultural identity. This equivalence is inherently contradictory because cultures are defined as equally different, distinct and incommensurable. Individual cultures are simultaneously variations of one model of universal 'culture', and also by definition, unique, original, authentic and radically incommensurable. As Bauman (1997: 131) notes, such a conception of culture functions as 'an anti-randomness device' which imposes order or frameworks of commensurability on societies. In effect, the concept of 'culture' is performatively produced in a moment of assumed transparency, recognition and equivalence or interchangeability between distinct cultures. These cultures cannot hold the status of identity prior to the process of recognition and naming. Yet their pre-constituted identity is required to generate that very concept of 'culture' which names them.

The model of culture that Stolcke (1995) describes is produced within and through a European framework constituted by the historical development of the modern nation-state in colonialism and capitalism. In earlier sections of this chapter I mapped out how the historical constitution of 'the individual' was fundamentally modelled around sexual, racial and class subordination. Overlaid with these formulations are contemporary discourses of cultural difference which may shift the struggle for definitions of 'culture' towards notions of 'ethnicity' as 'cultural belonging'. As I indicate in the next chapter, this shift in definitions is played out through the contested cultural legitimacy of the new middle classes and 'cultural intermediaries'. Such a definition of culture can be translated into a discursive shift in the terms of conventional European political affiliation of the nation-state towards the concept of cultural citizenship. With a new emphasis, ideas of cultural origins or ethnicity come to form the basis for formal political membership of a nation-state, generating a diffuse sense of exclusive belonging and entitlement. As I will go on to argue, this is based in part on discourses of consumerism. Notions of self-possessiveness, exchange, recognition and 'individual' status in consumerism articulate access to 'difference' as a consumer resource in the production of legitimate, politically validated identities. The following section addresses contemporary discourses of citizenship within Europe. I do not attempt to review the vast literature around citizenship, but instead aim to indicate some shifts occurring in the discursive framing of rights, obligations, belonging and exclusion in relation to difference.

The citizen and the consumer

Bryan S. Turner (1993) emphasizes that citizenship is the product of a range of discourses tied to social institutions. These discourses create a framework of inclusion (for some) and organise individuals' access to rights to resources; 'citizenship may be defined as that set of practices (juridical, political, economic and cultural) which define a person as a competent member of society, and which as a consequence shape the flow of resources to persons and groups' (*ibid.*: 2). Turner stresses that citizenship should not be considered a universal concept, but rather a variable framework which may be peculiar to the West. Within the West, Anna Yeatman (1994) argues, the constitution of the categories of the individual and the citizen interrelate through the process of creating the boundaries of a community. In effect, they operate through the universalisation of the notion of unitary individual status within Western nation-states in which 'the discourse of citizenship is universal: it extends the status of "individual" to all who fall under the state's jurisdiction and become counted as members of the state as a self-determining political community' (*ibid.*: 73).

Citizenship is, then, a 'shared order of being' held together by the assumption of the rational nature of all members (*ibid.*: 80). This group of citizens is then treated as a 'corporate individual' with 'a clearly bounded integrity' and identifiable shared will (*ibid.*: 81). This principle of generality extends the exclusionary constitution of 'the individual' to the citizen in terms of a contractual set of rights and obligations. Conventionally, these rights have been seen in terms of T.H. Marshall's (1992) influential evolutionary model of British civil, political and social rights which he first produced in 1950. He argued that civil rights developed first in the eighteenth century, establishing such rights as the ownership of property, the right to justice, and the right to freedom of speech, all of which were based around the concept of the unitary individual. Next, nineteenth-century political rights developed around parliamentary functions, including the vote and councils. Finally, in the twentieth century, social rights were established primarily around access to education and welfare (Marshall 1992). Later commentators have emphasized the importance of considering Marshall's account not as representative of the actual processes of the historical establishment of citizenship rights, but rather as indicative of how citizenship functions as 'one of the central organizing features of Western political discourse' (Hindess 1993: 19). In the following sections, I examine how contemporary citizenship relates to consumerism, another central organising feature of Western societies.

In the context of my focus on British and French advertisements and identities, the next section explores how the development of these principles of citizenship and belonging have taken different forms as organising features of political discourse in Britain and France. The historical British definition of citizenship has had little formal content due to the fact that there is no single-document constitution or basic law which sets out rights and obligations (Dummett and Nichol 1990; Evans 1993). This allows for a flexible interpretation and implementation of regulations by governmental bodies such as the Home Office and the Immigration Services (Dummett and Nichol 1990). In contrast, the post-revolution French *Déclaration des*

Droits de l'Homme et du Citoyen of 1789, and the French nationality code of 1889, had a more rigid structure and clearer regulations (Stolcke 1995). Despite these differences, Stolcke (1995) traces the shifts in legal citizenship and nationality linked to the indices of descent, birthplace and domicile. She demonstrates how immigration and citizenship came to be firmly linked in both Britain and France by the 1980s and 1990s.

The French Republican 'assimilationist' model of citizenship and nationality produced in the French code of nationality of 1889 conferred national status on those descended from a French father, and those born in France (*ibid.*). This code did not apply to the French colonies until after the Second World War, and after Algerian independence hostility from French nationals to immigrants, and particularly Algerians, grew (*ibid.*). From the mid-1970s, French nationality and citizenship became intrinsically linked to immigration policy and were centred around a more general idea of 'French culture' and who could legitimately belong (*ibid.*). As I develop in the final chapter, there was a parallel shift in French anti-racist discourse in the mid-1980s from ideas of *le droit à la différence* [the right to difference] (Taguieff 1992) to a more republican model of integration based on shared cultural values and demanding cultural assimilation (Stolcke 1995). In 1993, the conservative French government passed a law restricting automatic access to French citizenship for French-born children of immigrants, putting a new emphasis on descent as a legal requirement for the status of citizen (*ibid.*). This shift relocated citizenship rights to a concept of French ethnicity firmly rooted in shared cultural heritage.

In Britain, rights to citizenship have been tied to birthplace historically and have automatically required allegiance to the crown (Dummett and Nichol 1990; Stolcke 1995). Immigrants from the British colonies, therefore, had free access to citizenship as British subjects until 1962, when a series of restrictions resulted in the British Nationality Act of 1981 (Stolcke 1995). The Act limited the birthplace rules and linked together nationality, citizenship and immigration in a parallel to discursive realignments occurring in France. In this move, the Act reconfigured nationality and foreignness, redefining 'black subjects' as 'cultural aliens' (Stolcke 1995: 10) representing a shift from 'race' to cultural difference. This 'culturalist' move presented immigration in terms of a threat to the shared cultural heritage of Britain (*ibid.*).

The cultural fundamentalism identified by Stolcke, and the gendered nature of citizenship discussed by Yeatman (1994) and Lister (1997), highlight how 'the other' of the individual, and 'the other' of the citizen, are based both on shifting legal and cultural definitions. The fusing of citizenship laws and immigration policy indicates how the immigrant as 'alien' functions as the counterpoint which comes to define 'the citizen' of the bounded, ostensibly homogeneous political community. The exclusion of the foreigner as 'cultural alien' binds together a specific notion of national culture as unique and inherently valuable. The 'potential' of each culture is therefore framed as a right and duty to uphold 'cultural traditions' and to defend them against 'dilution', either through assimilationist strategies or through tight immigration controls.

According to the principles of cultural essentialism described by Stolcke (1995), all cultures are distinct and incommensurable, although theoretically equally 'authentic', and hence valued. Through the linking of citizenship and immigration controls within Europe, this notion of 'culture' has become almost synonymous with 'national culture'. But are all cultures equally valued? The colonial histories of Britain and France suggest that some cultures may be considered more 'compatible' than others, some ways of life and traditions less 'alien' than others. The shift away from biological ideas of 'race' and difference towards a cultural essentialism as the currency of commensurability and dialogue has produced an intensified focus on cultural difference. As I describe in more detail in later chapters, the terms of commensurability of cultures do not operate symmetrically for all, especially in the case of the relation of Islam to Europe. Brubaker (1992) notes that, in France, North African Muslims have become the prime target of exclusionary and discriminatory practices due to the perceived 'unassimilability' of Islamic culture to French culture. Other European nationals are considered more suitable candidates for immigration due to their imagined shared European cultural heritage (*ibid.*). This formulation is not exclusive to France, for as Soysal (1994: 114) argues, within Europe (and indeed other parts of the world, notably the United States) Islam has come to be seen as an explicitly 'ethnicized political identity'.[5] It becomes framed as stereotypically 'traditional', as opposed to Western 'modern' (Christian) democracy.

> Rationally defined goals and functions, and systematic management are considered modern organizational forms and as such are assumed to be alien to 'Islamic cultures'. The underlying assumption is that Islam cannot combine European organizational categories with its religious order, which does not provide for an autonomous hierarchical structure.
>
> (Soysal 1994: 115)

What Taguieff (1992) calls the 'culturalisation' of difference operates to highlight and redefine cultural, rather than 'racial', difference and installs the principle of 'equally different and differently equal'. Yet the example of Islam shows that, within this European discourse of identity and difference, some cultures are seen as more different than others. This is most visible when they fall outside a European 'cultural heritage' of capitalist democracy, Christianity, 'culture' and 'civilisation'. In the following the section I explore the links between these discourses of cultural difference and those of consumerism in relation to potential and individuality.

Consumer-citizenship

The notions of uniqueness and potential of both the individual and the Western nation-state draw on explicitly 'culturalised' processes of knowledge of difference and identity. These occur through contact and dialogue between self or nation and 'the other'. On an individual level, I have explored how this assumed 'dialogical egalitarianism' (Crapanzano 1991: 437) is in fact based on exclusion and hierarchy. On the related national level, I have shown how discourses of supposedly universal commensurability and dialogue operate on a Eurocentric basis which rejects certain cultures as incompatible with egalitarian 'dialogue'. In this section I am going to explore the contested terms of 'culture' in this newly culturalised discourse of identity and their relation to discourses of the 'inner depths' and potential of the self. I examine how the compulsory 'action' of the constitution of the 'individual' and 'citizen' comes to be articulated through discourses of consumerist choice. I argue that this 'choice' becomes framed by 'expert knowledge systems' which present ways of accessing, interpreting and actualising knowledge of (and the potential of) 'the inner self'.

Zigmunt Bauman (1992) relates shifts in forms of identity to shifts in the social groups who hold legislative authority over the mass of society. He argues that in the Western pre-modern, highly structured, hierarchical order of society, decisions were made by an elite, whilst the mass of the population led highly regulated lives. Indeed, identity and subjectivity in those periods did not exist in the ways imagined and experienced in contemporary society (Taylor 1994). Foucault (1988) maps a shift from these centrally regulating power structures to a more diffuse operation of power, in which the subject is encouraged to engage in self-monitoring through technologies of the self. This generates an interior discursive space to the notion of subjectivity, which is seen as an arena of self-knowledge and self-regulating work on the self. Taylor (1994) argues that the self then gradually comes to be seen as a repository of unique and authentic potential which must be realised through processes of discovery, expression, and thus self-actualisation. In contemporary Western society this self-realisation appears in one form as a process of active 'choice' framed in terms of consumerist engagement with the idea of self as project. The constitution of the self through consumerist choice is thus construed as a personal duty and responsibility (Bauman 1997, 1998).

Bauman (1992: 15) argues that the legislative authority of the elite in premodern times has been displaced by a growing group of 'trained experts' in the realms of surveillance, correction, welfare supervision, medicine and the legal system, producing a shift from 'legislation' to 'interpretation'. As I discuss in the next chapter, a parallel expansion has occurred in the area of 'cultural guardians', including publishers, art galleries and the managers of mass communications systems who function as 'interpreters' of culture, framing consumer choices through expert knowledges (*ibid.*: 17). In his suggestive but highly speculative thesis, Bauman argues that through 'expert knowledges', these interpreters present interpretative 'solutions' to the complex series of choices (or 'problems') on offer in societies where judgement values appear to become increasingly relative.

> The most salient problem in such a world [of pluralism and relativity] – one with which the ordinary competence of otherwise knowledgeable members cannot cope without assistance – is communication between systems of knowledge enclosed within their respective stocks of knowledge and communal systems of relevance.
>
> (Bauman 1992: 22)

The interpretation of culture, then, becomes 'an essentially hermeneutic exercise' in which culture is 'something to be mastered cognitively, as a meaning' (Bauman 1992: 23). Culture becomes available for such a flexible interpretation through its popular image as a repository of various traditions and meanings. In the next chapter, I explore Bauman's thesis in relation to the circulation of 'cultural' knowledges between advertising agencies, clients and magazines, but at this point I want to emphasise the diffusion of specific notions of 'culture' and their relation to consumerism.

> The vision of culture as, essentially, an activity performed by a part of the population and aimed at another part, is replaced with a vision of a spontaneous process devoid of administrative or managerial centres, free of an overall design and perpetuated by diffusely deployed powers.
>
> (Bauman 1992: 23)

Bauman (1990) argues that these shifts combine to produce 'the consumer attitude', in which life is viewed as a series of 'problems' which are one's duty to solve. In Taylor's (1994) terms, the subject is offered a range of choices for self-actualisation and realisation of one's potential. These choices are framed and presented by expert knowledge systems as options of realisation which can be purchased and 'consumed' (Bauman 1990). So in this way, culture becomes an explicit means through which people can imagine themselves and construct frames of meaning.

As I argue in the final chapter, such a view of culture may be usefully related to Stolcke's (1995) conceptualisation of a 'culture' as a distinct and bounded entity, incommensurable with others, binding together 'national community' and ethnicity. Ideas of unique potential and characteristics (as individuals and national communities) thus come to be defined through the particular ways in which identities can be actualised through the technologies of choice on offer. These discourses posit that individual particularity can be expressed and materialised through an active re-articulation of signs in consumer discourses. Or, in Bauman's terms, identity can be expressed and produced through a cognitive mastery of the discursive framework which defines 'culture'. As Stolcke (1995) argues, the concept of 'culture' is a product of complex intersections of particularity and difference. 'Culture' is then articulated through a system of equivalences and dialogue in which a white, male, Western, consumerist model of 'culture' comes to be understood as the generic form. This produces a contradictory discourse in which cultures are both fundamentally incomparable, and yet require forms of recognition from each other in order to generate cultural boundaries. Those that constitute the outside, the 'other' culture, the cultural aliens, are made available as options on a Western consumer 'menu' of cultural difference. Actualising one's potential as individual and citizen of a national community becomes intertwined as 'consumer choice', which comes to be seen as a right and a duty in order to express one's 'inner, authentic' essence.

In this way, 'choice' comes to mediate the terms in which certain subjects have access to the politically validated categories of 'the individual' and 'the citizen'. These discourses redefine the boundaries, status and role of the citizen in terms of potential contributors to the nation-state as consumers expressing rights of choice.

> For those who are legitimate members of the state, their shared identity is not that of the social citizens of the welfare state, but that of actual or potential contributors to the performativity of the competition state. The trend is thus to turn all nationals into contributors, ... and to define out of existence non-contributors.
>
> (Yeatman 1994: 111)

The emphasis on *active* contribution to the national community, or 'active citizenship', can be related to earlier discussions of contract and the compulsory recognition and reiteration of the category of 'the individual' in exchange (Diprose 1994; Pateman 1988; Yeatman 1994). 'The emancipation of the individual's freedom of action is what constitutes individuality, namely the freedom and capacity to act' (Yeatman 1994: 60). The repeated action of recognition, and exchange of this recognition, for example in the exchange of labour power in employment contracts, is required to performatively produce and maintain the system of equivalences and exchange. Amalgamated with discourses of consumerism and citizenship, the capacity to act comes to be defined as the potential to engage in processes of consumerist recognition, exchange and choice.

In Britain, the government White Paper *The Citizen's Charter: Raising the Standard* (1991) refigured the rights and role of the citizen as those of consumer of goods and public services and as taxpayer (Evans 1993; Miller 1993). The Charter restated the ideal of the autonomous, self-monitoring individual, increasingly detached from state intervention, engaging in the rights of access to knowledge and rights of 'informed choice'.

> The Citizen's Charter is about giving more power to the citizen. But citizenship is about our responsibilities – as parents, for example, or as

neighbours – as well as our entitlements. The Citizen's Charter is not a recipe for more state action; it is a testament of our belief in people's right to be informed and choose for themselves.

(HM Government 1991: 2)

'Choice' is the key term continually reiterated throughout the document, invoked alongside the other stated main themes of 'quality, standards and value', laying out the terms of citizenship rather like a supermarket's marketing strategy. The Charter draws on a notion that 'choice' is an inherently 'good thing' when allied with the information necessary for *informed* choice. Choice here functions as a 'natural' human capacity or potential which, according to our duty, we must express. As I develop in the next chapter, information operates as a natural 'need', necessary for the processes of interpreting and actualising this potential and expressing our 'rights'.

One result of this dissemination of the discourse of choice is that an appeal to the rights of the individual or citizen can only be articulated as yet another act of choice (to choose to take one's choice elsewhere); 'Whenever the client can exercise a choice, the most effective form of redress is the right of exit: the decision not to accept the service provided and to go somewhere else' (HM Government 1991: 50). In the Citizen's Charter's terms, dissatisfaction with a 'service' requires that 'the consumer' access the relevant information and choose another NHS doctor or school. This is an explicit example of citizenship articulated as a contract and, in the final chapter, I examine how 'The Third Way' in Britain is another instance of contractual models of rights and obligations. The knowledge needed to enact the contract is 'information' about services and the alternatives. Yet, more importantly, the citizen as consumer is defined as an individual who is *capable* of making that informed choice. For it is in the very act of choice that the individual actualises *himself* as chooser and hence citizen. In effect, an abstracted notion of 'choice', and the transparency of self and other, functions as the system of equivalences for the contractual exchange.

Yet, as I have argued, the transparency of 'self' requires the simultaneous signification of 'others' in an imagined 'dialogical egalitarianism' (Crapanzano 1991: 437). Women and overlapping subordinate groups have an ambiguous relation to the category of 'the individual', moving between and across the discursive boundaries of difference (de Lauretis 1989). Yet with regard to discourses defining 'the consumer', women hold an ambiguous status in 'an economic discourse in which the feminine is inscribed as the prototypical consumer' (Radner 1995: 3). The sphere of consumption is often associated with women, and advertisers recognise that women make a large proportion of all purchases (Leiss *et al.* 1990). Yet the status of women as neither fully inside nor outside the discursive framework of 'the individual' partially excludes women from the self-identical status required for exchange. The material consequences of such an ambiguous positioning are extremely detrimental to women. Nancy Fraser (1989) examines how the discourses of welfare programmes in the United States draw on notions of 'the individual', paid work (active contractual engagement) and the private sphere to position unemployed white, middle-class men as 'rights-bearers' and 'purchasing consumers'.[6] In contrast, unemployed women, racialised groups, or women with families, are positioned as lower-status 'clients' or 'beneficiaries of government largesse' (Fraser 1989: 149–53). The white, middle-class men are framed as receiving benefits that they deserve, which they have 'paid in for' through social insurance schemes (similar to National Insurance in Britain). This discursively qualifies them as active citizens, whereas women and racialised groups are seen as non-contributing 'dependants' on the state (*ibid.*). In Britain, the model of full-time paid work also defines the terms of access to welfare, positioning middle-class men as 'the norm' (Sassoon 1987). In this way, British welfare provision operates largely through a male breadwinner model, despite the fact that the majority of welfare recipients are women (Bryson 1992). This subordinate status means that women do not have the same automatic, 'natural' access as white, middle-class men to interpretative 'informed choice' as a means of agency.

This section has explored the relations between the discourses of 'the individual', cultural belonging, citizenship, 'choice' and identity and has signalled the fundamentally sexed and racialised nature of these discourses. The following section takes up the issue of self-present identity as temporally and spatially bounded and sets up questions about the nature of time, identity and difference which will form central themes of later chapters.

The temporality of identity

The Rousseau quotation at the head of this chapter states that, whilst females are bound to the (subordinate) category of 'Woman', men are granted a certain flexibility in relation to the category 'Man': they are only male at certain moments. In this last section, I want to consider the temporality of discourses of difference. What is the temporality of the spatial mapping of the self and the nation suggested by Anderson (1991), Kirby (1996) and McClintock (1995)? What is the temporality of the 'interiority' of the self?

In the previous sections, I discussed how actions are central to discourses of 'active citizenship' – for example, in the compulsory reiteration of the categories 'individual' and 'consumer' through enactments of recognition, exchange and choice. Judith Butler (1993: 244) argues that 'acts' in performative processes should not be conceived as 'intact and self-identical' or external to the processes of time. These multiple acts do not occupy or constitute the same units of time; they are not equivalent or interchangeable, and their boundaries are not impermeable. In addition, acts occur both within time and also constitute our understandings of time. At this point I want to return briefly to Diprose's (1994) discussion of contractarian concepts of identical self-presence. The instances of mutual recognition or dialogue as described by Diprose can then be conceptualised as performative 'acts'. These are not temporally 'intact', or impervious to temporal seepage between the past-self, present-self and future-self. Nor are they spatially secure in their boundaries between the self and the other.

Indeed, Butler (1993) argues that time has been overlooked in many theories of identity. She contends that the Foucault's genealogical mapping of the convergence of relations of power theorises the motion and space of such articulations, but does not fully address the temporal nature of such manoeuvres. It does not address the constitutively temporal nature of movement between levels, or dimensions, of discourse. This is particularly significant for my discussion of the ambiguous discursive positioning of women and other subordinated groups, as spatial and temporal motion forms the basis of those processes of positioning. De Lauretis' formulation of discursive inside/outside positioning stresses 'the crossing back and forth of boundaries' (1989: 25) which may afford women 'an eccentric discursive position' (1990: 127). This encourages an examination of the spatio-temporal motion and contact of discourses. What occurs in such moments of recognition and exchange?

Butler argues that the time of performative acts of identity merge in ways that we should explore – we should problematise 'the discrete identity of "the moment"' (1993: 245). She resists spatialising metaphors which map temporality as 'a simple succession of distinct "moments", all of which are equally distant from one another' (*ibid.*: 244). This confers on 'the moment' the status of a spatially bounded duration which is equivalent in content and in distance from all others, yet is simultaneously distinct from them. There are echoes here of Stolcke's (1995) concept of cultural essentialism, equivalence and the incommensurability of difference. Butler argues that the 'betweenness' that both separates moments (as distinct) and joins them (as identifiable as the genre of 'moment') is crucial to conceptualising 'the content' of the moment.

> What differentiates moments is not a spatially extended duration, for if it were, it would also count as a 'moment', and so fail to account for what falls between moments. This 'entre', that which is at once 'between' and 'outside', is something like non-thematizable space and non-thematizable time as they converge.
>
> (Butler 1993: 10n8)

This formulation of 'the non-thematisable' raises the issue of knowledge, or what can be known, which I will address in later chapters in relation to the visible, the transparent and the intelligible.

Following Butler, the constitution of the consumer-citizen can be formulated as the convergence of the non-thematisable space between the self and the not-self. Yet it is also the convergence of the non-thematisable temporality of the relations between the past-self, the present-self and the future/potential self. The consumerist discourses of self-actualisation frame the temporality of the self in terms of 'potential'. Indeed, the concept of potential is itself temporal in nature, because its future ideal is implicit in the temporal logic it proposes. The 'moments' of potential cannot be distinguished as distinct segments, however, as they are repetitively re-produced as their own future; potential can never fully be achieved, as its very nature continually looks forward to what it may be. Discourses of consumerist self-actualisation, then, encompass within their structure mechanisms for their own perpetuation.

In summary, I have outlined how 'the individual' is not a entity formed prior to an engagement in discourse. There is not a preconstituted, core self to be expressed or communicated in acts of consumption and display. The self is constituted performatively in the very action of acting, mediated through discourse. Social contract is a particular discursive structure which frames individual agency through citizenship, belonging, entitlement and consumerism. Yet, the shift towards 'consumer-citizenship' that I have outlined in this chapter does not merely unite the distinct discourses of citizenship and consumerism, but actively refigures their terms. In their joint performative articulation, the materialisation of the effects that they name reveals new forms of belonging and rights. In the following chapters, I draw on and develop this chapter's themes of temporality, potential, choice, individuality and cultural difference. In Chapter 3, I present the findings of my study of advertisements and explore how the categories of sexual, 'racial', ethnic, class and national difference function as a visual currency for the re-production of white, Western, classed, male selfhood and rights of belonging. And in Chapters 4, 5 and 6 I explore how the visual articulates with the 'materiality' of citizenship rights and examine the temporality of narratives of difference and exclusion. In the next chapter, I explore how interpretation, information and knowledge-circulation in the advertising industry produces certain targeted groups as categories through particular definitions of 'individuality'.

2 Advertising knowledges

In Chapter 1, I outlined how the interpretation of culture can be an exercise in which culture is 'something to be mastered cognitively, as a meaning' (Bauman 1992: 23). I argued that this interpretative process is performative – subjects are not preformed entities but rather are formed in the very process of engaging with culture. What, then, is the significance of advertising within this cultural context, and in what sense might advertising mediate individuality? What role does advertising play in the commercial circulation of cultural meanings about target markets of consumers? How does it establish a context within which viewers engage in practices of interpretation?

As I argued in the introduction, academic critics have considered advertising imagery as an ambiguous cultural form. Visual advertising is often imagined to be emblematic of capitalist societies, the visible manifestation or materialisation of the capitalist logics of exploitation, alienation and reification. For instance, Robert Goldman (1992: 2) argues that advertising is 'a key social and economic institution in producing and reproducing the material and ideological supremacy of commodity relations'. Goldman acknowledges that he is drawing on Judith Williamson's (1978) highly influential work *Decoding Advertisements*, in which she argues that the economic interests of capitalism and the symbolic form of advertising distil to produce a highly powerful cultural form. For Williamson, advertising mystifies us, deprives us of knowledge and appropriates our real needs and desires to serve the interests of capitalism. Following Williamson, Goldman (1992: 8) argues that advertising is a force which erodes the fabric of social life and functions as 'a form of internal colonialism that mercilessly hunts out and appropriates those meaningful elements of our cultural lives that have value'. From this perspective, the close textual study of advertising images is thought to reveal 'the underlying social grammar of meaning in ads' which in turn illuminates the deeper ideological significance of advertising (*ibid.*). Goldman acknowledges that the ideological meanings of advertising do not reside solely in images but are produced in circuits of cultural production, representation and interpretation. Nevertheless, his framework privileges advertising images as a 'unique window' on the logics of commodity relations (Goldman 1992: 2).

My concern in these debates is to consider the ambiguous ways in which advertising is presented both as the material form, or the embodiment of the essence of capitalism, yet also as a mere representation or symbol of the 'real issues' of ideological power and the circulation of capital. Within accounts such as those of Williamson and Goldman, advertisements are foregrounded as a privileged site for the study of capitalist societies. For Williamson, advertising is so significant that advertisements and ideology become coterminous. Advertisements are imagined as ideology materialised, and appear to gain a life of their own, organically rearticulating social meanings in line with their own interests: 'advertisements (ideologies) can incorporate anything, even re-absorb criticism of themselves' (Williamson 1978: 167, parentheses in original). Yet at the same time advertisements are seen as *immaterial* in the sense that they are merely the conductors of ideology – they are imagined to be the visible, outer shell of the inner logic of capitalism, having no *real substance* of their own. For instance, Williamson argues that 'analysing ads in their *material form* helps to avoid endowing them with a *false* materiality and letting the "ad world" distort the real world around the screen and the page' (*ibid.*: 11, emphasis in original). Here, the 'material form' of advertisements at once represents the materiality of capitalist relations and also misrepresents 'the real world' which is thought to exist somewhere beyond the 'immateriality' of the text on the screen or page.[1] So, in one sense, advertising is considered to represent or embody capitalism in a distilled form. It is seen as a visible, material form of capitalism, transparent in its aims to sell goods and to perpetuate capitalist ideologies of ownership and profit. Yet at the same time its actual force is imagined to be non-material, mysteriously hidden by the sophistry of its 'visual persuasion'.[2] As Mica Nava (1997: 34) argues in relation to such analyses, advertising has been 'framed', set up as '*the* iconographic signifier of multinational capitalism'.

Goldman makes his rather schematic case more forcefully than other critics, but I would argue that his analysis represents the assumptions implicit in many accounts of the relationship between advertising and society. Martyn Lee (1993: 18) describes one such view which sees advertising as 'an attempt to construct an economy of symbolic or cultural goods that is aligned sympathetically with capitalism's fundamental objective, namely its own successful reproduction'. Lee cautions against reductive approaches which gloss over what he sees 'the uneven and highly complex nature of the power of capitalism to regulate the cultural sphere' (*ibid.*). Nava (1997) echoes Lee's concerns, arguing that many accounts of advertising make untenable claims about the relationship between the economic and the symbolic. They simplify the cycles of production and consumption and assume a symbiotic, seamlessly symmetrical relation between them. These approaches have been fuelled in part by the way in which studies of advertisements as *products in themselves* have been sidelined as having no real 'substance' or contribution to the debate (Nava 1997). As a result, analysis of advertisements as products have tended to be bracketed out of frameworks for understanding consumer culture.

I want to approach the issues of the materiality or immaterialty of advertising images through debates about advertising's mediation of meaning and its role in the communication of identities. How does advertising 'act on' individuals, and how does advertising frame the actions of the individual? Colin Campbell (1997, 1999) has challenged conventional models for understanding the relationship between action, intent and meaning in advertising and consumerism. Action has long been a key site for social and cultural analysis, due to its imagined intimate relation with individual agency. Campbell (1999) argues that many such analyses define action as that which . possesses human meaning. This is distinguished from non-action, which is often understood as 'mere behaviour'. Meaning, Campbell (*ibid.* 49) argues, is 'a term that is usually identified with intentionality, or such cognate terms as goal-directedness or purposiveness'.[3] In the area of consumerism, these assumptions about meaning take the form of 'a communicative act paradigm' (Campbell 1997: 341). Campbell argues that in this typical model, consumer goods are considered primarily as signs (framed by advertising) which function as a mediating form of communication in the tasks of self-construction. This is frequently seen as a reflexive project of the self in which subjects are encouraged to monitor and work upon themselves in an ongoing process of self-management and development. Campbell suggests that analytic approaches which accept this communication-based model develop a particular theoretical framework which focuses primarily on symbolic meaning. It is assumed that consumers are aware of symbolic meanings in discourses of consumerism, and that they actively orient their consumption through them. The concomitant assumption is that consumers have intent to make use of these meanings as messages about their identities which they communicate to others. The corollary of these assumptions is that many consumer studies focus on an exploration of identity and lifestyle in which it is assumed that the aim or intent of consumer acts is to gain recognition for this identity (Campbell 1997). Campbell's primary criticism is that this communicative act paradigm reads 'conscious intent' into these various levels of engagement in consumer culture. This, Campbell suggests, is problematic, as awareness and intent are not coterminous and should not be conflated. The relationships between intent and awareness are multiple and may appear counter-intuitive:

> For individuals may intend to send a message and be aware that this is what they are doing; they may, however, be aware that they are sending a message, even though it is not their intention to send one, just as they may succeed in sending a message even though they neither intend to do so nor are aware that they have done so.
>
> (Campbell 1997: 349)

Campbell is here challenging the idea that intent and meaning are unambiguously embodied in the act of consumption. He is also criticising the idea that awareness has an unproblematic relation to intent. These frameworks, he argues, assume that acts of consumption are primarily about communication. The consequence of these assumptions is that consumer acts are studied primarily:

> not as physical events involving the expenditure of effort, or for that matter as transactions in which money is exchanged for goods and services, but rather as symbolic acts or signs, acts that do not so much 'do something' as 'say something', or perhaps, 'do something through saying something'.
>
> (Campbell 1997: 341)

I would agree that meanings in consumer culture are not solely the raw materials for individuals to communicate or 'send messages' about their identities. It is also clear that acts of consumption have significance across a range of physical, social and economic practices. However, it is possible to make the point that meanings, messages and intent relate to one another in complex ways and arrive at rather different conclusions. As Appadurai (1990, 1997) argues, the imagination is a social practice, and we can study this practice in ways which do not reduce it to a simplistic tracking of meanings in 'messages' about identity. Campbell wants to disengage from the idea that acts do not so much *do* something as *say* something or communicate something. As I have demonstrated in previous chapters, theories of performativity can be useful for exploring how 'saying something can be doing something'. This 'doing' is not necessarily about sending messages, but rather is the very action of constituting the self. Performativity looks at how speech acts produce the subject and aims to show how something as apparently 'immaterial' as speech can form what we understand as the very materiality of the bodily self. I have adapted this framework to consider the visual, and in the following chapters I explore how meanings and their relation to the awareness of the self produce complex forms of intent and responsibility.

If, as Appadurai (1990, 1997) suggests, the imagination is a social practice, what role does the imagination play in the social practices of advertising agencies and the imaginative practices of viewers of advertisements produced by those agencies? In the following section, I examine the circulation of knowledges about target markets of consumers between advertising agencies and clients. I argue that units of information generated by agencies about markets are not themselves objective, material facts; rather, they actively materialise those markets. In effect, the markets are a product of the imaginative practices of executives in advertising agencies. The knowledges generated by the agencies are oriented towards self-promotion, because agencies are forced to compete in order to present themselves to potential clients as experts in knowledge about the consumer. Specific advertisements and campaigns are products of this self-promotional imperative. Within this dynamic, I explore how certain forms of textual address are incorporated into campaigns and linked to the construction of social categories.

Advertising agencies and the circulation of knowledge

In this section I argue that advertising campaigns are the material products of imaginative processes of advertising agencies and are created within the constraints of commercial enterprise. This enterprise is directed towards persuading client firms that the advertising agency can effectively identify and target specific markets of consumers. As I explore in this section, agencies do not merely 'uncover' sections of society and present them to clients as a 'deliverable' market. In an active, imaginative process, agencies segment and rearticulate an ideal of the target market in terms of gender, age, income bracket, 'attitudes', etc. Agencies then mobilise this idea of the target market to imagine ways of 'reaching' or addressing this market. In aiming to 'speak to' certain groups (which they themselves have defined), agencies incorporate their concept of the market into the textual address of the advertising campaigns they produce. This differentiated textual address, or way of 'speaking to' specific sections of society, in turn offers viewers ways of understanding and redefining themselves. In effect, the textual address of advertising campaigns can materialise the social categories of consumers that it names. In what follows, I explore agencies' reflexive incorporation of imaginative practices into advertising campaigns and into the potential imaginative practices of viewing subjects.

Advertising not only promotes images to potential consumers, but also promotes the image of the client company and advertising agency. As Mica Nava (1997: 40) argues in relation to clients, 'advertising is as much about promoting the corporate image of a company (or institution) to its rivals, clients and employees as it is about selling commodities to the consumer'. Advertising agencies, too, have an imperative to engage with a view of themselves as marketable entities, and must create a rhetoric of legitimation for the services they claim to provide. These services crystallise around the identification, measurement and 'delivery' of specific target markets of consumers to clients. These are offered through strategies of advertising address which, they claim, tap into viewers' desires and motivations. In promoting these targeting skills to potential clients, advertisers are faced with several methodological problems: that of the accurate measurement, and hence legitimation of their 'expert' knowledge, that of the effects of advertising on sales, and that of the accurate measurement of the number of viewers or readers of advertisements.

In terms of the measurement of effects, it has been widely acknowledged that it is impossible to isolate the effect of advertising from other forms of marketing and promotion (Mattelart 1991). Michael Schudson (1993) suggests that marketing, sales personnel, distribution and various 'sales promotions', such as premiums, coupons and competitions, etc., all contribute to the promotion of goods alongside advertising, and the specific contribution of each area remains indeterminate. Yet, Schudson argues, there is a non-specific belief in the power of advertising which can materially affect the success of the product through increased support from investors, the behaviour of retailers and the confidence of salespersons in the product. In a self-promotional dynamic, the belief amongst companies' investors of the status and effect of advertising can encourage further investment. This in turn increases resources for all forms of promotion: 'Expensive, well-executed, and familiar ads convince the investors, as nothing in the black and white tables of assets and debits can, that the company is important and prosperous' (Schudson 1993: xiv). This self-fulfilling prophecy prompts Schudson to argue that it is 'entirely plausible, then, that advertising helps sell goods even if it never persuades a *consumer* of anything' (*ibid.*: xv). The relationship between advertising and increased sales is, then, highly ambiguous. Despite a general confidence in advertising's impact as (self-)promotion, the advertising agencies themselves and their clients share an ambivalence towards the legitimacy of measurement, targeting and the effect of advertising on sales. In response to this, both agencies and clients develop strategies for dealing with the uncertainty and the legitimacy of their own knowledges and practices.

Considerable effort is invested by advertisers in providing an accurate estimate of the numbers that any one advertising campaign will reach. Such mechanisms for measurement can operate on national and, simultaneously, transnational levels, linking British and French advertising in significant ways. For instance, in the 1980s, the transnational CCA (Centre de communication avancée de Havas) based in France produced a data bank of specific consumer classifications which they termed a 'socio-cultural mapping' of the consumer (Mattelart 1991: 165). In 1989 the CCA brought out the first encyclopaedia of European 'lifestyles'. It was based on 24,000 interviews in sixteen European countries and generated a range of consumer 'types' (*ibid.*). Other French–British advertising connections developed in the 1980s through the French based RISC (International Research Institute on Social Change) (Nixon 1996). In Britain, a range of such measurement frameworks developed from the mid-1980s: for example, VALS (values and lifestyles) (Davidson 1992).

Crucially, such estimates and targeting strategies do not merely describe a 'social reality', but actively *produce* the market as taxonomy:

> Contrary to marketing ideology, markets do not already exist 'out there' in social reality but are 'constructed': the selection of the advertising medium and the way in which audiences are segmented, that is selected to be addressed by advertising, are both ways in which social categories become transformed into markets.
>
> (Sinclair 1987: 97)

The British advertising trade paper, *Campaign*, consistently focuses on agencies' competing techniques of measuring the audience, and hence potential market. Yet, Mattelart (1991) argues, an emphasis on counting the numbers who are watching television or reading a newspaper or magazine cannot accurately represent the levels of attention involved in reception. He cites a well-known example of a self-promotional advertisement produced by the agency Howell Henry Chaldecott Lury in 1989. This promotion was an attempt on their part to debunk received wisdom (or open secrets) in the advertising industry and to present themselves as an alternative, insightful source of information,

> A self-advertisement for the agency in the *Financial Times* showed a couple making love in front of a television set, with the legend, 'Current advertising research says these people are watching your ad. Who's really getting screwed?' Thames Television were so appalled that they withdrew their £5m account with the firm.
>
> (Mattelart 1991: 153)

Mattelart reports that, despite Thames Television's response, the agency won several major contracts following the advertisement. This is an example of rhetoric of the legitimacy of knowledge in which the audience is seen as recalcitrant in advertisers' attempts to measure and package as a target market for clients. For advertisers, the audience can be disturbingly unpredictable, yet the audience is also seen as harbouring 'hidden depths' waiting to be tapped by insightful practitioners and innovative research techniques. For example, the presentation of focus groups[4] by advertising agencies as a sensitive and accurate means of gauging popular opinion (Lury 1989; Nixon 1996) can function as a way of attempting to legitimise advertising industries' 'knowledge' of target groups. In this sense, advertising agencies promote themselves as expert knowledge systems for interpreting and targeting markets.

Celia Lury and Alan Warde (1997) argue that producers of goods are continually in a state of anxiety over generating enough sales, and so turn to advertising agencies in a bid to create new markets or maintain established ones. Yet, Lury and Warde argue, knowledge of the consumer is a highly unstable and contested area – consumer behaviour and motivation can be opaque to both agencies' research and academic analysis. In this way, a space of uncertainty is opened which agencies attempt to occupy. They offer solutions to the effective targeting of consumers and attempt to manipulate 'producer anxiety' over securing markets (Lury and Warde 1997: 91). As agencies occupy a subordinate position of power in relation to their clients who hold the purse strings, they attempt to generate rhetorics of legitimacy for their knowledge. They 'sell themselves', particularly through producing myths of 'scientist modes of measurement and evaluation' (*ibid.*: 93). In this way, Lury and Warde argue against approaches which concentrate solely on advertising's role as providing a means to assuage consumer anxiety[5] over what product to choose by generating a framework for that choice. Instead, they argue that advertising functions to address producer/client anxiety over the efficient targeting of specific markets.

Advertisements can be seen as part of these material processes of production in which advertising agencies' commercial aims of competitive self-promotion are paramount. Yet these material processes are based on imaginative practices – target markets are imagined rather than 'discovered'. In the next sections, I want to broaden this framework of (self-)promotional discourses of legitimacy. I explore the reflexive circulation of knowledges between certain 'sites', namely, the clients/producers, the agencies, the viewers/potential consumers and the magazines in my sample. I approach this through investigating the measurement and evaluation of the viewers/readers (and their promotion as a market). I then consider this in relation to the measurement and promotion of the talents of 'creativity', 'individuality' and 'intuition' of advertisers. In order to examine the rhetoric of advertisers, I use examples from the British advertising trade paper, *Campaign*, during the period of my sample of advertisements (1987–95). I take the analysis of this material as indicative of certain trends in advertising rather than as comprehensively representative of the advertising industry.

Hidden secrets of the insecure client

In a *Campaign* article entitled 'Hidden secrets of the insecure client',[6] the uncertainty and insecurity of agencies is discussed in relation to clients' fickleness when choosing advertising agencies. Here the focus is on agencies' anxiety over the unfathomable decisions of clients. The article asserts that it is common knowledge that there is, at best, a tenuous link between advertising and increased sales. Richard Phillips, then a creative director at the agency J. Walter Thompson, is quoted as saying that a correlation between advertising and commercial success is very difficult to prove. From the article, it seems that this knowledge is shared by the clients, yet they appear to become complicit in rhetorics of legitimacy in this reflexive anxiety management. The article suggests that the key to the motivations of this complicity may in part lie in the need of executives at the client firm to justify their choice of agency (or indeed any agency, rather than in-house advertising) to their immediate bosses and investors, as this would reflect on their own managerial abilities. The article argues that, ironically, this insecurity is displaced onto a foregrounding of the significance of facts and figures generated from research, despite a general scepticism as to their accuracy.

> What a client would really like to say, when asked why he or she chose a certain agency, is: 'I have three filing cabinets full of documents which categorically prove that 17 years of research into the habits of the C2

gerbil means that our new agency is going to make all our shareholders and ourselves very rich the day after tomorrow'.

(Campaign 12 February 1988: 74)

The article goes on to argue that statistics from research are used as an alibi by executives representing the client firm for their 'subjective' decisions because, 'clients just love anything which doesn't make it apparent that all the decisions are subjective' (*ibid.*).

Clearly written from the perspective of the agencies, the article suggests that the base-line for clients' decisions is the impression made by the individuals, generally account managers and planners (Lury 1989), that the clients meet at the agencies. This, it is argued, is an unsaid acknowledgement of what agencies always knew, namely that 'advertising is a "people" business' (*ibid.*: 67). In this rhetoric, 'the individual' is the repository of intuition, imagination, creativity and self-promotional drive and comes to represent the nature of the advertising industry itself. Ideas of measurement are paramount, particularly in respect of the potential of information generated from this measurement to circulate as part of self-legitimising strategies. Clients are presented as difficult to gauge; paradoxically, consumers are seen as both measurable to the skilled interpreter and yet stubbornly opaque. At the same time, the measure of advertisers is located at the individual level in terms of self-presentation or promotion and certain definitions of creative intuition. Ironically, this complicity in knowledge and anxiety management, and the general scepticism about statistics, does not make redundant the perceived value of market research. Instead, the unspoken value of market research is its function as an alibi for clients' 'subjective' choice according of rhetorics of 'individuality'. In effect, these are forms of reflexive processes of measurement in circuits of self-authorisation and promotion. In the following sections I explore how these particular notions of maculinist 'individuality' are implicated in the growth of the new middle classes and cultural intermediaries and their search for self-authorisation and legitimacy. I go on to argue that particular views of individuality and legitimacy come to be incorporated into the textual address of advertising campaigns.

Frank Mort (1996) describes how advertising in Britain developed as a 'people business' in the 1980s, but argues that the 'people' who were allowed access to the most privileged and powerful positions in the industry were overwhelmingly young, male and university-educated. In the 1980s a growing number of humanities and social science graduates were entering advertising and marketing and were facilitating a dissemination of social and cultural theory, notably semiotic analysis, linguistic deconstruction and theories of the structure of post-industrial society (Mort 1996). Mort describes the hugely influential agency Bartle Bogle Hegarty as an 'intellectual voice within the industry' which had acquired 'a powerful reputation for conceptual thinking' (*ibid.*: 107). Most of its members were from 'creative' backgrounds, such as art directors and copywriters, and its creative director

John Hegarty placed a strong emphasis on 'flair', 'creativity' and 'attitude' (*ibid.*). Hegarty wanted to recruit 'new young people' who would foster innovation, and when interviewing prospective employees would always pose himself the questions, 'Is he our sort of person?', and 'Does this man have our standards?' (*ibid.*: 108). This gendered approach was not merely rhetoric-based, Mort argues, for the agencies had a very strong, structurally masculinist ethos. Women accounted for almost half of all employees in the advertising industry in the 1980s, yet comprised only 14 per cent of the membership of the boards of directors (*ibid.*). On one level, this exclusion operated through the working practices of the agencies: movement up the career ladder in part depended on a commitment to very long working hours and out-of-hours socialising and networking. Many women were unable to engage in such practices due to family commitments, or were unwilling to participate. Such practices were based on, and consolidated, informal working networks through which privileged inclusivity was fostered and important decisions made (*ibid.*). On another level, the very qualities of creativity, imagination and flair which were so highly valued were always already implicated in notions of 'male creative genius' (*ibid.*: 117), based on what Christine Battersby (1989) has called the aesthetics of virility. This masculinist definition of creativity was fostered through the fields of art and design education, which, in turn, were the chief recruitment pools for creative teams at agencies (Mort 1996). So, despite the rapid growth in the industry during the 1980s, women's position did not improve due to this structural bias, and indeed it was in the area of the creative departments of art direction and copywriting that women made least progress at all levels (*ibid.*).

Crucially, it was this creative area that was growing in importance, particularly since the widespread establishment of account planning (Lury 1989). Account planning integrated various financial, planning and creative aspects of advertising work, and the highlighted significance of 'creativity' fostered in advertisers an idea of adverts as 'artefacts, as abstract things' (*ibid.*: 18). This focus on creativity gave advertisers a new abstracted view of adverts as artwork, 'because you are viewing this communication really as entertainment rather than as something that will persuade you to change your habits' (Fletcher, cited in Lury 1989: 18). Yet, as Mort (1996) argues, this notion of creativity was strongly masculinist and produced an environment in which advertising *men* came to see themselves as 'style leaders', who were 'at the cutting edge of cultural as well as artistic change' (*ibid.*: 118). In the following sections, I explore how this structural stress on (masculinist) 'individuality', creativity and innovation operates in relation to specific legitimating strategies in advertising around the 'knowledge' of the market linked to the 'new middle classes'.

'New individualism': *savoir faire* and legitimacy

In a *Campaign* article (11 September 1987: 55–7) entitled 'Blueprint for a New Consumer', it is suggested that 'the era of adman as manipulator is coming to an end'. The article argues for the existence of a new media-literate consumer resistant to blatant 'manipulation', and outlines diverse agencies' competing rhetorics of what is seen as the measurement, understanding and targeting of this new consumer. The article draws on the agency Ogilvy and Mather's survey called 'Project Badge' based on group discussions with four generations growing up in Britain in the 1950s, 1960s, 1970s and 1980s. The 1987 findings of this survey mirror ideas which have since been widely discussed in academic circles[7] namely discourses of risk, the distrust of information received from authority figures and the sophistication of viewers of advertisements:

- Consumers have experienced increasing insecurity as the growth in living standards and the quality of life generally have come under attack.
- There has been the breakdown in the trust of external values and authority figures (a church leader was considered less trustworthy than Persil, according to one of those interviewed).
- Consumers have become far more visually sophisticated and aware that they are being manipulated by the media.

(Campaign 11 September 1987: 56)

The article maps how these results are interpreted differently by competing agencies in bids to claim legitimacy for their 'expert knowledges'. Ogilvy and Mather, who commissioned the survey, argue that the 'hard sell' is no longer appropriate for what they call the critical and discerning 'New Individualists' who do not want to be manipulated through stereotypical campaign addresses. In their view, the New Individual, as instanced in one of their shampoo adverts, is about 'expressing herself, becoming someone, being herself and choosing the brand to do it' (*ibid.*). They argue that advertising should present an address based on emotional 'fit' with the sensibilities of the potential consumer rather than an 'overt' attempt at manipulation.

In contrast, the agency J. Walter Thompson distances itself from what it says is a totalising rhetoric of 'New Individualism' and instead claims more efficiency in specific target marketing. The Henley Centre for Forecasting agrees with some aspects of Ogilvy and Mather's analysis of individuality, but focuses more forcefully on the anxiety involved in decision-making and the potential this offers advertising:

People want to keep apart from the Jones's … . It's the savvy society. People want to be seen to be clever. For the wide boy, that's savvy, for the middle class, it's *savoir faire* ... . People didn't have to think about it at all when authority knew best. ... But now they are more anxious than ever before, they are disoriented, they are being told everything can be questioned. There is so much to know, so much choice, so many pressures to feel accomplished in any field that there is an opportunity for brands to come in and solve people's problems.

(*Campaign* 11 September 1987: 56)

Here, the Henley Centre for Forecasting is presenting its capacities as a form of expert knowledge in tune with shifting attitudes which can address clients' anxiety about 'reaching' the market.

All these self-promotional advertising pitches attempt to distance themselves from 'old-fashioned manipulation' and instead emphasise the savviness of the media-literate and sceptical viewer. With this emphasis on the recalcitrant target market, the agencies are presenting to clients the necessity of their own savvy skills at targeting the market through being 'in tune' with assumed new formations of individuality. In these discourses of the ability to measure proposed new forms of individuality, advertisers claim a status of 'cultural intermediaries' in touch with both the working-class aspirations for 'savviness' and the middle-class aspirations for '*savoir faire*'. Advertisers are promoting their potential as intermediaries, or the *new* middle class, on the cutting edge of innovation, both in terms of their supposed capacities for mapping and interpreting cultural shifts and in terms of innovative forms of advertising address.

Mike Featherstone (1991) ties the emergence of 'the new middle classes' to that of 'cultural intermediaries'.[8] He argues that these intermediaries deal in symbolic goods and services and proliferate in, what I see as, the self-promotional areas of advertising, marketing and public relations: among them radio and television producers and presenters, magazine writers and the helping professions, for example, social workers, dieticians and marriage counsellors:

The emergence and expansion of sectors of the new middle class ... creates not only specialists in symbolic production and dissemination but also a potential audience that may be more sensitive and attuned to the range of cultural and symbolic goods and experiences that have been labelled postmodern.

(Featherstone 1991: 35)

They have emerged from the lower sections of society and so do not hold the established class status and privilege of the upper and established middle classes. Due to this insecurity, they must continually strive for self-authorisation and legitimacy, and attempt this through claiming an innovative, flexible style and attitude; they cultivate and disseminate ideas of 'lifestyle' and are in pursuit of 'new values and vocabularies' with a focus on 'choices not rules' (Featherstone 1991: 48):

> Theirs is a lifestyle which focuses very much on identity, appearance, presentation of self, fashion, design, decor; and considerable time and effort have to be expended in cultivating a sense of taste which is flexible, distinctive and capable of keeping abreast of the plethora of new styles, experiences and symbolic goods which consumer culture industries continue to generate.
>
> (Featherstone 1991: 108–9)

Featherstone sees a symbiotic relation between members of the new middle classes and a particular segment called cultural intermediaries, which reflexively re-presents and shifts ideas of the nature of individuality. In France a similar segment of *'jeune cadres'* [young executives] has developed through the 1950s to the present (Ross 1995). As in Featherstone's account, the *'jeunes cadres'* aspire to social mobility through the development of specific skills which require a 'sustained level of mental flexibility and psychological adaptability' (*ibid.*: 171). They are 'ideologically homeless' in that they have moved beyond working- and lower-class aspirations and jobs, but have not yet achieved a secure middle-/upper-middle-class status (*ibid.*). In Britain and France these cultural intermediaries are both artistic and cultural innovators and part of the new middle classes which form 'the audience'. As in the case of advertising agencies, cultural intermediaries in general reflexively incorporate a (masculinist, 'creative', innovative) image of their own aspirations and capacities which they claim to hold.

Featherstone's account of the rise and expansion of the new middle classes is wide-ranging and speculative. Critics have argued that the 'new' middle class has been around rather a long time, and, whilst the middle class is indeed fractured, specific consumer practices cannot be mapped onto segments of the middle class in a consistent pattern (see Longhurst and Savage 1996). My concern in these debates is less to chart the relationship between class and consumer practices than to consider the use by advertisers of a *rhetoric* of 'new' class fractions and cultural intermediaries. Individuals in agencies promote themselves as cultural intermediaries who can deliver expert knowledges of the ever-changing formulations of individuality. In doing so, individuals in advertising actively generate *in their image* a notion of the existence and expansion of the new middle classes. This imagined (although not necessarily imaginary) category of 'new middle classes', along with advertising agencies themselves, are seen to be trying to incorporate the residual working-class values of a street-wise 'savviness' together with new middle-class aspirations for a more culturally valued and sophisticated *'savoir faire'*. As I argue in later chapters in relation to irony in adverts, this image becomes reflexively incorporated into campaigns and disseminated as material from which viewers may indeed interpret themselves as innovative, flexible members of the new middle classes.

This uncertainty and anxiety over the measurement and legitimacy of the consumers can be seen to operate simultaneously on multiple levels; that of clients' anxiety over targeting the market, anxiety on the part of agencies attempting to predict the decisions of their unfathomable clients, on the level of magazines attempting to sell advertising space to agencies through 'delivering' pre-packaged target markets, and also on the level of middle-class consumers confronted with a vast array of choices from which to make the correct, self-validating, self-authorising choice. This is not to fully accept the interpretations of Oglivy and Mather's study, which argue that consumers are desperately in need of advice as to how to deal with consumer choice. Rather, I want to consider the issue in terms of a reflexive production of 'attitude'.

Bauman (1990) argues that the contemporary configuration of discourses on individuality and consumption combine to produce what he calls 'the consumer attitude'. This is an attitude through which life is seen as a series of problems to be solved, and hence can be anxiety-provoking in the face of a vast array of choices on offer. Expert knowledges such as advertising, Bauman argues, present a framework within which to make informed choices and so assuage anxiety. I want to suggest that this notion of a frame-work of 'attitude' and promotional, saleable capacities to negotiate the levels of knowledge are implicated on the four levels I indicated above. This notion of attitude is manifested through agencies' rhetoric of an attitude of flexi-bility and innovation which will be in touch with the cultural shifts, and on the part of executives of the client firm who adopt a flexible, calculated atti-tude towards the legitimacy of data in decision-making. Magazines, as I will discuss later, adopt an attitude similar to the agencies in their bid to sell their opinion-forming and target-market-forming capacities to the agencies. For (certain) consumers, the resulting framework for choice management offers a flexible notion of control which may detach the consumption of images of advertisements from the purchase and consumption of branded goods. If this can be seen as a 'consumer attitude', then it is an attitude involving self-control and a manipulation of the notion of 'choice' – this is a self-reflexive narrative of the capacities and potential of the self.

In the following section, I examine the institutional production of the consumer target market of 'youth'. Here, youth becomes detached from the characteristic of age, producing youth as an *attitude*. I have chosen to focus on youth, as the magazines *Q*, *Elle* and *Première* in my study target a market which can be seen in terms of differing definitions of 'youth'.[9] I consider how this production of youth as 'attitude' takes place and the way in which such an attitude is reflexively incorporated by agencies into their campaigns.

Youth is wasted on the young: attitude and innovation

The category of 'youth' as a target market is highly significant in the structuring of the magazines *Q*, *Première* and *Elle* in my study. As an imagined
demographic, it delivers to magazines considerable revenue from selling
advertising space to agencies targeting that market. I want to explore how
the strategic manipulation and marketing of the category 'youth' in terms of
innovation is related to agencies' self-legitimising rhetorics around their role
as new middle-class cultural intermediaries.

In academic debate, studies of youth culture have mapped the development of the category 'youth' as 'audience' in relation to media policy. Simon
Frith (1993) argues that during the 1980s a new alliance of television, the
music industry and global advertisers framed 'youth' as a pop audience. This
packaging of the category 'youth' meant that the music industry could claim
a position as an expert knowledge system which could 'deliver' the audience
to advertisers as a coherent market (Frith 1993). Frith argues that in this
way, 'youth' as a category became detached from age, for 'those people of
whatever age or circumstance who watched "youth" programmes became
youth' (1993: 75). Youth became disengaged from social status and was
articulated as an *attitude*; '"Youth" no longer described a particular type of
viewer, who is attracted to a particular type of programme but, rather,
describes an attitude, a particular type of *viewing behaviour*' (Frith 1993: 75).

In the advertising rhetoric played out in *Campaign* magazine, the age
range of the category of 'youth' varies widely between 15 and 24 (*Campaign*
13 May 1988: 26) and 16 and 34 (*Campaign* 29 September 1995: 13). 'Youth'
is seen as a difficult market to reach consistently, as its members are 'notori-
ously fickle' and have 'eclectic tastes in media' (*Campaign* 29 September
1995: 13). Advertisers and television producers appear to address this
problem by detaching 'youth' from age and therefore enabling an approach
which can mould and form tastes. An executive from the youth-music station
MTV is quoted as saying 'It's not about age but about attitude. ... Our
viewers have similar attitudes and lifestyles' (*Campaign* 29 September 1995:
13). In another article, Stephen Garrett from Channel Four argues that the
'youth' audience is an arbitrary group 'better characterised by an attitude of
mind; a curiosity, a thirst for knowledge and a search for the new' (*Campaign*
13 May 1988: 26). From the point of view of the advertisers, this article
concludes that traditional 'youth marketing seems to rely on an old-fashioned notion of youth as a discrete group which has communal interests
simply because of age' (*ibid.*). In fact, this article suggests the existence of a
fraction of 'youth' which is seen as 'ex-teenagers' and occupies the age
bracket 25–45. The significance of this rather elastic approach to age may be
a device for accurately measuring a lucrative market: in the eyes of advertisers, 25–45-year-olds have a well-documented track record of purchasing
tastes, and hence can be more easily tracked and targeted. In the 1988 article,
this idea of 'youth' presents the group as highly sophisticated with more

disposable income than ever before, and hence as a highly lucrative group willing to spend and exercise their 'curiosity' in a 'search for the new'. I would argue that the 25–45-year-old 'ex-teenagers' who focus on lifestyle and strive for innovation and knowledge and can be accurately seen as the new middle-class advertisers in their role as cultural intermediaries. They self-reflexively present narratives of their innovative and flexible capacities and align them with a lucrative imagined target market.

The advertising rhetoric in *Campaign* argues that new notions of 'youth' as 'attitude' are detached from all social categories, yet Frank Mort (1996) traces how these formations are structurally gendered. Ideas around television audiences and magazine readerships are intimately linked, for, as Mort argues, the success of the music magazine *Q*, which was launched in 1986, provided the touchstone for the development of the music television programmes in the 1980s.[10] It proved that music could be framed as a youth interest, and so would deliver a target market. Yet, Mort argues, this market was always already targeted as gendered, because *Q* was marketed to advertisers as a means for tapping into a young *male* market. *The Face, Arena*, and *GQ* had already created a self-consciously male target group, yet this self-consciousness was seen by advertisers and magazine editors to sit uneasily with the way men wanted to address an idea of their masculinity (Mort 1996). *Q* was to deliver to advertisers a male target market which could be framed as a music interest group in order to take into account the sensibilities male consumers (*ibid.*). Indeed, the media pack produced by *Q*, which is designed to sell the readership to advertisers as a market, refers to *Q* as 'the UK's most popular men's magazine', in which 'our witty and provocative style … has made us the dominant force in the men's magazine market today'. Music is presented as the root to this market; 'It's a fact that music is closer to men's hearts than almost any other subject'. This statement is made very forcefully, despite the readership figures presented later in the pack which state that over a quarter of all readers are female.

Mort (1996) argues that in the 1980s, ideas in advertising strategies shifted towards a notion of 'taste leadership' of certain segments of society. This, Mort indicates (and I have suggested earlier) positions 'creative' individuals in advertising as capable of tuning into innovative shifts in target-market tastes. The above conception of the innovative section of the population called 'youth' as masculine articulates with a masculine positioning of the creativity of agencies. This notion of agencies' qualities of innovation, imagination and taste leadership is projected back reflexively to the agencies by the media packs produced by the magazines. The magazines present their readership in terms of a lucrative market of 'style leaders', 'early adopters' and 'opinion formers' – precisely the way in which the agencies promote themselves to clients. This position of innovation, imagination and creativity is framed in terms of 'attitude', which can flexibly capture the working-class ideal of 'savviness' and the middle-class ideal of 'savoir faire'.

In this chapter, I have attempted to show that far from being 'immaterial' or mere 'representations' of the real issues in consumer capitalism, advertising images are material products. They are part of the circuit of production and consumption within which the imagination as a social practice plays an important role. Agencies have an imperative to demonstrate to potential clients their ability to effectively target and 'deliver' specific markets. In this self-promotional drive, agencies do not merely identify consumer markets; they actively select, segment and rework ideals of their imagined target market – markets are made, not born. In turn, agencies incorporate their imagined ideal of the market into the textual address of the advertising campaign they produce. This textual address is designed to 'speak to' specific sections of society and functions to offer viewers ways of understanding and redefining themselves. Through forms of textual address, advertising campaigns can materialise the social categories of consumers that they name. In effect, the imagination can be a social practice with social consequences.

In the next chapter, I explore the textual strategies employed by agencies in targeting advertising campaigns at particular market segments that they have 'imagined'. Through the address of specific campaigns, I explore the ways in which the 'attitude' produced through agencies is made available to certain men. A central concern of this chapter will be to problematise the differing availability of the structurally defined positions from which to convert social positioning into detached 'attitude'.

3 Advertising, texts and textual strategies

In the previous chapter I argued that consumer markets are not social facts which can be 'discovered' and targeted – they are generated or materialised in the very processes of marketing and advertising. I argued that the characteristics of these 'imagined' target markets come to be reflexively incorporated into the textual address of advertising campaigns. In this chapter my concern is to compare the forms of textual address found in female-targeted advertisements and in male-targeted advertisements. How is meaning created in a print advertisement? How is this meaning targeted at specific groups? How should we analyse images of gender in advertising?

Images of gender have long been the focus of feminist work. Early feminist studies were concerned with challenging the 'misrepresentations' or stereotypes of women in images. Across a range of sites, such as pornography, advertising, film and art, feminists aimed to set right 'inaccurate' or false images of women (van Zoonen 1994). Yet such critiques risked relegating women to the position of dupes seduced into accepting 'false' images of a 'natural' femininity. Such an approach immediately forecloses questions of female agency and subjectivity, and relegates women to a position of passivity whilst reifying a homogenised category of 'women'. This tendency is present in a range of analyses of consumerism and advertising. Many accounts of advertising emphasise notions of alienated, commodified identities and a 'pseudo-individuality' (Goldman 1992) divorced from an 'authentic' self. In accounts such as those of Haug (1986), Dyer (1992), Goldman (1992) and Williamson (1978), the logic of commodity aesthetics disrupts what are seen as the intimate relations between genuine needs and material use-value. Through processes of abstraction and alienation, exchange-value comes to displace use-value as the primary mode of relating to produced objects. In these accounts there is a sense of a loss of particular values in the relations between the production and consumption of goods through commodification. In analyses such as Dyer's (1992), 'false consciousness' resulting from the operation of ideology masks true capitalist relations of production, exchange and consumption. Human relations come to be defined in terms of the exchange of goods which abstracts human labour value from those processes through a 'privatizing discourse of consumer desire' (Goldman 1992: 14). Advertising is seen as 'the manipulation of social values and attitudes' (Dyer 1992: 2) through which 'false' needs and desires are disseminated with the aim of regenerating desire for the consumption of an ever-increasing volume and diversity of goods. In Judith Williamson's (1978) combination of a semiotic and a psychoanalytic approach, advertising is seen to tap into individuals' psychological depths and compel them to identify with what they consume. Within this framework, the representation of women in advertising is often seen as emblematic of more general processes of alienation and objectification (see Goldman 1992). 'False' images of women are thought to symbolise the manipulative ideology of capitalism.

Yet other feminist work has approached the gendering of images in different ways. Griselda Pollock's (1992) work on art has shifted the focus away from an 'images-of-women' approach to an analysis of gendered, embodied viewing and painting practices. Pollock argues that the referencing of masculinity in paintings occurs not only in the depiction of female bodies framed by the male artistic gaze. Even in abstract expressionist art, which depicts no human form, the 'purity of the visual signifier, seemingly emptied of all reference to a social or natural world, is still loaded with significance through its function as affirmation of its artistic subject' (Pollock 1992: 142). The combination of the creative gesture in painting and the trace of the creating subject 'secure by metonymy the presence of the artist' (*ibid.*). Underpinned by the 'bourgeois mythologies of the self-possessing and self-realizing individual', gender structures the very terms of the visual (*ibid.*: 144).

Following these insights, it is possible to approach gender in advertising in a multilevel way. A focus on stereotypes of women, false images of women or 'objectifying' images is only part of the story. In the sections and chapters which follow, I explore how the forms of textual address in advertising images connect with the ideal of the 'self-possessive individual' which I introduced in Chapter 1. What form of 'creative gesture' inheres in the practice of viewing images? How do the rights of 'the individual' frame the forms of knowledge produced in viewing advertisements? The next section explores methods of analysing texts and presents ways of considering gendered textual address.

Magazine advertising: methods of analysis

The original aim of this study was a comparative analysis of gender and national identity in advertisements. As I explore in later sections, the focus of the study shifted during the analysis from an 'images-of-nation' approach to an analysis of European visual rights or 'visual epistemologies'. At the outset, I selected print advertising in French and British popular magazines as the site of my analysis because this form of advertising provides a good indicator of changes in advertising in general (Leiss *et al.* 1990). Magazine advertising is a communication form which is very open to influences from other media and, due to the form of magazines' distributive circulation, is a prime site for national advertising (*ibid.*), allowing for a comparative analysis between Britain and France. For comparative purposes, I decided to select magazines with differing target markets. I focused on three French and three British popular (colour) magazines, including a glossy women's magazine, a popular culture/'youth' magazine, and a current affairs/business magazine. I chose *Elle, Première* and *L'Expansion*, selecting the nearest British equivalents as *Elle, Q,* and *The Economist*. These are not direct equivalents, as the French media market divides up its target markets of readers along different lines from the British media. *Elle* is a transnational publication with slight national editorial variations in the same vein as other magazines such as *Marie Claire* and *Cosmopolitan*. The media pack produced for potential advertisers states that *Elle's* readership is primarily 'young' (69.2 per cent are between 15 and 34) and have considerable spending power. The British and French editions draw on a very similar range of product advertisements, such as cosmetics and perfume, yet vary in terms of 'local' products, such as food and services. The French *Première* is a youth-targeted cinema and music magazine, drawing on advertising from a wide range of products including clothes, alcohol and cigarettes. I decided against the British edition of *Première* as a comparison, as its advertising focused almost exclusively on cinema and music products. In its place, I selected the youth-targeted music magazine *Q*, as its range of advertising reflected more accurately the range of products found in the French *Première*. *L'Expansion* is a business/current affairs magazine, and I selected *The Economist* as its nearest British model whose target market of readers is primarily middle-class, affluent businessmen. *The Economist's* media pack states that its readership is predominantly male (91 per cent), aged 35–55+ (80 per cent), university educated (86 per cent) and high earning (only 9 per cent earn less than £20,000 p.a.; average personal income is £68,000 p.a.).

Using a pilot study, I aimed to develop the most suitable methods of coding and analysing the main sample of advertisements. At this stage I focused on Leiss *et al.*'s (1990) combined qualitative and quantitative analysis, which I discuss in later sections of this chapter in more depth. I selected only French advertising, randomly sampling the April editions of the three magazines from the years 1988, 1991 and 1995, making a total of nine magazines. I developed three successive coding and interpretative frameworks in an attempt to integrate a systematic and comparative analysis with the sensitivity of a qualitative analysis. In the first analysis of the pilot study sample of advertisements, I divided the sample into three 'genres': first, branded commodities (with sub-divisions of cosmetics/perfumes, clothes, cars, cigarettes/tobacco, alcohol, accessories, computers, media products, sports equipment); second, services (insurance companies, tourist companies); and third, corporate advertising (promotion of corporate awareness, for example, regional councils promoting their area for tourism/business).

I charted the variables of product type, placement magazine, date, size (single page or double), images of social difference ('race', gender, ethnicity, class, nation) and ratio of visuals to written text.[1]

From an initial analysis of the sample I noted the presence of ironic or self-conscious forms of address in adverts. These drew my attention, as they were visually striking or puzzling in the same way as some forms of modern art. Yet advertising is not conventionally understood as art, and I was interested in the way that these ironic adverts reflexively drew attention to their status *as advertising*. I saw this as an emphasis on the self-consciously 'fabricated' or 'artificial' which ran counter to an emphasis on 'authenticity' and 'natural needs and desires' which underpins many academic accounts of advertising. I produced a working definition of 'reflexive' adverts as those which incorporate a self-consciousness as to their intertextual composition of signifiers. They draw attention to the way in which they were put together in a collage from multiple sources, and they display this to the viewer. In effect, these adverts are explicit about their position in popular culture and offer viewers a complicity in this knowledge. Irony was a frequent feature of this form of address in the sample adverts, typically drawing together signifiers of social difference in discordant formations, or configurations not conventionally recognised in the discourses of popular culture. This use of an ironic or knowing visual address, which I discuss more fully in Chapter 4, explicitly signals the *activity* on the part of the viewer in producing meaning. This is contrasted with other approaches which assume a static or literal location of meaning generated purely within and through the text. Distinctively, a reflexive address refers to intertextual popular culture signifiers and actively incorporates an assumption of the viewer's knowledge and competencies in situating and mobilising these signifiers. In effect, this *visualises* the articulation between advertising and popular culture and the relation between viewer, text and social context.

The results of my codings and charting of the intersections of variables was a highly intricate mapping of difference. The complexity of the patternings militated against my initial aim of systematising the data through Leiss *et al.*'s (1990) codings. In effect, this first coding produced nothing more systematic than an impression of diversity. Yet, through the codings of ironic/literal, I did identify what I saw as advertisers' attempts to anchor certain meanings to the production of certain target markets. This targeting, which simultaneously produced these markets as 'knowable', was particularly evident in terms of gender, class, 'race' and nationality. As I discuss in later sections, I found that adverts targeted at women were significantly less 'reflexive' than those targeted at men or a supposedly undifferentiated 'youth' market. Wanting to hold on to these insights and to develop a more systematic approach, I decided to alter the framework of the coding and analysis to parallel more closely Leiss *et al.*'s (1990) categories. I drew on Leiss *et al.*'s framework, which focused on the terms of viewer address rather than the specific type of product or specific representation of social difference. I imagined that this would enable a development of my interest in the literal/ironic address at the same time as allowing for a more systematic treatment of the codes. This framework has four formats, namely, the product-information format, the product-image format, the personalised format and the lifestyle format. I also coded the adverts in terms of 'literal' or 'reflexive' address and their representations of social difference. I attempted to code the pilot sample of adverts exclusively within these categories, but the boundaries of the categories were recalcitrantly more fluid than those which appeared in Leiss *et al.*'s (1990) study. I could not meaningfully separate certain adverts along the lines imposed by the framework, and I became increasingly aware of the *relative* and shifting nature of the form of address linked to images of specific differences. The four formats overlapped, shifted in relation to one another, and mobilised varying images of social difference in different codings. In respect of this fluidity, I also came to see the significance of the data as primarily qualitative rather than quantitative, as the analysis suggested complex interrelations between codes rather than broadly quantifiable, fixed 'results'. I felt that I could map these shifts most sensitively through a detailed qualitative analysis of certain forms of address, and so developed a third analytic approach to the pilot sample which I subsequently carried over into the main sample.

This third framework focused on dividing the sample according to the form of address and images of social difference and engaging in a detailed mapping of the specific textual devices used to produce meanings. This approach generated interesting readings of the textual cues which offer viewers interpretative positionings, including the unusual juxtaposition of signifiers and explicit intertextual references. The themes of individuality, choice and temporality which were generated in this analysis resonated with ideas I had come across in the literature on potential, choice and the constitution of 'the individual' in contract theory. I found these issues of particular interest as they challenged notions of 'authentic', atemporal selfhood and addressed the structurally political and hierarchical nature of the constitution of 'the individual'.

Satisfied that this framework was providing an approach sensitive to complex interrelations of codes, I set about collecting my main sample of adverts. I collected the sample from the six magazine titles discussed above between 1987 and 1995. I collected a sample of 135 French and 135 British adverts, totalling 270. I then coded the entire sample, according to my definitions of 'reflexivity', producing three primary categories: 'reflexive' adverts, 'unreflexive' adverts which included images of social difference, and 'reject' adverts which did not fall into either category. This coding enab- led me to chart the relation of images of social difference to 'reflexive/ unreflexive' forms of address, eliminating purely 'informational' adverts – for example, notice of sales promotions.[2]

Using this framework, I developed an analysis which integrated three levels of knowledge-production: a textual analysis of the production of meaning in adverts; an analysis of the advertising industry's operations in generating specific target markets, together with magazines' promotion of advertising space to advertisers; and an analysis of the implication of the viewer in the production of meaning. Through this combinatory approach, I was able to explore the relations between the levels. I examined how the advertising industry's imperative for the delimitation, and simultaneous production, of target markets of potential consumers related to the forms of textual address in specific adverts. These forms of address mediated the circulation of knowledge of the market between advertisers, producers and magazines, as discussed in the previous chapter. I could also explore how branded products or certain image combinations were not intrinsically gendered, 'racialised' or classed. Rather, these values were produced relationally in mobile formations which nonetheless reproduced forms of hierarchy. This coding framework enabled me to explore how these processes of dislocating and relocating the terms of relationality are tied to processes of vision and the printed image. Furthermore, I was able to theorise how the political constitution of 'the individual' operates as a framing matrix in these movements. Through this combination of analyses, I map out how 'the cultural' is implicated in conventional 'political' articulations of citizenship rights and belonging.

These modes of interpretation actively altered the terms of the research questions I had initially formulated. My interest shifted from charting stereotypes of women or gender roles to an analysis of gendered textual address and viewing positions. Also, my initial research questions had focused heavily on nation as pivotal site of difference. This is unsurprising, for, as Featherstone (1990) points out, sociological theory developed its critical framework taking the Western nation-state as foundational unit of analysis. The results of my coding of the main sample of advertising indeed revealed representations of nation, such as France, Britain and Germany. Yet they also highlighted the production of an ideal of Europeanness in opposition to non-European 'others'. I became more interested in the constitution of shifting ideas of 'Europe' and in the Eurocentric, exclusive constitution of the category of 'the individual'. This shift away from a rather formulaic notion of 'the nation' as foundational, albeit 'constructed', category altered the terms of my focus on national and transnational advertising, and I became less interested in the 'local/global' questions. For example, the question of the threat of homogenisation through America's supposed cultural imperialism appeared to re-produce a specific notion of the pre-eminence of 'the nation'. This theoretical insight prompted me to focus less on a comparative study between Britain and France – indeed, I found fewer differences than similarities in French and British advertising. Instead, I began to focus on the contested and multiple terms of 'culture': the idea of 'a national culture' (generally seen as coterminous with 'the nation'), culture as creative art-forms, and a notion of a specifically 'European cultural heritage' of democracy and 'civilisation'. As I argue in later chapters, such a shift of emphasis facilitates different insights into discourses of 'cultural belonging' and can chart the shifting relations between advertising, consumerism and citizenship.

Findings of the analysis

This section presents the findings of my analysis of the sample of advertisements and offers interpretative approaches to textual analysis. The small size of the sample, and the complications in comparative analysis between the British and French magazines and advertisements make me cautious about making general claims. However, my quantitative findings are strongly suggestive of certain trends in the advertising industry's textual strategies of viewer address and target marketing, and the use of specific images of difference. I explore these trends in the context of shifts in individual and group notions of identity and cultural belonging, and discuss what role advertising images play in these shifting discourses.

A total of 270 advertisements were randomly sampled from the British magazines *The Economist*, *Elle*, and *Q*, and the French magazines *L'Expansion*, *Elle* and *Première* In line with motivations I discussed in the previous section, I coded those advertisements which included images of social difference according to the categories 'reflexive' and 'non-reflexive' and a separate category for those which did not fit into the framework. I also charted the range of product type,[3] date and target market in relation to the placement magazine. In relation to these specific magazines, I identified the chief target markets of female, male and 'undifferentiated youth' through their form of address linked to the images of social identities mobilised. I have excluded the date of the adverts, as the sample showed no increase or decrease in frequency of unreflexive or reflexive adverts over the sampling period of 1987 to 1995 (see Appendix for a chart of the results). The primary conclusion that I drew from this mapping of target audiences was that neither the modes of address, nor the product types can be seen as intrinsically gendered – they must be examined through frameworks of the continual re-production of specifically gendered, classed and racialised target markets. The categories of 'reflexive' and 'unreflexive', and advertisers' strategic mobilisation of them, are relational rather than absolute categories, and rely for their meaning on the shifting definitions of social differences.

The advertisements in the 'reject' category were drawn in large part from the business/current affairs magazines *The Economist* and *L'Expansion* and used an 'unreflexive' form of address which did not incorporate images of social difference. For example, the advertisements primarily promote financial/corporate services, computer/office equipment and business travel services in a way which presented 'information'. In terms of the reflexive adverts, the product types were evenly distributed between the British and French adverts and gendered target markets, and comprised chiefly cars, toiletries, tobacco, alcohol, clothes/shoes, accessories (bags, etc.) in equal proportions. The small size of the reflexive sample makes it unfeasible to draw statistical conclusions about shifts in numbers of 'unreflexive' and 'reflexive' advertisements. However, the cultural significance of reflexive advertisements and their relation to definitions of 'unreflexive' advertisements (and their associated target markets of consumers) cannot be assumed to remain static. In later sections I will argue that the quantitative content analysis results from the sample are indicative of trends in shifting social meanings and can be usefully examined in order to map out the operation of discourses of belonging, rights, gender, 'race' and class.

As with the reflexive advertisements, there was no significant shift in numbers of unreflexive advertisements during the period 1987 to 1995. The product types, however, varied significantly according to gendered target market and the choice of gendered magazine for the placement of the advertisement. There were some products which remained relatively stable in their equal proportion of gender targeting, such as tobacco and accessories, but the main body of product type was polarised. The predominantly female-targeted advertisements were for cosmetics/perfume, clothes/shoes and various products such as painkillers, food, furniture, and were placed chiefly in the British and French *Elle* magazines. The unreflexive advertisements targeted at men were predominantly business-oriented, such as business travel/hotels, computers/telephone services, business services, corporate profiles of companies, plus some personal accessories. These advertisements were overwhelmingly placed in the business/current affairs magazines *The Economist* and *L'Expansion*. I will go on to discuss the significance of this division of unreflexive textual address, product type and gendered target market in the following section, along with comments on what I consider to be the key themes to be drawn from the data.

Images and social difference

The general findings of the analysis of the sample indicate a significant division in the use of reflexive advertisements to target men and women: there was almost double the number of male-targeted reflexive adverts in relation to female-targeted adverts. The 'raw' total of 'unreflexive' advertisements is much more evenly distributed between male and female target markets: 70 female and 64 male. However, the profile of the readership of the magazines they are placed in, together with linkages between modes of textual address and images of social difference produce significant gendered divisions within the 'unreflexive' category. The 'undifferentiated youth' category was heavily situated in the French magazines, highlighting French modes for delimiting target markets different to those exhibited in the British magazines which I discussed in Chapter 2. In later chapters I analyse the supposedly gender- and 'race'-neutral address of these adverts and argue that there is indeed implicit positioning and legitimising in this address.

As indicated above, the largest proportion of male-targeted unreflexive advertisements are in the business magazines *The Economist* and *L'Expansion*. As well as the business advertisements, there is a significant number of advertisements for personal accessories, which comprise a very stable core of products – chiefly watches, pens and cars. These products are associated in the texts with the display and re-production of a socially identifiable 'identity' (of class status, taste and wealth). *The Economist*'s media pack, which is produced for potential advertisers, presents its readership as one of 'outstanding quality in terms of corporate decision-making power, political influence and personal wealth'. The pack states that the majority of *The Economist*'s readers are male (91 per cent), have a university education, and in terms of age are in 'the dynamic middle years' (35–55+).

The above product types also appear in the male-targeted reflexive advertisements, but the images of social difference and 'status' and reflexive textual address are remarkably different. The accessories in the unreflexive advertisements are presented as conventional 'status symbols' tied to notions of tradition, exclusivity, craftsmanship and prestige. These codes evoke historically established hierarchies of social difference and offer a range of white and middle-/upper-class masculinities. The production of these masculinities is mediated through a fairly uniform mobilisation of images of upper-/middle-class masculinity, as well as images of national/European difference and historical tradition. The products mediated through these images of difference are presented as objects to be purchased and consumed as visible indicators of already existent social standing and wealth of the middle- and upper-class readership of those magazines.

In contrast, the accessories in the male-targeted reflexive advertisements are presented through a mode of address which offers images of social difference in unconventional configurations. The readership of the magazines in which reflexive advertisements predominate is chiefly male and young. This is a social group which does not conventionally hold the same social and financial standing as the established businessmen of the readership of the magazines in which an unreflexive address predominates. The media pack for *Q* magazine presents its readership as male (72 per cent), predominantly aged 15–34, and middle- or lower-middle-class. The 'status' offered by advertisements of the same product types as in *The Economist* and *L'Expansion* in comparison with *Q* and *Première* is presented in a significantly different manner. Readers of the young, male-targeted *Q* magazine are invited to engage in a process of rearticulating images of difference in an active, ever-shifting visual process. The images of social differences which mediate this meaning-production are predominantly those of national/ European difference, 'the exotic', masculinity and class, and 'youth' and national/European difference. The theme of active self-actualisation in relation to these differences will be taken up in later sections of this chapter and discussed in conjunction with gendered textual strategies for ironic address.

The 'unreflexive' category can be further segmented by examining product types in *Première* and *Q*, which are ostensibly addressed at a male market but in fact are actively targeted by advertisers at women. For example, aftershave advertisements are primarily targeted not at men, but at women – women account for the largest proportion of aftershave sales, because they purchase all their partner's/brother's/father's clothes and accessories either routinely or as presents for them. This division is shifting in advertising as young men are increasingly being addressed in terms of their masculinities. These masculinities are often presented as consumer projects to be worked upon rather than as fixed social identities taken for granted (Mort 1996; Nixon 1996).

The number of reflexive advertisements targeted at women (9) is strongly contrasted with the number of unreflexive advertisements (70). The self-actualisation, or identity re-production, in these unreflexive advertisements is offered in a form radically different from that of the reflexive and unreflexive male-targeted advertisements. As discussed in Chapter 1, women do not hold an equivalent position of social or legal status to men. Therefore, they cannot be addressed adequately through the socially established hierarchies of difference in the manner of the unreflexive, male-targeted advertisements. Nor are women discursively positioned to actively rearticulate signs of social difference in the socially authorised form which is accorded to the young, male middle-class readership of *Première* and *Q*. The female-targeted unreflexive advertisements offer self-actualisation through a quite stable core of repetitive images of conventional, or socially established, images of female beauty, self-control (through diet, exercise, etc.) and self-management (through make-up, clothes, etc.). These advertisements typically employ images of 'Woman' as icon produced in either diffuse or more direct ways through signifiers of national, cultural and racial difference. In contrast to the male-targeted reflexive and non-reflexive advertisements, explicit references to class were not generally present in my sample, suggesting that the classed nature of these advertisements operate in significantly different ways.

In summary, the results of my analysis indicate the fundamentally relational nature of the categories of 'the reflexive' and 'the unreflexive' advertisements and their gendered target markets. In order to explore this relationality, the following sections engage in a detailed qualitative analysis of sample adverts beginning with a discussion of the nature of 'reflexivity'.

Reflexivity and difference

Reflexivity has become a key term in diverse areas of social and cultural theory. It is increasingly used to describe social forms such as newly evolving structures in organisations in which flexibility is the key characteristic (Martin 1994; Lash and Urry 1994). Reflexivity has also been foregrounded in ways of writing about the objects of study: for example, in

forms of feminist ethnographic research which makes explicit the researcher's position and her role in the production of knowledge (Skeggs
1995). Yet, as Donna Haraway (1997) cautions, reflexivity should not be
seen as an inherently transformative, positive force – reflexive practices also
have the potential to reinscribe supposedly 'universal', yet in fact hierarchical, norms. I explore how this reinscription can occur through advertising
images in Chapters 4, 5 and 6. As I discussed in earlier sections, reflexivity as
an *explicit* mode of address became a particular focus of this research
through my identification of a certain category of advertisements which
directly and self-consciously displayed their mechanisms of signification.
These advertisements mobilised a 'knowing' form of viewer address which
made explicit advertising's relation to the viewer and advertising's position
in popular culture. Arguably, advertising's address is always explicit, in that
it is generally understood that advertisements' purpose is persuasion, and
this understanding frames the reception of the advertising 'message'.
However, the advertisements in the category that I initially described as
'reflexive' incorporated in their structure textual and intertextual strategies
aimed at eliciting a complicity between the viewer and the advertisement.
This complicity is a self-conscious incorporation of the viewers' potential
modes of interpretation of the advertisements. By highlighting each element
of their visual codes and the way in which the codes work together to
present meanings, reflexive adverts draw into their very structure the acts of
interpretation of the viewer. Trinh T. Minh-Ha (1991) discusses the concept
of reflexivity in representation in relation to the frame of meaning,

> The 'core' of representation is the reflexive interval. It is the place in
> which the play within the textual frame is a play on this very frame,
> hence on the borderlines of the textual and the extra-textual, where a
> positioning within constantly incurs the risk of de-positioning, and
> where the work, never freed from historical and socio-political contexts
> nor entirely subjected to them, can only be itself by constantly risking
> being no-thing.
>
> (Minh-Ha 1991: 48)

In relation to reflexivity in advertisements, the reflexive play within the
textual frame of the advertisement makes explicit the borderline quality of
the frame itself. This highlights the advertisement's relation to the extra-
textual, drawing attention to the link between text and viewer whilst also
foregrounding advertising's position in popular culture. The reflexive advertisement knowingly mobilises a play on the 'within/outside' of its frame in
order to establish a complicitous link with the viewer by a movement back
and forth across the borders of the frame. This mobile, reflexive mode of
address is strongly associated with male-targeted advertisements in the
study. Yet, as discussed in Chapter 1, mobile positioning forms the basis of
de Lauretis' (1989) conceptualisation of women's discursive positioning as

shifting inside and outside discourse or representation. These ambiguous gendered relations to reflexivity and mobility will be more closely examined in later sections of this chapter.

In my study, almost double the number of the reflexive advertisements were male-targeted as opposed to female-targeted. Here I want to draw explicit links between the textual and extra-textual operation of reflexivity in advertising, and the reflexive constitution of the self. In Chapter 1 I discussed how distance between the self and the other is crucial for the creative production and maintenance of the boundaries of the self. Diprose (1994) describes how influential discursive models of the self and citizen (and, by extension, the consumer) deny this capacity for creative distancing to women and others subordinated in terms of race, class and sexuality. This distance is crucial for a perspective on the self and its boundaries, and necessary for processes of recognition of unitary selfhood by others. It is the means by which the individual reflexively confers the status of recognition of selfhood on others, whilst simultaneously being affirmed and constituted in *his* own selfhood.[4] Drawing together these arguments, I propose that the interior of the unitary self is bounded by its frame. The reflexive play on this frame in moments of mutual recognition spatially expands and contracts boundaries of the self and other. By extension, the self can also be considered to be temporally bounded, requiring forms of framing between the past-self, present-self and future/potential-self. This is necessary in order to maintain both a narrative of unity of each unique self and forms of temporal segmentation which mark the past/present/future as distinct. I will argue that the narrative of unity which binds together these elements is the discursive concept of 'potential' which projects the boundaries of the self into the future. This occurs through a self-reflexive engagement with facets of selfhood in the past and present in order to rework possibilities of self-actualisation of the future/potential self. These affirm both uniqueness of that self and belonging to certain social and national groupings. The potential for unitary selfhood is thus inscribed through these processes as a capacity for spatial and temporal distancing and self-creative moments of recognition. This relational, creative move is reflexive in that it requires an explicit process of imagined 'mutual recognition' – it requires and reflects upon the spatio-temporal boundaries and relations between the self and the other.

The advertisements targeted at women were overwhelmingly 'unreflexive' in that they did not display this form of explicit distancing and self-conscious presentation of the advertisement's relation to the viewer. However, the definition of 'reflexivity' in the terms described above may not be capable of representing varying forms of reflexivity which operate in discursively marginal ways. De Lauretis argues that not only are women discursively positioned through a movement inside and outside discourse, but that they are, 'conscious of being so, conscious of that twofold pull, of that division, that doubled vision' (1989: 10). This may be a different form of self-consciousness, or in de Lauretis' (1989) terms, a kind of 'unusual knowing'. What forms of complicity, distance and knowledge might this involve? How might this be articulated, and in what terms are women and other subordinated groups offered modes of self-actualisation? What occurs in this different mode of the 'reflexive interval' of representation? These questions will be addressed in detail in Chapter 5, but the discussion at this point raises issues of the relational nature of 'the reflexive' and 'the unreflexive'. The generation of reflexivity is reliant on a play on the frame or boundaries of the 'unreflexive', requiring a form of movement and recognition in order to regenerate its meaning continually. From an analysis of the advertisements in the study and of the discursive constitution of selfhood, I will argue that these processes are founded on shifting definitions of gendered, racialised and classed difference. The following section explores the specific ways in which 'the literal' and 'the ironic' operate in frames of reflexivity to generate gendered, racialised and classed target markets of viewers.

The literal and the ironic

Within the category of 'reflexive' advertisements I further isolated a genre of those that were 'ironic', comprising 15 of the total 38 reflexive advertisements. In previous chapters, I created a working definition of reflexive advertisements as those which incorporated a self-consciousness as to their intertextual composition of signifiers. They offer viewers a complicity in this knowledge and are explicit as to their position in popular culture. Irony was a typical form of address in reflexive advertisements and is of particular interest, as ironic advertisements simultaneously hold various levels of discourse, or frames of meaning, together in tension. This is a useful site of analysis to map out the shifting formations of gendered, classed, racialised and national target markets between and across different levels of discourse.

Irony is a term which appears in feminist theory across a range of contexts. Rosalyn Diprose (1994) argues that women's discursive position is fundamentally ironic: women are both required for processes of (white, male, classed) self-constitution, and yet also negated. Women are construed as identical to men, yet positioned as radically other. Irony for Diprose (1994: 40) is ' "the otherness of the other", that incalculable residue of difference which cannot be subsumed under any universal'. On the level of social practice, consumerism offers women an ironic position of being negated as active subjects and simultaneously being offered the possibility of *acting* through forms of consumerist self-actualisation (Radner 1995). These perspectives on irony emphasise contradiction, tension, distance and difference, neatly summarised by Donna Haraway (1991: 149), 'Irony is about contradictions that do not resolve into larger wholes, even dialectically, about the tension of holding incomparable things together because both or all are necessary and true'. Haraway's use of the terms of 'both or all' highlights that such contradictory difference may not be restricted to dual oppositions, such as male/female, but incorporates multi-dimensional, mobile complexes of many forms of difference. These differences cannot be straightforwardly combined to form a unified, coherent, mosaic-like whole. Their sum is more than their parts – each intersection of differences forms a fusion which cannot be dissected and regarded separately, nor can it be seen as simply equivalent to other fusions of difference. This perspective disrupts the stable framework of pairing differences in complementary opposites such as male/female, or white/black, and focuses on the tension which holds the pairings or mosaics in place. In this sense, irony operates by suspending levels of incommensurability instanced in the discourses of universal yet unique 'individuality', or discourses of a distinct yet shared notion of national culture.

I was interested in examining how the tension between the (male-associated) 'reflexive' and the (female-associated) 'unreflexive' advertisements operated. How do advertisers mobilise this tension to re-produce specific gendered, racialised, classed and national/European target markets? The reflexive and the unreflexive require each other for their meaning, yet should not be seen as symmetrically opposed. If their contradictions do not resolve into a unified whole, where does irony fall in this dual mobilisation? Is irony's position that of a juncture, a fault line, a space of residue of irreducible difference? How are women and subordinated others positioned in this 'space'?

Tension between levels of discourse forms the basis of Linda Hutcheon's (1994) interpretation of irony. She argues that irony has a dual character in that it is 'the making or inferring of *meaning* in addition to and different from what is stated, together with an *attitude* toward both the said and the unsaid' (1994: 11). In the context of my study, the 'unreflexive' advertisements can be seen as the 'literal' or 'said' meaning. They draw on conventional, widely recognisable configurations of social difference in popular culture, for example, the sign 'Woman' (white and classed) as icon of beauty. The 'reflexive' advertisements can be seen as 'the unsaid', as their juxtaposition of 'literal' signifiers must be actively and self-consciously rearticulated to generate their meaning. Ironic meaning is made possible by the mobile interaction between the said/literal and the unsaid/reflexive, creating a meaning which is more than, and qualitatively different from, the sum of those parts. Hutcheon argues that irony 'happens' and, in effect, is a performative event requiring both the literal/said and the reflexive/unsaid for its constitution,

> [irony] happens in the space *between* (and including) the said and the unsaid; it needs both to happen. What I want to call the 'ironic' meaning is inclusive and relational: the said and the unsaid coexist for the interpreter, and each has meaning in relation to the other because they literally 'interact' ... to create the real 'ironic' meaning. The 'ironic'

> meaning is not, then, simply the unsaid meaning, and the unsaid is not always a simple inversion or opposite of the said ...: it is always different – *other than* and more than the said.
>
> (Hutcheon 1994: 12–13)

Hutcheon (1994) argues that irony has three main features: relationality, inclusivity and differentiality. Irony is relational in that it occurs between meanings, and differential in that these meanings are founded on difference. It is inclusive, as it is not a mere substitution of meanings but is a rapid movement between meanings. None of the meanings is negated in the process – they are held together in tension.

Irony, then, does not inhabit a specific locus, but rather occurs in and through a movement between levels of meaning. In this light, de Lauretis' (1989) formulation of women's discursive movement across and between discourses can be seen as an ironic oscillation between diverse points within a range of discourses. If such a movement takes the form of a reiteration (of the legal status of 'the individual', of the relational nature of reflexive/ unreflexive or literal), as discussed in Chapter 1, then each reiteration is also an alteration. Each demarcation of a boundary actively restates the terms of that boundary (Butler 1993). The constitution in these 'moments', 'acts' – or perhaps, better, 'events' – is continually shifting, such that the mutual generation of categories such as male and female, 'the individual', 'the consumer' is always subject to disruption or rearticulation. Yet this constant alteration paradoxically operates within frameworks of stability. Minh-Ha (1991) argues that such repetition focuses on the space between the events of repetition,

> Repetition sets up expectations and baffles them at both regular and irregular intervals. It draws attention, not to the object (word, image, or sound), but to what lies between them. The element brought to visibility is precisely the invisibility of the invisible realm, namely the vitality of intervals, the intensity of the relation between creation and re-creation.
>
> (Minh-Ha 1991: 191)

The visibility of the interval, or space between, will be discussed in later chapters. For the present, I will focus on the space of the 'betweenness'.

In Chapter 1 I discussed Butler's problematisation of 'the discrete identity of "the moment"' (1993: 245). Butler argues for a fully spatial *and* temporal understanding of 'the moment' which examines the 'betweenness' of moments as a convergence of 'non-thematizable space and non-thematizable time' (*ibid.*: 245). This betweenness is the space of the constitutive 'moment' of imagined mutual recognition between the self and the other. In that mutual recognition of self-presence, there is assumed transparency of self and equivalence between the two. This forms the crux of the contradictory discursive position of women and subordinate others. There is an inherent contradiction at work in the requirement of a preconstituted, prediscursive self to recognise another *in order* for those very processes of constitution to occur. Butler calls this contradiction 'the non-space of cultural collision' (*ibid.*: 124), characterised by repetition and ambivalence. I will argue in the following chapters that this non-space is held together in tension by 'potential', which is articulated through discourses of consumerism and self-actualisation. This spatio-temporal matrix, or 'non-space', will form the basis of the following section which examines how the concepts of the 'moment' and irony might be formulated in the context of media images and the relation of these images to the viewer.

The non-space of images

As I argued earlier, reflexivity can be considered as a self-conscious play on the textual frame, bringing into focus the nature of the frame as boundary. A close analysis of the textual devices in advertisements targeted at male and female markets is a way of examining how the discursive representation and re-production of the categories of sexual, racial, class and national difference operate through dimensions of intersecting difference. The frame of the categories of the literal/non-reflexive and the reflexive sets the borders of this re-production of difference in my study of advertisements. What is 'beyond' the frame of the literal/non-reflexive advertisements targeted at women, as compared to the reflexive, and particularly advertisements targeted at men? What forms of textual 'elsewhere(s)' are generated, and what are the dimensions of this 'space'? What are the forms of movement of signifiers within and beyond the frame? How do these textual devices articulate modes of potential, self-actualisation and choice differentially available to certain groups?

Margaret Morse's (1990) concept of 'non-space' has the potential for expanding ways of thinking about the 'moment' of recognition, assumed transparency and mutual constitution. Through 'non-space', the moment can be imagined as occurring in a multi-dimensional matrix, a spatio-temporal convergence of discourses of difference and identity. It resists a purely linear and reductive, or binary oppositional, approach, and emphasizes fluidity and contradiction. It disrupts the terms of 'the boundary' and offers different ways to map the boundaries of categories of difference and of the interiority of the self. In this way, the moment of the constitution of 'the individual' and of difference could be formulated as occurring in a kind of 'elsewhere'/'elsewhen', or multiple 'elsewheres'/'elsewhens' of discourse.

Morse (1990) theorises what she calls 'non-space' in a discussion of sensory experiences of contemporary forms of television, the shopping mall and the freeway. In the context of the media, Morse argues that non-space is not an identifiable, concrete locus, but is a 'ground within which communication as a flow of values among and between two and three dimensions and between virtuality and actuality ... can "take place"' (*ibid.*: 196). Morse argues that media forms like television – and, I would argue, advertisements in magazines – draw on the 'liquidity' of signifiers. This liquidity is facilitated by the increasingly rapid flow of signifiers of difference which move across national borders in the form of flows (Appadurai 1990). The deterritorialisation of media networks 'transposes new and abstract electronic space across earlier physical and social geographies' (Robins 1991: 28). This produces a '"placeless" geography of image' (Robins 1991: 29) in which signifiers become detached from their socially embedded historical, geographical, political and cultural contexts. Signifiers then can operate through fluid connections and become potentially interchangeable. This liquidity can result in

> the exchange of values between different ontological levels and otherwise incommensurable facets of life, for example, between two and three dimensions, between language, images, and the built environment, and between economic, societal, and symbolic realms of our culture.
>
> (Morse 1990: 194)

This problematises the boundary between the literal/the ironic, between social differences and between the visual and the 'materiality' of citizenship rights and obligations. The fluidity of non-space disrupts the mapping of the boundaries of the self and of the nation which I discussed in Chapter 1 in relation to the work of Anderson (1991), Kirby (1996) and McClintock (1995). Notions of boundary, interiority, exteriority and 'authentic' inner selfhood are explicitly called into question. In the following section, I explore how the terms of the categories of the ironic and the literal can function to stabilise certain meanings momentarily and so generate the necessary boundaries of gendered, classed and racialised selfhood.

Elsewhere(s), irony and distraction

The above conceptualisations of non-space and irony share the characteristics of holding different levels or dimensions together in a productive tension. None of the elements is negated, but rather they are suspended together with the potential of being rearticulated in new formations. Non-space is not the simple inverse of 'space', but is premised upon a movement between and across dimensions, encompassing a vast range of possible combinations of spatiality and meaning. This movement can be seen in parallel with de Lauretis' (1989) formulation of women's position as shifting between and across the borders of discourse, in which a concept of 'elsewhere' is a tool to theorise moments of slippage in discourse. De Lauretis stresses that this discursive movement is not from the realm of representation to that of a 'real' outside of discourse, and that 'elsewhere' is neither a mythic past nor utopian future (*ibid.*: 25). The elsewhere, she argues, is the blind spot of discourse, that which is not represented but is implicated in the discursive manoeuvre. Drawing on film theory, de Lauretis uses the concept of the 'space-off' as a metaphor for the elsewhere: 'the space-off' is that which is not visible within the frame, yet is implied by the frame. The space of representation, then, articulates with the non-represented, the space-off, or blind spot:

> These two kinds of spaces are neither in opposition to one another nor strung along a chain of signification, but they exist concurrently and in contradiction. The movement between them, therefore, is not that of a dialectic, of integration, of a combinatory, or of *différance*, but is the tension of contradiction, multiplicity, and heteronomy.
>
> (de Lauretis 1989: 26)

Again, irony and the elsewhere share the features of tension between levels of discourse, and the production of a supplementary, different, meaning. Like irony, the elsewhere is not a specific locus or material form. It is not, Butler argues, 'an ontological thereness', and can only be imagined or visualised 'at and as its most tenuous borders' (1993: 8). I would argue that non-space is the weightless zone which occurs in the rapid movement, or oscillation, between the borders of discourse (what is represented) and the elsewhere (the space-off, the unrepresented yet implied). It is in this movement that the borders of discourse/non-discourse are both constituted and can be imagined and visualised. As I argued in Chapter 1, this movement or action generates the systems of equivalences and transparency of knowledge necessary for the production of the ideal of selfhood. This is a zone in which discourses are reformulated continually to re-produce categories of sexual, racialised, national and classed difference. This movement, de Lauretis (1989) stresses, is not dialectical or symmetrical, but multiple and contradictory. The movement across and between discourse, together with the tension which locks the realms together, is the force which generates the very borders of discourse.

Distraction as a mode of viewing constitutes one means of negotiating this fluid movement between frames of discourses in the context of a non-space of mobile images. In his essay, *The Work of Art in the Age of Mechanical Reproduction*, Walter Benjamin (1982) describes a shift in modes of perception at the beginning of the twentieth century from contemplation to distraction. Contemplation, he argues, involves the studied absorption into the art form of the solitary viewer. In contrast, distraction – which was associated with the growth of mass media – operated in a more diffuse, kinetic manner. It was a mechanism used to buffer the self against the unaccustomed force and speed of the images produced by changes in urban life and new media forms, particularly film. Michael Taussig describes Benjamin's concept of distraction as a 'type of flitting and barely conscious peripheral vision perception' (1992: 143). Taussig's emphasis on the movement of flitting and peripheral vision draws a parallel with de Lauretis'

(1989) notion of mobility between discourse and the 'space-off' or else-where(s).

Morse's (1990) analysis of distraction focuses on television and the experience of shopping malls and the freeway, but can be usefully related to the experience of reading or flicking through magazines, as all these media forms draw on overlapping pools of mobile image resources. Morse argues that these media forms make available distraction as a mode of viewing which is 'an attenuated *fiction effect*, that is a partial loss of touch with the here and now' (*ibid.*: 193). This loss is only partial in that the different levels of 'reality' do not negate each other, but are held together in tension,

> Ultimately, distraction is related to the expression of two planes of language represented simultaneously or alternately, the plane of the subject in a here and now, or *discourse*, and the plane of an absent or nonperson in another time, elsewhere, or *story*.
>
> (Morse 1990: 193–4)

This formulation of distraction can be closely related to the definition of irony discussed earlier in its simultaneous suspension of different levels or dimensions of discourse in a discursive tension. In later chapters I will explore how the temporal nature of these narratives or stories may operate not only in a dual or binary framework but also in a multi-dimensional form facilitating movement in many directions. Morse argues that distraction is possible through the generation of non-space as a form of free-floating zone of sign exchange disengaged from socially embedded structures. Distraction, too, operates through spatial fluidity and a movement between boundaries:

> Distraction as a dual state of mind depends on an incomplete process of spatial and temporal separation and interiorization. The automobile, for instance, is connected to the world outside via the very glass and steel which enclose the driver. However, the dualism of the outside/inside within these separate realms means that a connection with 'outside' drifts between a 'real' outside and an idealized representation.
>
> (Morse 1990: 202)

Morse here stresses both connection and distance in the process of distraction. This is a 'de-realised' mode of experience, in that it has a disembedded relation to socially recognised discourses of reality which are suspended in tension with the 'idealized representation', or mediated view. Morse argues that this process of experiencing car travel and viewing the media is a mobile, shifting encounter between different levels or dimensions of 'reality'. It can fundamentally alter the experience of self-awareness, producing an 'unanchored mobility' of the self (*ibid.*: 204).

This refiguring of the experience of a mobility between dimensions can be usefully considered in relation to forms of the aestheticisation of everyday life implicit in Morse's discussion. Mike Featherstone (1991) argues that a range of cultural phenomena, including the erosion of the strict distinction between 'high culture' and 'popular/mass culture', has led to an increased aestheticisation of everyday life which elevates the significance of consumerism in people's understandings of themselves. One aspect of this has been advertising's self-reflexive, explicit presentation of its position in popular culture in Britain and France. Featherstone (1991) argues that the aesthetic sensibilities made available in this shift operate by switching between involvement and detachment in the mode of viewing. This requires a kind of 'controlled de-control of the emotions' (Featherstone 1991: 80). This calculated de-control enables the individual 'to enjoy the swing between the extremes of aesthetic involvement and detachment so that the pleasures of immersion and detached distantiation can be both enjoyed' (*ibid.*: 81). As Morse (1990) stresses, this aesthetic experience has achieved new dimensions, interrelating discourses of 'the real' and the 'idealized representation' in new ways.

Whilst Featherstone (1991) relates this aesthetic to the rise of the new middle classes, he does not engage in an analysis of differential discursive access for women and racialised groups. In the following section I will examine the textual address of one male-targeted reflexive advertisement and one female-targeted 'unreflexive/literal' advertisement. My analysis draws on the codes and forms of address which I developed during the main analysis of my sample. During that part of the research I became sensitised to certain configurations of images of difference and developed an interest in 'frames' and planes of meaning as conceptual tools for tracking the movement of meaning within and beyond the borders of print advertisements. In the following I analyse how certain forms of address tied to the discursive status of 'the individual' allow for a privileged movement between and across the boundaries of discourse.

Irony and simultaneity

In this section, I analyse a Becks beer advertisement (Plate 3.1)[5] to demonstrate how irony operates as a textual strategy. I selected this advertisement as it is typical of the category of ironic advertisements within the larger category of reflexive advertisements: the advert arranges images of social difference in discordant formations, that is, in formations not conventional in discourses of popular culture. In effect, there is a jarring of textual planes which, in this case, takes the forms of discordant juxtapositions of historical periods. Typically of this type of advertisement in my study, the Becks advert is male-targeted – the product type and the placement magazine indicate that its primary target market is young men.[6] On one level, the use of a reflexive, ironic textual address may merely reflect the restrictions placed by the British Advertising Standards Authority on advertising for certain product such as alcohol and tobacco.[7] For example, alcohol advertising may not present drinking as 'a challenge', nor must it use models who appear to be under 25 years old. In addition, 'advertisements should not suggest that any alcoholic drink can enhance mental, physical or sexual capacities, popularity, attractiveness, masculinity, femininity or sporting achievements'.[8] These regulations obviously present certain challenges for advertising which aims to attach positive associations to its brand. Yet the regulations do allow alcohol advertising to promote distinction of taste or style; 'a brand preference may be promoted as a mark of the drinker's good taste and discernment'.[9] It would be possible to argue that these restrictions discourage the use of 'conventional' forms of address such as the model/product-image/tagline format found in many print advertisements. Indeed, the regulations could be said to encourage the use of a reflexive address which abstracts the advertising 'message' from specific images of social difference which may fall foul of the regulations: e.g. images of sexually attractive young people. Following such an argument, the significance of the use of a reflexive address would not be seen in relation to the gender-targeting of the advert, but rather would be seen merely as product of advertising restrictions. However, I will argue in the following section that the impositions of the regulations only partially account for the prevalence of this form of address in advertisements. Indeed, this form of address was present in my study across a range of product types such as cars or walking boots, not purely in alcohol and tobacco advertising. The ironic address of the Becks advertisement relies on gendered and racialised privilege in order to 'make sense' and speak to its (male) target market. The textual address draws its significatory power from the forms of historical privilege that it references – in effect, the advert frames privileged viewing positions and re-produces those very forms of privilege.

The Becks advertisement (Plate 3.1) uses a black-and-white photographic image of a group of white men in colonial Africa, drawing associations of military conquest or colonial exploration. The advert forms part of what the company calls its 'World Heritage Series', which takes 'real' historical photographs and uses them in contemporary advertising. The photographic image is framed by a black line at the top of the advert with the text 'Africa 1901' in red, and a red line at the foot of the advert with the text 'Brewed in Germany. Drunk all over the World' in black. To the right of the photographic image, there is the text 'On the jungle juice again' in green. These three colours echo the colours of the small image of Becks beer at the bottom right of the frame.

Several planes of meaning are generated in this advertisement; the photograph of the men drinking beer draws on Western popular culture's image pool and elicits associations of European histories of African exploration, taking tokens of 'civilisation' (in this case, European beer) to distant lands.[10] These associations are positioned as ahistorical and timeless through the use of the black-and-white photograph, situating it in a 'bygone age' now inaccessible except through images. The association of the photograph's

Plate 3.1 Becks advertisement, 'On the jungle juice again'. *Source: Q* magazine, April 1990 (courtesy of Scottish Courage Ltd).

'capturing of history' is further emphasized by the white background and framing black and red lines which 'place' the image as if it were a mounted photograph in a display or collected in an album. This dimension of the background functions as a device which focuses on the borders of the image, making it identifiable as a photograph, distinct from its mounting. Simultaneously, it *connects* the 'old' photographic image to the background dimension, that is, the context of a contemporary display or album. As in Morse's (1990) discussion of the glass of a car's windscreen simultaneously connecting the occupant to the outside world *and* separating her/him from it, the 'framing' of the photograph signals concurrent and divergent onto-logical statuses of the image and the viewer's relation to it.

These temporal and spatial dimensions are disrupted in two ways. Firstly, the taglines 'On the jungle juice again' and 'Brewed in Germany. Drunk all over the world' lift the historical meanings of the photograph into the contemporary. Secondly, the historical tone of the black-and-white photo-graph is jarred by green, red and black colours of the bottle of Becks. The colour of the bottle of Becks visibly flags its difference from the sepia-tint of the 'old' photograph. Its positioning between the two framing lines above and below the photograph functions to literally 'brand' the movements and connections between the historical and contemporary dimensions. This juxtaposition of temporally and culturally disjunctive signifiers draws atten-tion to the textual frame or boundary by making explicit the ways in which the text's signifiers interact to produce meaning, 'it invites the perceiver/reader to follow what the creative gesture has traced, therefore rendering visible how it can be unmade, restored to the void, and creatively re-made' (Minh-Ha 1991: 195). In effect, these self-conscious and explicit textual moves enable the addressed viewer to engage in a creative rearticula-tion of signifiers. As I argue below, this is mediated by specific textual devices focusing on both borders within the textual frame, and borders between the viewer and the text.

These spatial and temporal dimensions do not negate each other, but operate simultaneously in tension. This tension occurs on multiple levels; between the categories of literal and ironic adverts, between the borders of the textual and the bodily vision of the viewer, and between the diverse ontological statuses of the planes of meaning within the text. The 'literal/non-reflexive' elements are the signifiers of white, male colonial explorers, historically embedded in recognisable popular culture discourses. The reflexive framing of the coloured bottle and humorous tagline in disjunctive juxtaposition enables a continual movement between and across dimensions – this makes a particular humorous, ironic interpretation of the advertisement available. This irony requires 'the literal' in order to signify its distinction from it and, hence, its existence. It is through the use of 'literal' or conventionally established signifiers of African cultural difference and a 'colonial past' that the existence of certain categories of contemporary, European, middle-class men are performatively produced as viewers.

'Civilisation', here represented by the drinking of beer, becomes the key marker of cultural status through a continual movement between images of a 'real history' and a rearticulated 'idealized representation'. This fluidity of signifiers operates as a kind of non-space, or zone of contact between images which are uprooted from conventional contexts and are available for rearticulation in new formations. In Morse's terms (1990), the 'real outside' (the literal signifiers) is the material reality of a destructive colonial history. Through a flexible rearticulation of signifiers, this can be cleaned up/whitened up and 're-anchored' to (an idealised representation of) contemporary white, European, middle-class viewing masculinities who are enabled to view the image ironically.

The layering of the textual planes, and the discordant formation of signi-fiers, form an explicit acknowledgement of the viewers' interpretative capacities of movement between levels of meaning. This acknowledgement is incorporated into the text through its explicit address, which Robert Goldman calls a 'knowing wink' (1992: 181). This elite knowingness is branded by the Becks image and colours which aim to transpose themselves across the different ontological levels of the frames. As I indicated earlier, the British Advertising Standards Authority allows that 'a brand preference may be promoted as a mark of the drinker's good taste and discernment'. The discernment produced in this advertisement, which is typical of those in my study, is the discernment of irony and the capacity to use an ironic address to switch between levels of meaning.

I would argue, however, that the textual strategies for the production of difference, together with the discursive limitations of gendered, racialised and classed representation discussed earlier, serve to limit the availability of privileged ironic interpretations to certain groups. As discussed in Chapter 1, the discursive constitution of 'the individual' relies on systems of distance and difference which utilise women and subordinated others as a currency of equivalence and exchange. This discursive operation denies the subordi-nated groups the status necessary for full discursive representation, suspending them in an ambiguous position of 'elsewhere', shifting in and out of representation. In contrast, white, middle-class men are accorded the necessary discursive status to negotiate the crucial distance between the self and the other for the successful re-production of boundaries of the self. In the Becks advertisement, this movement can be traced as the kinetic relation between planes or dimensions of meaning in the text, and between the text and viewer. The non-space which occurs in the interaction of dimensions in this (white, middle-class) male-targeted advertisement is not the symmetrical equivalent of the 'elsewhere' of ambiguous discursive status accorded to women and other subordinated groups. The non-space of ironic tension between dimensions tied to male discursive status enables the shifting rela-tions of detachment (and distance) and immersion (contact and exchange) in those dimensions through distraction as a mode of viewing. This 'controlled de-controlled' as Featherstone terms it (1991:80), may generate pleasure (and in this case humour) as well as reiterating status as an *interpretive sign*.

The textual production of 'the literal'

'The literal' functions for the advertising industry as a means of demarcating the boundaries of (and so producing) target markets of consumers. At the same time, 'the literal' also offers ways of imagining modes of femininity available to women. However, the ambiguous and mobile discursive positioning of women 'elsewhere' problematises readings of this femininity. De Lauretis (1989: 25) argues that it is not that feminists have failed to produce 'a view from elsewhere' which theorises the operation of differences, but rather 'that what we have produced is not recognizable, precisely, as a representation'. By this, I take her to mean that the attempts to theorise difference have been subsumed under sameness, in which women and subordinated others cannot be thought of as different to (white, heterosexual, middle-class) men. Alternatively, women have been rendered invisible and unthinkable due to their radical difference which is beyond the frame of discursive representation.

To illustrate the operation of specific textual strategies and ambiguous discursive positionings of the category 'Woman', I have chosen for analysis a Guerlain advertisement for the perfume Un Air de Samsara (Plate 3.2).[11] I analyse other female-targeted advertisements in Chapter 5. This advertisement is present in both French and British samples in my study and is typical of the format of female-targeted literal/non-reflexive advertisements; it is promoting a 'female' product (others include cosmetics and clothes), and it uses images of a woman textually linked to images of the product, plus the product names and taglines. I selected this advertisement both for its typical format, and for the prominent way in which it mobilises certain characteristic textual devices. As such, it serves as a clear illustration of the often more diffuse ways in which this genre of advertisement generates its meaning.

Advertising's function as an expert knowledge system frames modes of self-actualisation for its diverse markets of consumers. For this, it requires the (at least temporary) stabilisation of categories of social difference in order to delimit the boundaries of specific target markets. These are, in turn, tied to manufacturers' gendered, racialised and classed target marketing of product-type. This imperative for continually re-producing identifiable markets requires the use of textual strategies in advertisements which actively function to stabilise certain meanings, for example, the regeneration of images of white, middle-class femininity linked to the sign 'Woman'. As each repetition of the sign 'Woman' is potentially an alteration of the previous, the process of stabilisation involves a constant rearticulation of boundaries of difference and the use of textual devices to anchor (temporarily) those boundaries.

Plate 3.2 Un Air de Samsara advertisement, 'Ni tout à fait la même, ni tout à fait une autre'.

Source: French *Elle*, April 1995 (courtesy of Guerlain).

Typically of the non-reflexive/literal advertisements, this Un Air de Samsara advertisement draws together conventionally articulated codes of difference and functions through the assumption that viewers will recognise and appropriately situate these codes. I will argue that this arrangement of signifiers of difference is achieved through highly structured textual strategies which operate through the use of frames and planes of meaning in a very different way from the reflexive advertisements. The advertisement features a female figure sitting on a rock engraved with an 'Eastern' text, an enlarged image of a perfume bottle, and the brand name of Guerlain. To the centre right of the frame the tagline reads '… not quite the same, not quite another …'. The colours are rich reds, blues, mauves and a sandy yellow. Viewers are invited to follow, and participate in, the flow of meaning around the advertisement through the textual arrangement of the shapes and lines formed by the figure and the placement of the perfume bottle and captions. The spatial orientation within the frame of the advertisement is crucial for organising, or managing, the meanings produced. The captions 'Un Air de Samsara, New Eau de Toilette' and 'Guerlain, Paris' function to fix the associations of the image firmly to a product and brand name. This is achieved by transposing their texts over the images and laterally organising (or 'squeezing') the planes of meaning as a textual strategy to achieve a degree of closure of meaning. The aim is to attach the meanings of the image to the perfume bottle and to make it function through the tagline '… not quite the same, not quite another …'. The captions operate by 'centring' and mediating the gaze (the form of the texts is literally centred). The established designer name gives status to the product name, whilst simultaneously the imagistic associations of the product name in the context of the advertisement build on the layers of meaning incorporated in the designer name. This textual move 'brackets' and brands the image and its levels of associated meanings between the captions.

In effect, these textual devices privilege certain possible meaningful interpretations of the advertisement by mediating the flow of meaning through the branded product in highly structured ways. Cultural and national difference is crucial in this advertisement for the signification of white femininity and Parisian chic. The text inscribed on the rock elicits associations of Eastern exoticism by invoking signifiers which have become part of the Western media's repertoire of images of cultural difference. The textual strategies discussed above organise the flow of meaning into a circular narrative movement linking the Eastern exoticism of the perfume bottle to the white, Western female figure via the text. Through the tagline '… not quite the same, not quite another …', the advert aims to produce a sign of feminine exoticism and beauty mediated through the product name. Here, European consumer discourse relocates its established signs of Eastern exoticism and maps them onto white 'Woman' as sign, momentarily fixing the category as a legible target market.

This mapping of the (not quite) same and (not quite) other can be seen in terms of the distance between the Western 'individual' and the Eastern 'other' in the processes of the constitution of the category 'individual'. The 'moment' of imagined recognition between self and other occurs, or performatively 'happens', in the context of signifiers' ambiguity. The process of constitutive recognition requires the establishment of a system of equivalence through which each self confers the status of selfhood on the other. As I have outlined, this process is contradictory, as women and subordinated others are discursively denied the necessary status to participate, and indeed function as the currency of exchange in the system of equivalence. However, the residue, or constitutive outside which is beyond the frame of sexual and cultural difference, cannot be subsumed within the terms of the discourse. The attempted establishment of equivalence (the fixing of meaning) cannot be a symmetrical move which binds together all possible meanings in an unambiguous totality. The partial stabilising of 'Woman' as sign (and market) through its textual linkage to signifiers of Eastern, 'feminine' mystery, cannot restrict other possible meanings. Indeed, these meanings can materialise through a movement between and across the textual frame and the elsewhere of that frame.

In summary, the (predominantly female-targeted) literal/non-reflexive advertisements in my study use specific, highly structured spatial and sequential devices to produce a flow of meaning. This flow joins conventionally articulated signifiers of difference in the advertisement through textual association. Contrasted with this, the reflexive (predominantly male-targeted) advertisements do not mobilise textual associations in conventional (literal) ways. Rather, they generate their meaning by attempting to elicit from certain addressed viewers an active rearticulation of disparate signifiers which are disembedded from their conventional contexts. These disparities in textual address represent one way in which the advertising industry can use images of social difference to actively (re)produce the boundaries of its target markets. The continual re-establishment of these boundaries require a certain coherence of form in the repetition of the visual category 'the literal', and I will examine this stability and repetition in Chapter 5.

The interpretative moves involved in the reflexive advertisements produce a new sign of cultural distinction tied to white males. The proportionately small number of reflexive advertisements in my study reflects the elite nature of this group. The group has a disproportionately large discursive influence through their framing by advertising agencies as a market of 'taste leaders' (as discussed in Chapter 2), and hence in the generation of new configurations of images of cultural difference and belonging. These differences in textual address suggest that the modes of consumerist self-actualisation on offer may differ significantly between social groups. The difference in focus on the frame/boundary and its relation to the self between the two categories of advertisement indicates variance in the discourses of the 'interiority' of the self according to gender, race, class and nationality. The modes of reflexive engagement with discourses of this interiority, or inner depths, may offer different perspectives on self-constitution. In the next chapter, I engage with the relations between 'the visual' and the temporality of narratives of self.

4 Branding vision
Advertising, time and privilege

In this chapter, I expand my focus on textual analysis with an emphasis on processes of vision and the constitution of 'the seeing European'. As discussed in Chapter 2, Colin Campbell (1997, 1999) has challenged conventional models for understanding consumer acts as 'communicative' acts. Such acts are often considered to communicate messages about identity – goods (mediated by advertising) are considered primarily as signs to be manipulated in a process of self-construction. Campbell suggests that the relation between a subject's intent, action and the meanings in advertising and consumerism should not be approached in a deterministic manner. We should not read 'conscious intent' into acts of consumption in a simplistic way – awareness and intent should not be conflated. Campbell argues that the assumptions about the subject's awareness and intent lead many theories of consumption to consider consumer acts primarily in symbolic terms. Understandings of action are reduced to the symbolism or meaning of the acts rather than the 'doing' of action. In this framework, acts do not so much ' "do something" as "say something", or perhaps, "do something through saying something" ' (Campbell 1997: 341). Campbell wants to move beyond this communicative framework to consider the *action* of acting. As I have outlined in previous chapters, theories of performativity can be useful for considering how *saying* something can be *doing* something. This 'doing' is not so much about communication – the action of speech actively constitutes the self, rather than expresses the self's communicative intent. In this chapter I examine the action of viewing advertisements through an adaptation of performativity. Using a framework of visual performativity, I explore the relations between awareness, intent and the action of vision. How does a reflexive form of textual address in advertising frame visual performativity? How are identities constituted and reworked in visual performativity? What forms of privilege are produced and re-produced?

Through the analysis of a sample advertisement, I will illustrate how colonial history and the sexed, racialised discourses of 'the individual' continue to benefit certain groups in contemporary society by affording privileged viewing positions. I argue that vision and time form the subject – they produce the conditions of possibility for vision and re-produce the privilege of certain seeing subjects. Linked to the textual address of certain advertising campaigns, vision can draw on colonial and sexual privilege, but can avoid acknowledging responsibility for both past and present power inequalities. Significantly, this approach to the visual is not an analysis of images of Europe or Europeanness. It is an analysis of ways of *seeing through* European privilege and how the historically generated privileges of 'the individual' are accessed and mobilised in contemporary visual culture. Advertising attempts to *brand* these moments in which the subject is formed and aims to produce 'the consuming citizen' through acts of vision. Yet the combination of time, vision and the commercial brand in the masculinised, 'European' visual realm does not completely erase women and other subordinated groups. I argue that there are 'blank spaces' or 'elsewheres/ elsewhens' in vision which can barely be imagined in conventional ways. Women and other overlapping subordinated groups may be offered ways of developing different, resistant subjectivities through the possibilities that this opens.

The previous chapter developed an approach to textual analysis which focuses on how the literal (or 'the said') and the ironic (or 'the unsaid') operate as relational rather than absolute categories. They have permeable boundaries which are held together in tension, requiring one another for their own constitution. I examined how this tension operates in parity with de Lauretis' (1989) concept of 'the elsewhere' or 'space-off'. That which is represented (for example in the discourses which constitute 'the individual') articulates with, and requires, that which is beyond the frame of representation, in the space-off or elsewhere. In this chapter I make connections between this tension and space-off and discourses of visibility and invisibility in the context of my study of advertisements. My aim is to map out how visual images can be formulated by advertisers to generate 'legible' social signifiers. These are required in order to delimit and continually redefine diverse target markets of potential consumers. I argue that this marking of boundaries points to the relation between the visual and knowledge and the capacity to generate social meanings tied to institutional power. What can be known, by whom, when, and with what discursive weight? This focus on knowledge emphasises the question of boundaries – that which is beyond the frame of representation can nonetheless be implied from what is visible within the frame. This indicates the existence of different relations or levels of contact between knowledge and the visual. In terms of images, the visibility and invisibility of different forms or levels of knowledge frame the differing availability of narratives of the self.

I establish links between the production of the visual and the discursive, performative constitution of irony. I argue that the visual can be imagined as performative of self, constituting the seeing subject through discourses of transparency and temporality. As I discussed in the previous chapter, irony is explicit in its address, self-consciously drawing attention to its mechanisms for producing meaning. In advertising, it achieves this explicit form of address by engaging conventionally recognisable visual codes in unusual or discordant configurations, highlighting the availability of another (ironic) level of meaning. These visual codes gain their meaning from established discourses of the relation between the visual and knowledge – what certain images signify – but also from that which cannot be visibly represented in a conventionally recognisable form. Certain images are therefore seen as 'explicit', in that they highlight their status as 'self-evident', as having a supposedly direct relation of signifier to signified. For example, an image using specific codes to produce the visual concept of a beautiful, white woman in an advertisement can be conventionally situated in the discourses of popular culture as having a direct relation to 'ideal femininity'. This relation is seen as visible and 'evident', drawing together what can be seen and what can be known. Such images of women are not conventionally imagined as 'self-conscious' or reflexive in the way in which certain male-targeted advertisements can be. This invites a focus on issues of discursive status and its links to visibility and transparency which I discussed in later sections of this chapter. Like irony, the visible holds different levels of meaning together in tension. It is performatively constituted in a continual movement or oscillation between these levels. The visible articulates with 'the invisible' situated beyond the frame, in the space-off or the elsewhere of representation. Later sections will address how this constitutive articulation occurs through a movement in space and time, back and forth between the boundaries or frames of these zones.

To understand the visual as tied to the human capacity of sight is not to understand the visual as a universal, unchanging, 'natural' means by which individuals relate to the external world. There has been considerable interest in tracing the development of historically and culturally specific relations of visuality to the experience and conceptualisation of selfhood (Benjamin 1982; Burnett 1995; Crary 1993; Jay 1993; Stafford 1991). As discussed in the previous chapter, Walter Benjamin (1982) argued that a shift from modes of contemplative viewing to modes of distracted viewing occurred in the early twentieth century. Benjamin's formulation draws together institutional structures of changing art forms and transformations in the speed of city life to imagine new ways that the visual operates in individuals' and groups' understandings of the world and themselves. In the contemporary context of an ever-increasing aestheticisation of the everyday (Featherstone 1991), and the velocity and density of signs in media 'non-space', I argue that the visual is a key zone of contestation of selfhood. Images of difference, and the shifting, disembedded relation they have to their original signifieds, form the site of new configurations of 'knowledge' of the identity of individuals and groups and ideas of difference, belonging and entitlement.

Vision, knowledge and transparency

I want to emphasise the importance of the concept of transparency in the context of my study of advertisements and my analysis of the constitution of 'the individual' and 'the citizen'. In Chapter 1 I discussed Diprose's (1994) argument that the positing of the self as 'transparent' to others is required for constitution of both self and other. It establishes a system of equivalences, or means for translation, which ensures the (hierarchical) discursive 'dialogue' between the self and the other. That is, transparency enables the process of recognition to occur, which, in turn, confers the status of selfhood on (certain) entities (Diprose 1994). Transparency, then, functions as a visual metaphor for the legibility or the 'absolute understanding' of the other (*ibid.*: 54). In these processes, the assumed dialogue and recognition which occurs is in fact 'a monologue which subsumes differences under norms already in place' (*ibid.*). This monologue refuses women, racialised groups, lesbians and gays and the working class the status of full selfhood in their own right. They form the space-off, or 'elsewhere' of representation, beyond the discursive frame of conventional knowledge. Yet their presence can be implied from what is visible within the frame and from the movements back and forth over its boundaries. This is a space of contradiction; these ambiguous entities are both assumed to be 'transparent' and ultimately 'knowable', yet also invisible in their own right. In a discussion of the widespread invocation of 'the feminine' in the signification of male subjectivity, Elspeth Probyn (1993) argues that this contradictory discursive production of femininity does not allow a space for theorising the ontological and epistemological complexities of 'being women':

> the isolated feminine *becomes* that which can allow for the masculine decentred and postmodern self. The joke is again on women as we are presented as both 'utterly knowable' ... and also the guarantee of 'the limits of knowledge'.
>
> (Probyn 1993: 46)

Across a range of discourses, the boundaries of the category 'Woman' as 'the limits of knowledge' have been produced as the discursive frame for visual legibility. This is particularly evident in the development of artistic conceptions of the body (Betterton 1987, 1996; Pollock 1988, 1992; Nead 1992). Lynda Nead (1992) examines how the female body has historically been regarded in art as unformed, undifferentiated matter which is situated at the borders of human embodment, sexual difference, art and obscenity. The dangerously amorphous status of the female nude requires forms of control which place it within the 'securing boundaries of aesthetic discourse' in which 'the distinctions between inside and outside, between finite form and form without limit, need to be continuously drawn' (Nead 1992: 2, 11). As the frame of knowledge, then, 'Woman' is continually re-produced as 'utterly knowable' and rendered transparent in the processes of vision and knowledge. Yet those very discourses simultaneously produce 'Woman' as opaque and mysterious, as her amorphous form cannot be fully contained within those borders. 'She' is literally framed as artistic product and forms the frame of that which is knowable. De Lauretis (1990) argues that para-doxically 'Woman' is

> displayed as spectacle and still unrepresented or unrepresentable, invis-ible yet constituted as the object and the guarantee of vision; a being whose existence and specificity are simultaneously asserted and denied, negated and controlled.
>
> (de Lauretis 1990: 115)

This historically generated liberal discourse of boundaries and difference operates simultaneously, although not symmetrically, with the production of categories of 'race' and cultural difference. In the context of contemporary formulations of cultural diversity and cultural difference, Homi Bhabha (1990) argues for the need to place an analysis of the discursive production of transparency at the centre of understandings of identity. Western 'civili-sation' imagines itself through what Bhabha calls 'a transparent norm' (*ibid.*: 208) or frame of knowledge: that is, the assumed neutrality and centrality of the white, middle-class, heterosexual male. It requires the difference of others as a discursive frame in order to generate its self-identity, whilst simultaneously requiring this difference ultimately to be transparent. This discursive manoeuvre subsumes difference and invokes a return to the same. The proliferation of cultural diversity does not signify a radical form of difference, but rather a menu of signs of the exotic for the Western consumer.

> In fact the sign of the 'cultured' or 'civilised' attitude is the ability to appreciate cultures in a kind of *musée imaginaire*; as though one should be able to collect and appreciate them. Western connoisseurship is the capacity to understand and locate cultures in a universal time-frame that acknowledges their various historical and social contexts only even-tually to transcend them and render them transparent.
>
> (Bhabha 1990: 208)

This framing of knowledge of the (white, male, heterosexual) Western self and his transparent others generates the '*creation* of cultural diversity and a *containment* of cultural difference' (*ibid.*). In later sections, I will argue that this production of diversity can function for some as a consumer resource, or repository of malleable signifiers, in the rearticulation of social privilege.

Transparency as a visual metaphor, therefore, has considerable discursive weight. It points to the ways in which knowledge, power and the visual have been historically articulated in the diverse areas of art, medicine, technology and philosophy (Crary 1993; Jay 1993; Stafford 1991). The status of trans-parency as metaphor is crucial for appreciating its performative role in the generation of knowledge tied to the visual. Metaphor requires a distance and difference between two signs in order to signify a new amalgam of meaning, and yet collapses difference in that moment of fusion. Drucilla Cornell (1993) argues that metaphor is not merely one linguistic trope amongst many, but rather, a central mechanism in the operation of language. 'The real' is not immediately available to us through the ostensibly transparent medium of language; our access to 'the real' is mediated in one form by the 'detour' of metaphor. In reaching out to the real through metaphor, we are paradoxically held at a distance from it:

> philosophy needs metaphor to reach the real and yet metaphor always takes us away from 'it' by performing on 'it'. Metaphorical transference, in other words, is a mechanism by which we attempt to reach the literal, understood as the necessary or essential property of things.
>
> (Cornell 1993: 68)

In the next chapter I critically assess the status of metaphor, arguing that, contrary to Cornell's emphasis, metaphor should be seen as only one, albeit significant, form of access to meaning. Furthermore, in the context of my study of adverts, the 'literal' quality that metaphor attempts to reach should be seen as relational and shifting, rather than as a stable structure. As discussed in the previous chapter, the sign 'Woman' as metaphor is mobilised by advertisers as a visual bridge reaching out to 'the literal'. This is required in order to function as an anchorage point for the availability of ironic inter-pretative moves targeted at male consumers. The imagined transparency of the sign 'Woman' as a frame for knowledge-production promises access to 'the literal' or 'the real', and yet always remains *elsewhere*, and from this distance 'performs' on 'the real'. In visual terms, then, metaphor (under-stood as the 'would be' or the 'as if' linking two signs) forms a constitutive part in the processes of vision. 'The "as if" of the imagination is implicated in the very act of "seeing" the real' (Cornell 1991: 169). Yet, I propose that the terms of the literal and the non-literal (for example, the ironic) continu-ally shift in 'seeing the real'.

The role of the imagination in processes of vision is not a universal framework which is suspended from historical and political contexts, but is firmly rooted in situated, embodied perspectives. Donna Haraway (1991: 189) argues that the idea of 'infinite vision', or transparency and legibility from a 'neutral' perspective, is an illusion which functions in mechanisms of oppression. All vision, Haraway argues, is embodied, situated and partial, and is implicated in the production of forms of knowledge. There are no 'innocent' or objective perspectives. Not only do others become legible to us through this structure of assumed transparency, but we also gain access to understandings of ourselves.

> Vision is *always* a question of the power to see – and perhaps the violence implicit in our visualizing practices. With whose blood were my eyes crafted? These points also apply to testimony from the position of

'oneself'. We are not immediately present to ourselves. Self-knowledge requires a semiotic–material technology linking meanings to bodies.

(Haraway 1991: 192)

That we are not immediately present to ourselves can be seen in terms of Hegelian dialectics of self-present identity (Diprose 1994), which I discussed in Chapter 1. Here the self is formulated as a unity having the same origins in time and space. This is not a static state of being but must be actively achieved through dialogue with the other in terms of distance and differ-ence. This dialogue involves assumed transparency which requires the discursive constructions of the 'sexual difference' of women (the bodies of women) and racialised, classed and sexually 'deviant' others in order to generate the distance and difference necessary for the re-production of white, male Western selfhood (Diprose 1994). Images of the self form a fluid semiotic grid of visual codes which link knowledge of 'difference' and self-hood to particular material, *male* bodies using the currency, or system of equivalence, of the sexual difference of the female body. Sexual and other differences are not, then, static natural codes, but are continually re-produced through systems of knowledge, transparency and the visual.

The visual and its relation to knowledge should not be imagined simply as shifting between binary poles of the visible/the invisible, the internal self/the external other, etc. It should be seen as a complex, contradictory process which may operate simultaneously on diverse levels of discourse. 'The topography of the subject is multi-dimensional; so, therefore, is vision' (Haraway 1991: 193). This multidimensionality encompasses the visible and knowledge-formation, for, as Ron Burnett (1995) points out, what is visible may not be legible, or wholly transparent to processes of knowledge which link signifiers and signifieds. Furthermore, Burnett argues that 'the visible in an image is ... merely a fragment of what is signified' (1995: 70). Therefore, there are significant disjunctures and 'blank spaces' or 'elsewhere(s)'/'else-when(s)' between the visible, embodied processes of vision, and the production of social meanings. The following section examines how vision and the production of the visible are performative 'events' which involve movement, distance and difference. The seeing subject is not a preformed entity who expresses 'his' agency and intent through reading off meanings in images. The seeing subject is formed in those very processes of vision.

The visual as performative

In Chapter 1 I discussed how the category of 'the individual' is performa-tively constituted in a continual generative process of recognition and expression of self-identical presence. In this process, the expression of the rights of 'the individual' in a range of contracts, including the citizenship contract, come to produce the category of 'the individual'. However, neither the rights nor the fully constituted individual stand in temporal priority one to the other: it is a mutually generative enactment. Performativity is, then, a discursive manoeuvre which in expressing itself, produces itself. Sedgwick and Parker (1995: 16) propose that exploring performativity involves asking the question of how 'saying something can be doing something'. What I want to explore is how *seeing something can be doing something*. The 'doing' of the speech act or the act of vision is the action of self-constitution – the performative process constitutes the self and the other through discourses of transparency and their relation to legibility. This process is both embodied and embodying – it spatially and temporally organises one's sense of 'self', or identity, through the bodily sense of sight. This generates a means of visually 'understanding' the relation or distance between self and other, performatively re-producing those boundaries. In the next chapter I address these issues in terms of reiterative narratives, pleasure and temporality. But for the present I will focus on the spatio-temporal constitution of visuality and the production of narratives of the self.

As indicated above, processes of vision are not linear or symmetrical movements between the assumed fixed points of reference, or perspectives, of the 'self' and the visual image. Nor are images immutable 'containers' of meanings to be accessed, decoded and deployed in the reflexive project of the self. Burnett (1995) suggests that the movements of perception do not operate in a simple translation of vision to language, from visual image to naming that image.

> It may be more useful to think of the relations between mind and vision as a series of hypotheses leading to destinations that randomly connect and disconnect, constructs more dependent on temporal distortion than linearity. *The time of vision may not link up to the time of thought or understanding.*
>
> (Burnett 1995: 26, emphasis added)

Burnett's emphasis on the idea of disjuncture in the operation of different levels of knowledge production and perception may open up a way of imagining 'the elsewhere(s)' or space-off and 'the elsewhen(s)' in a visual sense. The elsewhere(s) or space-off is formulated as the multidimensional zone of 'the invisible' or unseen. Both the invisible and the visible are performatively generated in a continual oscillation between shifting points of reference which signify 'the visible' and 'the invisible'. I would like to argue that this oscillation is composed of the reiteration of 'moments' of contact which are seemingly random temporal and spatial connections and disconnections of diverse elements. In Chapter 1 I initially problematised the assumed temporal and spatial boundedness of 'the moment', exploring Butler's (1993) idea that the 'betweenness' which separates moments also constitutes the interiority or content of those moments. If this 'betweenness' is composed of random connections and disconnections, as well as temporal and spatial 'seepage' or contagion between moments, then the boundaries of the visible and the invisible are in a continual, fluid rearticulation. As Butler (1993) indicates, each reiteration is also an alteration. Therefore, not only do the boundaries of the visible and the invisible shift, but so also does the spatio-temporal matrix of the 'moment'. This continually re-produces different modes for imagining space and time. In this way, the generation of the ideal of transparency and legibility shifts constantly in both spatial and temporal terms between and across the categories of the visible and the invisible. In Chapter 6 I address how this movement is articulated in one form through the concept of 'potential' tied to consumerist self-actualisation, but what I want to emphasise at this point is the mobile nature of these processes in relation to vision.

As discussed in the previous chapter, this mobility is overlaid by the contemporary media 'non-space' of fluid images which are disconnected from their previous social contexts (Morse 1990). Signifiers are disembedded, potentially interchangeable and available for processes of continual connection and disconnection with each other. This is not, however, a wholly unstructured play of signifiers lacking possible fixity. Certain viewers of images are offered modes of momentarily freezing and fixing particular meanings.

> Yet these are not processes lacking coherence as a result of all the variables; quite the contrary, we are able to temporarily unify the parts and in doing so articulate defined moments in which certain categories of explanation work or in which an interpretative strategy is acceptable. At each moment, if we grant the temporal a central place, a variety of new and potentially radical associations arise that yet again transform what had seemingly been fixed.
>
> (Burnett 1995: 27)

These interpretative strategies which enable a certain (temporary) fixing of meaning are not universally available, but are constituted through the exclusivity of the category of 'the individual', that is, white, middle-class, heterosexual and male. In the previous chapter I argued that advertisers employ textual strategies to actively delimit and generate target markets of consumers. I explored how one such strategy of the literal and the ironic operate in tension, producing fluid connections between privileged viewing modes and white, middle-class, heterosexual masculinities. In the next section I develop the theoretical relation between vision, knowledge and 'moments of exposure'. In doing so, I map out how certain modes of ironic interpretation or viewing are produced by advertisers as both signs of distinction and narratives of self-constitution.

Time and the advertising image

The complexities of perception discussed above indicate that new ways of conceptualising the visual image are necessary in order to move beyond the idea of a preconstituted self viewing a self-contained, although polysemic, advertisement in a singular, uniform 'moment' of interpretation. Acts of vision do not express the agency and intent of the seeing subject – vision is one performative process (amongst many) which actively constitutes the subject and its capacities for vision. Burnett (1995) argues that images are not fixed sets of visual codes, but instead occur in the space between the photographic/graphic print (in this case, an advertisement) and the viewer. Through this framework, I have argued that the process of image-generation occurs performatively. It is mutually constitutive of the meaning of the print and the viewing self, and ways of understanding the relation between the two. This image-production generates forms of self-consciousness or self-knowledge which can only be achieved through processes of knowing 'the other'. This in turn is achieved through the establishment of a system of equivalence and assumed transparency and legibility. This transparency and legibility, Burnett (1995) stresses, is not a symmetrical process directly linking temporal modes of thought and vision. Nor indeed, I would argue, is the process symmetrical in terms of social difference, as women and other subordinated groups are discursively produced as lacking the same constitution of self-consciousness as white, middle-class, heterosexual men. Yet, as de Lauretis (1989) argues, women are *conscious* of their ambiguous discursive positionings and the continual movement between and across borders of discursive 'elsewhere(s)'. What forms this consciousness might take will be addressed in the next chapter.

Viewing as a form of perception, then, introduces notions of two-way constitution, self-consciousness and ambiguity. Burnett (1995) argues that problematising of the processes of viewing puts into question the idea of the printed photograph or advertisement as self-contained repository of meaning. Instead, it opens up the question of the viewer's (and, of course, the researcher's) understanding of the print as a *product* of viewing processes.

> Sight is a mental construct, since the connections between seeing, perceiving and knowing are at best only available to us through hypotheses about the results of their interaction. When we speak then of seeing, are we speaking of a process? Or products of that process? And as the word *process* suggests, the maelstrom of visual activities accompanying the viewing of a photograph [or advertisement] cannot simply be reduced to the technological instance represented by the print.
>
> (Burnett 1995: 65)

Burnett here stresses temporality in our self-conscious access to processes of seeing. 'A sight' is the end product of the articulation between vision and knowledge. Paradoxically, it is also the starting point for imagining this very relation between seeing and knowing in which the printed image is, in a sense, *witness* to the temporality of vision. Paul Virilio (1994) situates this question in relation to debates around the 'objectivity' of the image and its material form. He argues that the locus of meaning of an image has shifted from its printed or celluloid materiality. Now an image's meaning is produced in the temporality of viewing that image.

> The problem of the objectivisation of the image ... largely stops presenting itself in terms of some kind of paper or celluloid *support surface* – that is, in relation to a material reference space. It now emerges in relation to time, *to the exposure time that allows or edits seeing.*
>
> (Virilio 1994: 61)

The location of meaning shifts away from the apparently tangible site of paper or screen. Instead, the time of seeing becomes the privileged mode of meaning-making. The image disengages its exclusive referentiality to the printed material – its meaning is no longer fixed to the conventional back-drop of ink on paper or light patterns on a screen. Instead, images explicitly draw on a temporal connection with the viewer in the 'exposure time' of vision. In effect, the reference point for the meanings of images becomes the exposure time of vision rather than the material surface of paper or screen. I would argue that this visual exposure should be seen as situated in time, but also as constitutive of our understandings of time and of our own temporal narratives of self. As Judith Butler argues, we should interrogate the assumption of 'the discrete identity of the moment' (1993: 10n8), and explore the 'betweenness' of moments which also constitutes the interiority of those moments. This 'betweenness' functions both to separate moments as distinct from each other. Yet it also draws connections between moments in a broader temporal sequence or cohesion against which distinct 'moments' are legible. Discourses of vision and knowledge, I suggest, link moments through narrative devices which mobilise visual metaphors such as transparency. So, the 'betweenness' of moments, the narratives of both connection and difference, are constitutive of processes of visually under-standing the relation of self to other.

Metaphor, then, does not merely become temporalised by contagion through its engagement in narratives between moments. It is itself temporal and reworks temporalities. Cornell (1993) argues that metaphor, in the form of the conjectural 'would be' or 'as if', is the condition of interpretation (or viewing). It functions through retroactively engaging its future-oriented meaning, casting into the future and into the past in order to produce modes of understanding.

> Interpretation, then, is retrospective in the sense that we always begin the process of interpretation from within a pregiven context. The process is also prospective, because it involves the elaboration of the 'would be's' inherent in the context itself. ... The 'as if' is oriented toward the future in that we project the proposition onto a future

situation to draw out its meaning. The future is implicit in the act of interpretation.

(Cornell 1993: 27–8)

What I am proposing is that, in explicitly engaging the viewer in the temporality of vision, 'the sight' can offer up temporal narratives of that viewing self. Processes of vision draw on the right to see – the historically established privileges of the category of 'the individual'. In effect, we 'see through' the rights accrued in discourses of transparency and equivalence which function to marginalise certain groups and privilege others. As Haraway (1991: 192) argues, 'vision is *always* a question of the power to see'. In visual performativity, the self is constituted in that time of vision by drawing on those histories of privilege, power and exclusion. In this understanding, the fusion of vision and knowing in the moment of exposure points to the *performative* nature of the self's constitution in visual moments.

Yet as Burnett (1995: 26) emphasises, 'the time of vision may not link up to the time of thought or understanding'. In the context of narratives of the self, this disjuncture means a continual and dislocated play between time frames: the impossibility of unitary selfhood in the temporal present attempts to authorise itself by drawing on a coherent narrative biography of a past-self. This past-self, in turn, can only be understood through projecting the present-self onto the future through metaphors of 'as if' and 'would be'. In the context of my study of advertising, these metaphors draw their significatory power from the continual re-production of the categories of 'Woman' and racial and cultural difference. These form the frame of knowledge within which the (Western, white, male, heterosexual) self can be structured, restructured and contested. In the following sections I will argue that it is these narratives of self-constitution which are generated in the moment of exposure that advertisers attempt to *brand* through certain textual strategies. In doing so, they produce that moment of vision/interpretation/self-constitution as a sign in itself. It is a sign of cultural distinction (of difference and belonging) which advertising then re-presents to the 'self' for consumption. The following analyses of advertisements explore this interplay of vision, knowledge and self-constitution in relation to irony and metaphor.

'A horizon is nothing save the limit of your sight'[1]

In this section I illustrate the above arguments with an analysis of a Marlboro advertisement for cigarettes (Plate 4.1).[2] I selected this advertisement because it mobilises themes typical of the reflexive advertisements in my study – that is, masculine 'individuality' and signifiers of privilege. These, I have argued, are discursively linked to ironic modes of address targeted at a male, white, middle-class market. As I indicated in the previous

SMOKING CAUSES CANCER

Chief Medical Officers' Warning
13 mg Tar 0.9 mg Nicotine

Plate 4.1 Marlboro advertisement. *Source: Q* magazine, April 1995 (courtesy of Philip Morris Ltd).

chapter, the use of a reflexive, ironic textual address may merely reflect the restrictions placed by the British Advertising Standards Authority on advertising for certain products such as alcohol and tobacco. For example, tobacco advertising 'should never suggest that smoking is safe, healthy, natural, necessary for relaxation and concentration, popular or appropriate in all circumstances'.[3] It should not aim to appeal to young people, nor should it be associated with 'social, sexual, romantic or business success', and it should not link smoking with people who are 'evidently wealthy, fashionable, sophisticated or successful'.[4] These regulations obviously constrain the images permitted in tobacco advertising, yet the regulations do allow such advertising to use humour and to link the choice of a brand to 'taste and discernment'.[5] As I suggested in the previous chapter, these restrictions may discourage the use of 'conventional' forms of address such as the model/product-image/tagline format found in many print advertisements. Indeed, it has often been noted that a 'cryptic' form of address is typical of tobacco and alcohol advertising for this very reason (Cutler and Nye 1997). The use of a humorous, ironic address might then be seen merely as a consequence of these restrictions and not, as I have argued, primarily as a medium of masculine viewing privilege. However, I argue in the following section that the impositions of the regulations only partially account for the prevalence of this form of address in advertisements. Indeed, this address was present in my study across a range of product types, such as cars or walking boots, and not solely in alcohol and tobacco advertising. The ironic address of the Marlboro advertisement relies on gendered and racialised privilege to target its (male) market. The abstract, 'cryptic' textual address draws its significatory power from the forms of historical privilege that it references – these privileges are themselves invisible or naturalised. In effect, the advert constructs privileged 'abstract' viewing positions and re-produces those very forms of privilege.

The advertisement presents a sepia-tinted photographic image of (what can be assumed to be) rugged North American landscape cut across by a railway track, apparently surveyed by someone wearing worn jeans and boots. The discordant red colour of the ant on the boot, together with the health warning at the foot of the frame, signals to viewers with a knowledge of widely circulating images in popular culture that this is an advertisement for Marlboro cigarettes. This advertisement is situated in a wider context of a non-space of circulating signs in which discourses of unitary, unique selfhood are articulated in new, more fluid formations. Through these discourses, the (male, white, Western) self is produced as unique and distinct from others through distance from them. Yet, simultaneously, the self requires 'sameness' in the form of coherent narratives of temporal self-identity in which the self can be identified as a discrete, bounded entity across time. Following Butler (1993), I have argued in previous sections that this is a continual re-generative process articulated through the reiteration of moments of contact with the other. According to Butler, these spatio-temporal moments sediment to the point of indistinguishability, producing what she calls 'non-thematizable space and non-thematizable time as they converge' (1993: 10n8). This convergence of difference and distance is potentially destabilising for the re-production of unitary selfhood. And it also disrupts the advertising industry's imperative continually to re-generate categories of difference in order to delimit specific target markets of consumers. The following analysis of the Marlboro advertisement addresses how advertisers attempt to prise apart these sedimented moments of 'identity' and produce coherent narratives of self in order to stabilise their target markets.

In this analysis I focus on how certain discourses of historically and culturally specific difference can be viewed (by some) from a contemporary European context. This viewing may engage simultaneously with different ironic and literal levels of meaning. This multidimensional suspension of signifiers allows for an active rearticulation of meaning, identity and narratives of the self. These narratives are guaranteed through the 'frontier' metaphors which act as the frame for the historical and contemporary production of Western knowledge. In this way the tropes of 'the Wild West', conventions of 'Western' films, and discourses of 'Western (European) civilisation' are held together in tension. Indeed, I will argue that they can be refigured to produce new meanings and new identities.

The textual structuring of the Marlboro advertisement (Plate 4.1) operates on several planes of meaning. It produces modes of address which continually shift between what is visible within the frame of the text and the referents beyond the frame. This potential fluidity is initiated by visual codes which draw into question the ontological status of the visible within the frame: the discordant juxtaposition of the red of the ant in sepia surroundings signals the possibility of multiple, potentially ironic levels of meaning. The sepia-tinted print draws its textual reference from the genre of nineteenth- and early twentieth-century photography of 'frontier' America. Moreover, its status as photograph lays claim to an assumed unmediated representation of a past reality. In a discussion of the genre of Marlboro advertisements, Michelle Henning (1995) argues that the context of contemporary advertisements requires a more complex understanding of their ontological status than that provided by Roland Barthes' influential conceptualisation of photographs.[6] Henning (1987: 44) cites Barthes' view that photographs lay a claim to representational 'reality' from their quality of 'having-been-there' and engaging in imagined direct spatial and temporal contact with the materiality of the past. Henning (1995: 219) questions this in relation to images in contemporary advertising; 'how common is it, in the ad-saturated West, to expect or require that advertising has the status of a document?'. She problematises the ontological status of 'the real' in advertising whilst disputing the validity of theories which, as she puts it, argue that contemporary society can be characterised by 'the loss of the real' in which individuals can no longer distinguish between 'reality' and its copies (*ibid.*: 219). This reality was never accessible to us, she claims, and our task now is to interrogate the modes of understanding in the form of narratives of the past which are made available to us.

I suggest that several levels and temporalities of meaning are textually produced in this Marlboro advertisement. In effect, these narrate the available understandings of the ontological status of both the photographic (advertising) print and the viewing self. The assumed certainty of the mimetic 'reality-status' of the sepia photograph is disrupted by the dissonant presence of a red ant. Its colour lifts the image from its embedded state in historical 'facticity' and opens up narratives of the past to potential reformulation. The ant's referents are both the contemporaneity of the moment of interpretation, or moment of exposure, and the complicity of the viewer engaged in this ironic shifting of levels of meaning. This movement is the generative drive for the production of a sign of interpretation as cultural distinction. The ontological disruption is, of course, a commercial break. The red of the ant is the visual signifier of the absent brand Marlboro, effectively *branding* the ironic interpretative manoeuvre.

However, the claim of the sepia photograph to a mimetic status of historical facticity is overlaid with explicit reference to popular culture narratives of 'the Wild West'. These have a dual recognised status of fiction situated within more general context of assumed historical accuracy. The double-page panoramic view of the landscape elicits references to the popular genre of Western films. This cinematic scope is emphasized by the band at the foot of the frame (containing the compulsory health warning) which functions to highlight the status of the borders of the photographic image as 'frame'. On this level, the visible within the frame refers to explicitly fictionalised narratives (we know that this is only an advert), together with the genre of fictionalised Western films. At the same time, the referents beyond the frame are narratives of assumed historical facticity.

The ironic oscillation between these levels of meaning and their ontological status is articulated through the relation between the visible and the production of knowledge. As Diprose (1994: 54) argues, a structure for producing an 'absolute understanding' of the other is required for the generation of 'the individual' and this occurs through the production of structures of 'transparency'. As I have argued above, the 'transparency' of the image in terms of ontological status is already disrupted through shifting levels of ironic meanings. At this stage, I would like to explore how moments of stability can occur in these shifts in order to generate the difference and distance required for the production of 'the individual'. As I argued in the previous chapter, the production of the ironic requires the (at least temporary) stabilisation of 'the literal' as referent. I would like to consider this in relation to the visibility and invisibility of signifiers in the Marlboro advertisement. I will argue that the white, European masculinity of the figure in the advertisement is not visible within the frame of the image in conventional terms. However, it is the implicit universal which mobilises specific narratives of historically constituted difference to generate its presence or identity.

   The railway track cutting across the landscape takes as its reference point the European colonial expansion in North America in the eighteenth, nineteenth and early twentieth centuries. During this period, railways opened up the West to mass European expansion and conquest, and as Edward Buscombe (1995) argues, framed certain features of the landscape as resources for tourism. In order to promote tourism, railway companies commissioned many of the photographs of the West's landscape with the aim of aestheticising the desert and demonstrating their technological capacities for surmounting difficult terrain (Buscombe 1995). In doing so, they evoked

> a future of limitless progress which could be delivered by the unstoppable combination of technology and capitalism. Landscape was no longer solely an object of contemplation but a barrier to be overcome. In taming its awesome proportions it could be possessed, made manageable, even domesticated, and turned into a source of profit.
>
> (Buscombe 1995: 99)

In the Marlboro advertisement, the track's position in the foreground of the frame situates it as 'the horizon of civilisation', a physical and epistemological vantage point from which the visual and understandings of the colonial self and indigenous other are articulated. From this perspective, the 'imperial eyes' (Pratt 1992) of the coloniser can align the technological ideals of progress, European democratic traditions and capitalist expansion and accumulation with historically situated discourses of individualism, rationality and potential. Bhikhu Parekh (1995) explores the discursive relation between European, and particularly Lockean, discourses of rationality tied to land ownership and sovereignty which were articulated in that era precisely in relation to colonial expansion. Parekh outlines how during the seventeenth-century European expansion into the Americas, John Locke developed concepts of European rationality, as opposed to the 'irrational' nature of the colonised North American Indians. Locke defended, and indeed endorsed, the confiscation of Indian lands on the grounds that the Indians were not 'industrious'. They were thought to waste the natural resources of their land, as they did not cultivate or use this land in ways familiar to Europeans. This jarred with European concepts of private property and rationality, for 'a truly rational society established the institution of private property and provided incentives for industry and the accumulation of wealth, without both of which men could not discharge their duty to develop the earth's resources and create a prosperous society' (Parekh 1995: 84). For Locke, this lack of industry demonstrated that the Indians were not 'rational' beings. This excluded them from the category of human, denying them access to other human rights, such as freedom from violence (*ibid.*). The Indians were failing in their use of their 'human capacities' or potential as defined by Locke, and therefore, they did not earn the liberal right to respect (*ibid.*: 97).

Through this capitalist framework of expansion, potential and rationality, the discursive concept of the European, rational 'individual' of 'civilisation' was produced in opposition to the North American 'savage'. As discussed in Chapter 1, this production also partially excluded women from that category of rationality, generating a universal 'individual' whose particularities (white, European, male, middle-class) were, in effect, invisible. In the Marlboro advertisement, then, the figure with the panoramic vantage point (and the complicit viewer with the privileged perspective on the advertisement) can be identified as white, European, middle-class and male although specific visual signifiers are absent. It is, in Bhabha's (1990) terms, 'a transparent norm'. This naming can take place not only through conventional masculine 'Wild West' tropes of rugged individuality, self-sufficiency, adventure and discovery (Bright 1989). It can also occur through the linking of those specific semiotic codes of (white, European) masculinity to the sexed bodies of men and women which are framed by discourses of 'the individual' and 'the citizen'. Indeed, the signifiers of 'individuality' shift not only according to gender definitions, but more broadly in relation to the cultural climate. For instance, Henning (1995) argues that cigarette advertising now rarely promotes smoking as 'relaxing' (as it did in the past), due to public awareness of health risks and shifting norms of social acceptability. In the Marlboro campaigns, the advertisers respond to this shift by using the compulsory health warning together with themes of rugged, unpredictable nature to produce an aura or frisson of danger. This functions to frame consumers' 'individuality' in terms of insouciance in the face of risk and public censure (Henning 1995). The Marlboro landscape makes reference not only to classic Western films, but also to the new genre of art-house/road movies which rework myths of the Wild West, for example, *Bagdad Café* and *Paris, Texas*. These films, Henning (1995: 224) argues, evoke an atmosphere of 'life lived at the margins' and 'risky living'. This address in terms of risk is, I would argue, another way in which advertisers attempts to elicit and brand a complicitous relation with viewers who are smokers.

To return to the visual signifiers of these differences, Henning's (1995) concern with the ontological status of images in advertisements is focused primarily on the question of how certain technological advances may make advertising texts more or less open to multi-layered meaning. Whilst addressing key issues of technological innovation, this approach leaves intact a notion of the viewing self as the preconstituted Western individual endowed with certain interpretative skills. My focus is on the ambiguous and shifting ontological status of certain advertisements in terms both of their acknowledged and widely accepted role of commercial 'persuasion', and shifting 'fictionalised' narratives of popular culture and 'historical' context. This emphasis leads me to ask different questions. I suggest that it is not the veracity of a 'real', historical past that is the primary point of significance. Nor is it the form of the narratives of that past which are now available to us. Rather it is the relation of narratives of those different levels of meaning to the formation of a category of (white, Western, male) 'individual'.

Modes of 'distracted' viewing, I argued in earlier sections, allow for what Morse (1990) calls a 'drifting' between levels of meaning and their relation to 'reality'. This can be seen as an oscillation between and across what is visible within the frame and what is invisible, or elsewhere, yet implicated in the production of the visible. In the Marlboro advertisement these flows are articulated through the shifting formations of the invisibility or assumed 'neutrality' and transparency of the norm of 'the individual' as white, Western and male. This norm is invisible and unintelligible as anything other than the politically universal 'individual' of Locke's ideal. Yet the performative re-production of this ideal relies on the historically specific partial exclusion of certain groups: women, racialised others, 'non-Europeans', the working class. The performative enactment forms the *doing* of *seeing* in its capacity of constituting the seeing, agentic self. The movement between and across zones of visibility and invisibility is not a symmetrical, self-identical mirroring. As Burnett (1995) argues, the visible may not be legible, and may indeed only be a fraction of what is signified. The partial discursive presence of 'the others' of 'the individual' and their relation to discursive 'elsewhere(s)' are disjunctures in these processes of representation. I do not mean this in the sense of fractures in otherwise uniform, coherent 'blocks' of meaning. Rather, I am referring to blank spaces, 'spaces-off', other multi-form dimensions of discourses of visibility, presence and flows of coherence. These shifting spatio-temporal zones and flows of movement actively rearticulate conventionally situated narratives of the historical past which are visibly presented as a form of knowledge.

These shifting claims to reality and knowledge disrupt the unproblematic 'transparency' or 'absolute understanding' (Diprose 1994: 54) of the (colonial) other which is required for the production of (white, Western, male) selfhood and the targeting of consumer markets. However, the framing of certain modes of (ironic) interpretation as a sign of cultural distinction can temporarily stabilise these meanings. Indeed, it can provide the potential for actively rearticulating the meanings of white, middle-class, European masculinities. In this sense, there is not a 'loss of the real', or privileged 'forgetting' of a violent colonial past. Rather, these historical narratives articulate with popular culture discourses of frontier America – they are held together in (ironic) tension with contemporary (gendered, racialised and classed) discourses of consumerist individuality, potential and self-actualisation. Contemporary motifs of rugged individuality, discovery and finding one's true essence in nature (and realising one's unique potential) can be consumed and enjoyed on a literal level, on the level of ironic detachment, and through a dimension of shifting between these levels. This mobility between levels is visualised in the Marlboro advertisement primarily through landscape which, Homi Bhabha (1994: 143) argues, has historically articulated with tropes of nation. 'The recurrent metaphor of landscape as the inscape of national identity emphasizes the quality of light, the question of social visibility, the power of the eye to naturalize the rhetoric of national affiliation and its forms of collective expression'. So, on one level, the trope of landscape provides a visual currency for transforming the space and time of America and 'turning Territory into Tradition' (*ibid.*: 149),

> the political unity of the nation consists in a continual displacement of the anxiety of its irredeemably plural modern space – representing the nation's modern territoriality is turned into the archaic, atavistic temporality of Traditionalism. The difference of space returns as the Sameness of time, turning Territory into Tradition, turning the People into One.
>
> (Bhabha 1994: 149)

In the context of the historical production of America as landscape in photographic and filmic genres, Buscombe (1995) describes how images of deserts and canyons replaced earlier images of mountains. In response to French, British and Danish competitive production of early twentieth-century 'Western' films, American film companies attempted to create the 'authentic' American Western using images of mountains. Yet mountains were a common feature in many European countries. As a marketing device, later American 'Westerns' started to use images of canyons and deserts as 'authentic local colour' to represent the 'real' America (Buscombe 1995). The corollary of this has been the inscription of a particular form of American landscape in the contemporary popular culture imaginary as 'wide-open possibility, a sense of vistas infinitely open in time and space' (Shohat and Stam 1994: 118).

In this way, the Marlboro advertisement plays on the discursive elasticity of space-time and expands and contracts those matrices to generate particular forms of 'nationness'. The advertisement produces a framework of transparency and equivalence by visualising and temporalising the space of the landscape as a linear narrative of the becoming-nation of territory invaded by European colonisers. In this sense, the American West was 'less a place than a movement, a going west, a moving horizon' (*ibid.*: 117–18). It is a mobile frame for the drama of the constitution of 'the individual' and *his* rights.

The central issue in relation to these discourses is how the contemporary (white, male, heterosexual) viewer within Europe can engage simultaneously with divergent meanings of the constitution of privileged selfhood. As discussed in the previous chapter, Featherstone (1991) has called this interpretative engagement a calculated de-control between pleasurable immersion and detachment. It is not so much a dialogue as a 'monologue which subsumes differences under norms already in place' (Diprose 1994: 54). This interpretative move between levels may not involve a direct ('literal') reading of European colonial expansion and the constitution of 'the Western individual'. Yet it requires the privileged discursive position which has been engendered by those discourses in order to produce its interpretative flexibility.[7] This is a performative, visual enactment which in expressing itself (as a privileged male subject), produces itself. The 'invisibility' of the (racial, sexual) other is produced through a mutually generative enactment with the historically constituted transparent norm of the white, male, heterosexual, Western 'individual'. The privileged (ironic) interpretative position of 'the individual' is precisely that which allows the (re-)production of 'the individual': the rights of 'the individual' performatively articulate with, and *express*, the category of 'the individual'.

For European (white, male) viewers, the Marlboro advert offers a range of levels of discourse which can be actively rearticulated. Fluid 'moments' of contact between signs can be (temporarily) stabilised as reference points for the production of a unitary self. Moments of 'frontier' contact with North American Indians (mediated both through the 'fictionalised' 'Western' genre and through imagined historical facticity) can be held in tension with contemporary (European, white, heterosexual) masculinities. Through this ironic shifting between detachment and immersion, contemporary tropes of North American popular culture can be used by European white, middle-class men as a image-pool of resources. These then act to reflect the cultural distinction of an ironic European perspective.

In conclusion, the 'moment of exposure' in visual contact is a form of spatial and temporal connection between the temporalities of the printed advertisement and the temporalities of the self. Histories of privilege and the discursive status of 'the individual' connect with the time of vision. This articulation draws on privilege to authorise the seeing subject and reworks that privilege in the very time of vision. Printed images should not be imagined as static, immutable 'containers' of meaning which are decoded and used by viewers to construct and communicate their identities to others. Images and time have complex and multidimensional relationships. Virilio (1994) argues that the impact of print advertisements, or their 'suggestiveness' as he puts it, has conventionally resided in their quality as 'phatic' imagery. This is high-definition imagery with precision print quality, making a high visual impact. Such imagery forces our attention, grabs the eye, and 'strives, through our gaze, to attain depth' (*ibid.*: 62). However, this attention-grabbing effect of the print quality is now being eroded, and print advertisements are attempting to reconsolidate their impact through the temporality of certain forms of visual address.

> The graphic or photographic quality of the advertising image, its *high definition* as they say, is no longer a guarantee of some kind of aesthetic of precision, of photographic sharpness etc. It is merely the search for a stereoscopic effect, for a third dimension. ... The phatic image that grabs our attention and forces us to look is no longer a powerful image; it is a cliché attempting ... to inscribe itself in some unfolding of time in which the optic and the kinematic are indistinguishable.
>
> (Virilio 1994: 62–3)

I am arguing that this stereoscopic effect, or third dimension, is the spatio-temporal 'zone/time' of the moment of interpretation or exposure. This is, in Burnett's (1995) terms, 'the image' which is generated between the print and the viewer. It is this moment of interpretative vision or reflexive engagement in self-constitution between the advertising imagery and the viewer that advertisers attempt to brand. In the Marlboro advertisement, the temporal linking of the optic and the kinematic[8] through movements of ironic disengagement and immersion disembeds and rearticulates multiple temporal narratives of self. The present, or moment of exposure, invokes retrospective and prospective narratives of self which mobilise metaphors of difference. Historical narratives of the constitution of 'the individual' through colonial encounters articulate with 'present-tense' moments of self-constitution. These, in turn, mobilise the 'rights of the individual' accrued in these and other hierarchical encounters and project them onto the future/potential-self mediated through metaphors of 'the other'. In Homi Bhabha's (1990) terms, these historically and geographically divergent discourses become a form of malleable resource (for some) of 'cultural diversity' which ultimately contains difference.

This reinvention of self and rights through shifting narratives can be seen in terms of Cornell's concept of 'natality'. This is 'the demand to renew oneself in every effort to maintain an "I" over time' (Cornell 1993: 41). Through the ironic suspension of different levels of discourse, the (white, male) 'I' can enjoy the rights of the ideal, unitary self-present identity. Simultaneously, he is authorised to flirt with multiple and contradictory positions. It is these interpretative moves of performative constitution that advertising attempts to brand and define in terms of a commodity or service. These mobile narratives of self draw on metaphors of its others. In doing so, they momentarily sediment and make visible in certain circumscribed terms 'the literal' categories of sexual, racial and cultural difference. In Chapter 6 I explore how 'history' and narratives of the 'origins' of the self offer dislocated relations to citizenship obligations and rights and what Judith Butler (1995) has called historical responsibility. In Chapter 5 I elaborate concepts of narrativised selfhood and explore the ways in which women have access to the discursive category of 'Woman'. Women and overlapping groups subordinated in terms of class, 'race' and sexuality have never been enabled to claim the status of unitary selfhood which underpins the discursive manoeuvres available to certain groups of men in the West. I address what forms of narratives of self-constitution and modes of self-reflexivity are available to women in the temporality of vision. What resources might 'Woman' as sign offer in which the visual metaphor 'performs on' the real? Through concepts of reiterative movement and performance, I will consider how women's practical magazine use and pleasure can generate models of selfhood which are 'beyond' the discursive frame of conventionally articulated space-time, yet which can be imagined through different forms of visibility.

5 Female visions

Advertising, women and narrative

The previous chapter challenged the idea that the viewers straightforwardly 'express' their agency in interpreting advertising images. Some views posit that the subject uses the advertisement's meanings as raw materials – or signposts directing their material acts of consuming goods – to construct 'messages' which are designed to communicate ideas about their identity to others. I argued instead that the subject is produced performatively in acts of vision. This disrupts a conventional notion of agency residing in the subject, awaiting expression through the interpretation and appropriation of signifiers in advertising. I examined the implications of the contemporary fluidity and dereferentiality of signifiers – their detachment from their original signifieds opens the field of signification to rearticulation. For Virilio (1994), this dereferentiality manifests itself in an untethering of the image from a material 'support surface' (print or celluloid). Instead, it engages a self-consciously temporal connection to the viewer in order to generate meaning. These moments of contact and interpretation, I argued, are branded by advertising in an attempt to articulate consumerist identities through specific commercial products. Framed by advertising, these interpretative manoeuvres reconsolidate the status and rights of the (white, male, heterosexual, middle-class) 'individual'. Simultaneously, they reiterate the uneasy positionings of 'others' between and across the borders of discourses of presence, visibility and 'individuality'. In effect, these positionings marginalise such groups in conceptual 'elsewhere(s)' and 'elsewhen(s)' and operate to 're-centre' the exclusive category of 'the individual'. Yet the theoretical approaches used to examine the shifting discourses of 'the individual' cannot be directly mapped onto an exploration of the elsewhere(s)/ elsewhen(s). This requires an approach to temporality and the 'betweenness' of moments which attends to the disjunctures in these spaces/times. In this chapter I examine the forms of self-temporality available to female viewers of advertisements in magazines. Through an analysis of narratives of self, distance, contact, tactility and performance, I explore the textual address in advertising targeted at women and consider what forms of marginalised agency may be available to them. I examine this in the context of advertising in women's magazines and draw on studies of gender and popular culture (e.g. Nava 1992). I explore how women's magazines may offer possibilities for resistant viewing strategies of advertisements, and I consider what forms of subjectivity this resistance may offer. In this approach, I develop ways of thinking about the discourses of individuality which many advertising campaigns draw on. I argue that campaigns' focus on individuality and rhetorics of choice coexist with women's exclusion from the political category of 'the individual' which I addressed in previous chapters. This makes for an uneasy relation between expectations and the reality of free (consumer) choice.

Using analyses of advertisements, I review and develop previous studies of women, popular culture and consumer discourses by exploring ideas of narrative and metaphor in relation to the visual. I argue that thinking about the visual as performative, together with an emphasis on vision as a tactile, sensuous experience, allows for a more nuanced methodological approach to gender and vision. It offers ways of imagining forms of female subjectivity that have previously remained 'invisible' or unthinkable. Yet the resistant possibilities of vision are not available to all women, as they pivot on the historical construction of privileged, classed, white, European viewing perspectives. Also, I contrast the forms of resistant subjectivity available to certain women with the previous chapter's analysis of male subjectivity. In the context of my study, the latter is based on a flexible and reflexive relation to images and identity in which certain men are endowed with a privileged access to the rights of 'consumer-citizenship'.

This capacity to translate cultural rights into political and economic privilege is a central theme of the chapter. Nancy Fraser (1989, 1997) argues that the discursive status and rights of 'consumer' is denied women and other subordinated groups who are relegated to the status of 'beneficiary'. This discursive positioning has *material* effects, she argues, as it grants white, middle-class men automatic rights of access to welfare benefits and other social privileges, whilst excluding other groups. Fraser's argument suggests that material changes in women's increased access to paid work may not in themselves grant significant citizenship benefits if the underlying discursive construction of rights continues to disadvantage women. I expand this argument to consider how performativity, vision and advertising interrelate with consumer rights and the privileges that this entails for some.

Referentiality and materiality

As I explored in the previous chapter, 'the image' is not a static, fixed container of meanings – these meanings are produced in the time of vision. These momentary productions of 'the image' can no longer rely on their material support surface, as Virilio (1994) argues. Instead they reach out for an explicitly temporal connection with the viewer. Therefore, we must pay close attention to the relation between the temporalities of self in moments of vision and the multidimensional connection of differences (gender, 'race', sexuality, nationality and so on) to the material body of the viewer.

Judith Butler (1993) argues that the body should not be seen as the support surface, or epistemological alibi, for the supposed materiality and naturalness of sex, over which a supposedly cultural, and hence constructed, 'gender' is laid. The material in this sense does not refer to a zone of reality beyond the frame of discourse that can be accessed and made intelligible in conventional terms. What we come to think of as 'the material' is constituted in and through discourse.[1] In relation to the construction of sexed bodies, Butler stresses that this discursive constitution does not hold a causal status. Nor does it fully delimit the totality of the subject of discourse.

> To claim that discourse is formative is not to claim that it originates, causes, or exhaustively composes that which it concedes; rather, it is to claim that there is no reference to a pure body which is not at the same time a further formation of that body. In this sense, the linguistic capacity to refer to sexed bodies is not denied, but the very meaning of 'referentiality' is altered. ... Indeed, to 'refer' naively or directly to such an extra-discursive object will always require the prior delimitation of the extra-discursive. And insofar as the extra-discursive is delimited, it is formed by the very discourse from which it seeks to free itself.
>
> (Butler 1993: 10–11)

Butler here stresses that the process of referring to 'the material' is implicated in the continual redrawing of the boundaries of 'the discursive'. The implications are that a reference to the 'elsewhere(s)' and 'elsewhen(s)' is always already in the here and now. However it is constantly shifting, just as referring to 'the natural' is held in a shifting tension with the boundaries of 'the artificial', 'the literal' with 'the ironic'.

In a discussion of fashion in 1980s Britain, Caroline Evans and Minna Thornton (1989) argue that women are paradoxically positioned as 'nature' in relation to male 'culture'. Yet in the arena of fashion in which the supposed cultural overlay of gender expresses 'natural sex', women are associated with the artificial and men with neutrality and naturalness. In this way, shifting fashion codes can disrupt the idea of a natural, sexed body as material support surface for a cultural play, – for instance in the 'androgynous look' in Britain in the 1980s, 'The (essentialist) association between nature, identity and the body is disturbed when the idea of gender becomes coded rather than natural in fashion fantasy. The body can be made, through dress, to play any part it desires, as gender coding is displaced from the body on to dress' (*ibid.*: 62). In the context of their discussion, sexual difference becomes 'a pure signifier, detached from biological difference' (*ibid.*: 64). Yet this fluid play on identity is only enabled by a foundational schema of difference; it is only possible because 'sexual difference waited in the wings, always ready to re-emerge as a 'naturalized polarity' – man or woman' (*ibid.*).

Yet this schema of difference is not static and unchanging. In Butler's (1993) argument, each act of delimiting 'cultural' gender (as fashion or dress code) from biological, 'natural' sex re-materialises ideas of the sexed body and gender in continually mutating forms. Each time naturalised sex makes its triumphant re-emergence, its terms of reference become altered. So in the movement between the detachment and reattachment of signifiers through the temporality of vision, shifts occur in the terms of referentiality – what differences mean at any one 'moment' can change. As I discussed in Chapter 3, in the mobile relation between 'the literal' and 'the ironic', the sign 'Woman' functions as the necessary 'literal', 'unreflexive' foil to the reflexive, active ironic possibilities offered to (some) men. 'She' functions as a metaphor of stability, transparency and intelligibility, yet she always remains 'elsewhere' or at a distance from this staging of 'herself'. As metaphor, 'she' is mobilised in an attempt to reach out to 'the real' or 'the literal' under-stood as some essential femininity required to stabilise sexual difference. Yet the 'detour' of metaphor paradoxically reiterates that very distance by 'performing on it' (Cornell 1993: 68). Each invocation of 'her' literal or natural status as touchstone shifts the referentiality of sexed difference and alters its meanings.

The dereferentiality of signs in media non-space generates a new fluidity of meaning. It allows increased possibilities of 'ironic' readings of signifiers in new metaphoric combinations. Simultaneously, it threatens to destabilise those very possibilities by unanchoring the necessary 'literal' referents. This dislocation of 'the real' or the literal destabilises the metaphor. In effect, it creates another dimension in the detour between the metaphor and 'the real' on which it performs. This elasticity in the relation of signifiers to signifieds, together with changes in the spatio-temporal zones of meaning-generation, can no longer guarantee even a partial closure of meaning. I would argue that in spatial and temporal terms, this dislocation of 'the real' does not translate as a further step *away from* a foundational reality. Rather, it gener-ates another dimension through which we produce understandings of 'the real' and visual images or legible reality.

The discourses of presence, legibility and visibility cannot, in Butler's (1993) terms, exhaustively compose that which they concede. Inevitably, there exist significant disjunctures or blank spaces/times. Yet access to understanding these spaces/times can only be articulated in the available terms which continually re-produce shifting boundaries of their status as 'reality'. In the following sections I argue that we can begin to imagine these spaces/times by examining the betweenness of the moment, or the else-where(s) and elsewhen(s). These become partially visible in the movement between and across their boundaries (de Lauretis 1989). In these moments of visual contact which make available narratives of self, it may be that forms of knowledge (for the researcher as well as the viewer) shift the terms of their referentiality, that ' "knowing" something becomes displaced by a "relating to" ' (Taussig 1993: 26). In the previous chapter I explored how this 'relating to' is framed for white, middle-class, male viewers as a self-affirming process. The process restates the contact and connection with the rights of 'the individual' which have been historically accrued in relation to subordinated 'others'. Through the use of the ironic, this connection is presented as explicit and self-conscious. Yet female viewers' discursively ambiguous 'self-presence' does not grant access to self-consciousness or self-reflexivity in the same terms. This ambiguous positioning forms the foundation of de Lauretis' (1989) question – how do women relate images of 'Woman' to their self-image, and what form of knowing does this encompass? What forms of self-consciousness or self-reflexivity might this offer? In the following sections I address these questions in terms of visual contact, narrative and temporal contact, tactility and texture.

The female times/spaces of magazines

Women's magazines have been seen as forming a 'private space and private time' (Winship 1987: 53) for women in which they can relax and legitimately address explicitly 'female' pleasures (Hermes 1995). This space, I will argue, articulates with the highly mobile dereferentiality of signs in media non-space, but exists marginally to it. That is, women's magazines are located in a discursive dimension which is implicated in the deferentiality of non-space, but which cannot be totally defined or made intelligible through it. I will explore what forms of female selfhood these spatio-temporal zones may allow and in what terms they may be articulated and made visible.

In the academic study of popular culture, women's magazines are often located on the margins of what are generally considered as the more significant and interesting areas of television, cinema, video and music. In this way, women's magazines seem to inhabit a kind of 'elsewhere' to popular culture, and also a kind of stagnant 'elsewhen', as they are seen as lacking innovation, perpetually re-producing the same genre of editorial approach. This is contrasted with significant proportions of male-targeted magazines which, Frank Mort (1996) suggests, operate through innovative approaches. The fact that women's magazines' target readership is exclusively women[2] may serve to reinscribe by association a notion of these magazines as the lowest and least interesting form of popular culture, as in the case of television soap opera (Brunsdon 1991). Yet this apparent marginality belies the significance of women's magazines evident in their high circulation figures, even larger readership, and financial investment from advertising.[3]

The notion of a 'female space' in popular culture was developed in Janice Radway's (1987) study of women reading romance fiction. In the context of my interest in space and time, the most significant aspect of Radway's research was her shift of emphasis away from the purely text-based aspects of novels to the *activity* of reading. In my approach, which should be distinguished from reader studies, the notion of situated activity can be translated onto several levels: the articulation of the time and space of the reading self in specific contexts, the time/space of the activity of reading/interpreting/viewing (or the 'moment of exposure'), and the spatio-temporal narrative formations of the magazine text. Joke Hermes' (1995) study of readers of women's magazines highlights the significance of how women fit the activity of reading into their daily routines. This focus on practices and an engagement with narratives enables me to explore how certain advertising images can articulate a range of narratives of self that traverse different zones or dimensions of self, context, historical location and text-based image. I address this in terms of the narrative structuring of magazines, magazine-reading as a space/time of female pleasure, and of the space/time of 'the image' generated between advertising print and viewer mediated through metaphor.

Narrative structuring

The structure of the typical women's magazine allows for multiple reading strategies and the possibility of constructing multiple narratives which connect meaning in diverse combinations. Hilary Radner (1995: 132) argues that women's magazines generate 'a thick discourse which invites repeated readings regulated by different regimes of attention'. This, she proposes, produces a multilayered, or 'heteroglossic' discourse offering multiple read-ings (*ibid.*: 128). Ellen McCracken (1993) argues that these repetitive readings of magazines are characterised by delay and interruption, and continually shift between different modes of attention. Initial readings may involve flicking through the pages, scanning the combined impression of advertisements, articles and fashion photo shoots. Subsequent readings may engage a more selective in-depth reading of articles and looking at images, followed by readings which involve an oscillation between both reading strategies (McCracken 1993). Indeed, Hermes (1995) found these very strate-gies played out by her interviewees as they fitted moments of relaxation into their daily schedules, picking up magazines at irregular intervals, flicking through them or reading in more depth. This fragmented and repetitive approach is mirrored in the magazines' narrative format, in which standard notions of sequence are disrupted:

> [the magazines' format] is constructed not on the model of a regulated 'flow' but in terms of a disorder that is ordered by the reader. ... A magazine has numbered pages, hence a certain order, but is architec-tured rather than narrativized. ... The articles and photographs may have a preferred order, but it is so unsystematically inscribed that it is only an active reader who can recreate this order, or some version of it. For example, since articles rarely appear in sequence, the reader must search out the concluding pages, in the process reading other pages, and

perhaps abandoning the initial article for one that holds more interest for her.

(Radner 1995: 133)

Here, Radner favours the concept of an 'architectural' structure over a 'narrativised' structure, yet does not fully develop the difference between the two. My emphasis will interrogate this approach to narrative and its stress on a conventional temporal notion of linear, future-oriented logical sequence. Once a sequential notion of narrative is displaced, I discuss how the activity of the reader/viewer in ordering the narratives is opened up in different ways.

Narratives have been seen traditionally as meaning-making structures which produce a form of order (Riessman 1993). Margaret Somers and Gloria Gibson (1994) define narrative as a structuring device reliant on relationality, which is constituted in time and space and involves a certain logic of structure. 'Above all, narratives are *constellations of relationships* (connected parts) embedded in *time and space*, constituted by *causal emplotment*' (*ibid.*: 59, emphasis in original). In this approach, the notion of causal emplotment involves a sequential order in which certain elements are produced as logical consequences of others. This order cannot be disrupted if the meaning is to remain coherent (Riessman 1993). In this view, narratives are seen as 'discrete units, with clear beginnings and endings', whose flow of meaning, or causal emplotment, is ordered by the question 'and then what happened?' (Riessman 1993: 17).

Yet Paul Ricoeur's (1981) approach to narrative challenges the seemingly linear, causal structure of these definitions and focuses on the activity of the reader and the temporalities of interpretation. Ricoeur argues that narrative involves a particular *directedness* and development in which the reader is positioned so as to respond with expectations as to the culmination of the narrative process. The reader is encouraged to develop a prospective anticipation of the conclusion; 'the 'conclusion' of the story is the pole of attraction of the whole process' (*ibid.*: 277). Yet the status of the conclusion is highly ambiguous and requires of the reader a retrospective ordering of events. This retrospection is only authorised by the future-oriented impulses in the reader's expectations when following the narrative order.

But a narrative conclusion can neither be deduced nor predicted. ... So rather than being *predictable*, a conclusion must be *acceptable* Looking back from the conclusion towards the episodes which led up to it, we must be able to say that this end required those events and that chain of action. But this retrospective glance is made possible by the teleologically guided movement of our expectations when we follow the story. Such is the paradox of the contingency, 'acceptable after all', which characterises the understanding of the story.

(Ricoeur 1981: 277)

So interpretation is a multi-levelled, temporal activity in which 'to follow a story is already to "reflect upon" events with the aim of encompassing them in successive totalities' (Ricoeur 1981: 279). Hence, in Ricoeur's account, sequence is not reliant on fixed structures of 'logical order'. Rather, its focus is on the active interpretative work of the reader in which the 'logic' of causal emplotment is destabilised. In later sections I develop how this schema is comparable to Cornell's (1993) formulation of 'recollective imagination'.

Magazines do not present a series of coherent, bounded, 'logical' narratives of causal emplotment in the forms of articles, editorials, fashion shoots, letters and advertisements. Rather, the structure and content of the magazine provides the potential for a diverse range of 'stories of coherence', or narrativised accounts; of readers'/viewers' relation to the magazine structure, of the female time/space of reading pleasure and relaxation legitimised through the magazines, and of the relation of female viewers' self-image to the images of femininity offered to them. In defining these multiply available stories as narrativised accounts rather than 'narratives', my aim is to emphasise the activity of the reader/viewer in meaning-making. By using the concept 'narrativised accounts', I want to indicate the presence of other (and multiple) times/spaces beyond the terms of their discourse. In doing so, I aim to open up questions of female subjectivity to multiple and seemingly contradictory insights.

Ricoeur (1981) argues that the conclusion of a narrative forms the focal point of retrospective and prospective interpretation in which the conclusion becomes 'acceptable'. Yet in contrast to this 'ends-oriented' or teleological imperative, Hilary Radner (1995) emphasizes the significance of *motion in itself* in the production of female identities. In this movement there are 'itineraries of dissatisfaction but also of pleasure in the movement itself, of returning and departing, only to return again – in the activity of "shopping around"' (*ibid.*: xiv). Drawing on Janice Radway's (1987) work, Radner locates this repetitive formula specifically in relation to the structure and activity of reading romance novels. She argues that the narrative does not generate a riddle or enigma to solve, for the resolution or conclusion is always 'a given' (Radner 1995: 70). The pleasure of the novels lies primarily in the experience or activity of reading, in the knowledge of the narrative formula and the repetition of that formula (*ibid.*). Radner contrasts the romance format with that of women's magazines', arguing that the latter's more loose, 'architectural' structure allows for more disjointed readings. However, following my points regarding the nature of 'sequence', I suggest that we need a different approach to temporality in narrative if we are to open up questions of the available horizons or ends of female selfhood. I propose that an adapted version of the repetitive narrative formula which Radner outlines in relation to romance novels can be seen usefully in relation to magazines. The style and content of both British and French editions of *Elle* in my study are remarkably consistent over time: the subject and content of the articles remain very constant, focusing primarily on personal, and largely (heterosexual) romantic relationships. In the advertisements, the product types, images of femininity and forms of address vary little over the span of my study (1987–95). These conventionally disjointed, or non-sequential, multiple narrativised accounts paradoxically produce a very coherent version of the ideal white European, middle-class, heterosexual femininity. This multiply disjointed effect is in itself a formula with which women readers are familiar (Hermes 1995). So, in this sense, the repetitive reading strategies employed by women readers may allow for the reiteration of conventionally 'non-sequential' narratives.

I suggest that this emphasis on strategies of repetition of formulae is a response to women's ambiguous discursive positioning. As discussed in Chapter 1, in the available political, social and cultural discourses of female identities there is no narrative of base or origin of self-present identity from which to orientate retrospective and prospective lines of interpretation as in Cornell's (1993) account. De Lauretis (1990: 115) articulates this as the 'nonbeing of woman' which is 'the paradox of a being that is at once captive and absent in discourse, constantly spoken of but of itself inaudible or inex-pressible'. It is a position in which self-image and images presented to the self continually operate in disjuncture. In effect, a focus on conclusions becomes less significant when the origins of the female self can never achieve the discursive weight necessary to rearticulate formally the narrative structure. A female reader cannot, in Ricoeur's (1981) terms, retrospectively *accept* the conclusion defining her in relation to certain femininities by conceding that 'this end required those events' when her agentic status is so *inconclusive*. In the face of this paradox, repetition may function as a means of negotiating this ambiguity. In a parallel fashion, the use of magazine-reading may offer the possibilities of providing a narrativised structure of the legitimacy of a specifically female time of leisure and space for addressing her own desires rather than the demands of family or work.

In contrast to this inconclusivity, (white, Western, middle-class, hetero-sexual) male subjectivities are positioned so as to operate from a discursive position of presence and privilege. As I argued in the previous chapter, they are positioned in such a way as to actively rearticulate narrative potential. For certain men, relationality to the conclusion (or 'moment' of self-authorisation and branding) of narrativised accounts of self inhabits a paradoxical position. It is both a 'foregone conclusion' (their historically generated status guarantees this) yet also enables fluidity and flexibility (they are granted a privileged discursive movement between identities). This conclusivity is not foregone in the sense of a projected and subsequently achieved intentionality or agency of the (male) self – as Ricoeur argues, the conclusion cannot be predicted. Rather, it is a foregone conclusion in that the projected and retrospective interpretative moves are authorised by discourses of self-present origin. These will always retroactively confer self-authoring status and will produce an ideal of a 'self-made man'. This myth of self-constitution will be dissimulated, and male subjectivity can be granted a self-authoring, heroic status. The genuine origins of this self (those produced in contradistinction to 'the others' of women, black people and other subordinated groups) will not be visible. The idea of self-origin will be produced at the very moment of constitution through a 'semiotic-material technology linking meanings to bodies' (Haraway 1991: 192).

In effect, the rights of 'the individual' performatively bring the (white, male, classed) individual into being. In this sense, the performative expression of those rights in the self's production of flexible, narrativised 'autobiographies' is 'a logical narrative', or self-fulfilling prophecy. The narratives of self which are generated always have an 'acceptable' conclusion: they are self-authored manoeuvres and will logically reflect and simultaneously call into being the wishes, opinions, rights, etc. of that self before he even 'knows them' in a conventional sense. This 'knowledge' of self-present identity (that is, the relations between self and other) is on the one hand self-conscious, flexible, explicit and often ironic. On the other, it is a form of knowledge-production which articulates the conventional terms of 'consciousness' and 'intentionality' in new ways. This is the zone/time of knowledge which advertisers attempt to brand, and might be seen as a new form of what Vance Packard (1956/1981) once called 'depth manipulation'. This does not *predetermine* the wishes, actions and motivations located in 'the depths' of the self. It *displaces* them to the time-space of 'the image' generated between the print and the viewer through which the self becomes performatively constituted. As such, 'the seen image', with the printed image as its witness, mediates the narrativised accounts of the relation between self and other before *he* can 'know' them. In the next chapter I explore what this mediation and displacement of intent means in terms of citizenship rights, obligations and more diffuse senses of 'cultural belonging'.

So, in relation to women's reading practices and narrative ordering, a notion of 'activity' is opened up to scrutiny. This activity is generally seen in terms of the active role of turning the pages and scanning the paper. This allows for a level of temporal control of the narrative processes that is not available to such a degree in genres such as television (although video affords some control) or cinema (McCracken 1993). In relation to this notion of control, Radner (1995) argues that the fragmented nature of the 'architecture' of the magazine enables women to imagine the process of reading and their role as reader in new ways, in what I interpret Radner to mean as a *self-conscious* process. I am suggesting that the formulation of narrative as 'sequence' which underpins these approaches does not address the multi-dimensional and shifting nature of narrative structuring of both texts and of the reader's 'self-conscious', reflexive understandings of herself through texts in the moment of exposure. The notion of sequence employed by Radner and McCracken does not adequately question the temporalities of narrativised accounts. Indeed, their notion may reinscribe a notion of temporality based on an assumed equidistant spatial and temporal relation of 'moments' which form the narrative whole. An assumed spatio-temporal symmetry of sequence subsumes difference. It forecloses an exploration of the specificity of the 'betweenness' of moments, that is, the possibilities of different forms of temporality. As discussed in relation to Butler (1993) in Chapter 1, the 'betweenness' of moments constitutes the interiority of moments, that is, the 'content' of biographical identity situated in and constituted by time. Narrative devices such as metaphor simultaneously separate moments as distinct and join them in a recognisable narrative form through reiteration. So, if reiteration through repetitive reading strategies is one form which re-produces the betweenness of moments (for example, the narrative-structuring devices, such as metaphor), then we need to address the temporality of certain metaphors in relation to reading/interpretation. As the non-space of media images disrupts the relation of signifier to signified, this temporality of metaphor may be in a state of flux. In the next section I approach these metaphors and narratives through Cornell's (1993) formulation of 'recollective imagination' which I initially introduced in the previous chapter.

Metaphor and image

In this section, I examine the pleasurable viewing/interpreting experience of repetition on several levels: in terms of the repetitive engagement with the shifting terms of the metaphor 'Woman' in advertisements, the repetition of the engagement in a female space of pleasure, and temporalities of the self in the moment of exposure. The repetition of certain configurations of images, often as metaphors, can be seen in parallel with the time-scales of specific advertising campaigns and the alterations made to the images. In my sample of female-targeted advertisements, the conventional or 'literal' images of the sign 'Woman' tend to have very long-running campaigns, such as a Samsara perfume campaign which ran in British and French magazines over the whole timescale of my sample (1987–95). In Chapter 3 I discussed the related advertisement Un Air de Samsara (Plate 3.2). Such campaigns are punctuated by minor changes in the arrangement within the advertisement's frame of the conventional elements of product image, brand-name, tagline and photographic image. For instance, the French advertisement for the perfume Dune (Plate 5.1) appears in my sample in several forms: in the form of Plate 5.1, and in other versions of a close-up image of a female face.[4] Typically of such shifts in the same advertising campaign, the images are recognisably related, in that they use the same basic metaphoric combinations of signifiers and that the use of colour tends to remain constant. The *relation* of this metaphoric combination shifts over time in the temporal lapses between different modes of reading, different times of viewing and narratives of self.

Plate 5.1 Dune advertisement, 'Un souffle d'évasion', late 1990s version of earlier Dune advertisements found in the sample.

Source: (Courtesy of Parfums Christian Dior).

This repetitive, extended time-scale can be contrasted with the male-targeted advertisements which have a much more rapid turnover in campaigns and more radical shifts in images and image combinations within the same campaign. For instance, the Marlboro advertisement (Plate 4.1) discussed in Chapter 4 is part of a campaign of print advertisements which mobilise a very broad range of signifiers in different metaphoric combinations: for instance ants, chillies and 'redneck' cowboys. Their only constants are the colour scheme (sepia with a touch of red), the North American landscape, and the ironic form of address. This rapid turnover suggests that the shelf-life of irony in specific image combinations is short. In this context, irony's value to advertisers lies precisely in targeting (and simultaneously producing as a market) male members of 'the new middle classes' for whom a rapid and skilful ironic response to innovation in image combinations confirms and re-produces their elite status.

For women, the repetitive, formulaic campaigns do not offer the same status, but may produce a different form of metaphorical space. According to Cornell (1993), metaphor's elasticity can open up different ways of imagining femininity.

> Metaphor as transference and analogy always implies both the like and the not like. The definition of the feminine ... *is* only a metaphor. Metaphor, in turn, allows both for expansion of meaning and for reinterpretation. The characterization cannot be cemented in stone precisely because it is designated as metaphor. Therefore, the realization of 'feminine being' as metaphor is what allows us to reinterpret, and, more important, to affirm, the feminine as other, and *irreducibly other*, to any of the definitions imposed by patriarchy.
>
> (Cornell 1993: 133–4)

So, mobilising this formulation, the metaphor of 'Woman' is used as currency to re-produce specific forms of European male identity. At the same time, a time/space is generated for women which allows a play on the designated metaphors of femininity. Yet, contrary to Cornell's account of a generic 'femininity' as 'irreducibly other', I suggest that these metaphors of femininity may only operate through specific discourses of 'race', visibility and privilege, as I discussed in Chapter 4. Furthermore, Cornell privileges metaphor as the primary mode of the signification and rearticulation of female subjectivity. Whilst I agree that metaphors are highly significant, they must be seen as merely one trope, and thus as one point of access to understandings of femininities. Moreover, the significance of metaphor should not be seen as a relativising universal but must be addressed in specific contexts in terms of visibility and invisibility. For instance, visual metaphors in women's magazines have a different discursive status, temporal operation and availability of access and intervention to metaphor in legal structures which are discussed by Cornell. In addition, metaphor as a trope has an 'explicit' status, in that it functions through drawing a self-conscious link and displaying this link between what Cornell terms 'the like and the not like'. Yet, in the context of my study of visual metaphor in advertisements, the explicit/implicit and literal/ironic are relational rather than absolute in their implication in the production of 'the like and the not like'. Many of the female-targeted advertisements are visually understood as 'explicit' or literal in their conventional or 'natural' linking of ideal white femininity to the sign 'Woman'. This explicit status precisely refuses a self-conscious linking of the like and the not like: they appear to be fused into one in a seemingly 'natural' relation. Conversely, many male-targeted ironic advertisements actively display their explicit ironic status and function to reformulate the conventionally understood terms of certain metaphors. This paradox must be seen in relation to the structures of visibility and invisibility in which the relation between the visible/invisible and the legible/illegible is continually refracting. In the Dune advertisement (Plate 5.1),[5] the play on 'the like and the not like' takes the form of the visibility and legibility of the metaphor of white 'Woman' as sand dune: the form of her hair echoes that of the grasses on the dune, and her skin is coloured to the same tint as the sand. In another, earlier version of this Dune advert, a woman's face is seen horizontally in profile. The contours of the female figure's face and her eyelashes function as visual referents for the dunes and grasses, signifying 'nature'. This is a play on the ontological status of 'Woman' as sign. Here metaphor functions as the frame within and beyond which are articulated ideal femininity and its relation to women's lived experience and activity of reading/interpreting.

Metaphor simultaneously separates and engages the two terms in a way which emphasizes, in Cornell's terms, the like and the not like. In parallel with the betweenness of moments discussed above, the terms of the metaphor are produced as both distinct *and* fused together in tension. The metaphor offers viewers narrativised access to ideas of both ideal femininity and readers/viewers' visual experience of it. In de Lauretis' (1989) terms, this is the disjunctive relation between representations of self and self-representation. This tension, or elastic gap, between 'Woman' and 'dune' allows for a performative relation between them. The 'naturalness' of white femininity (its 'literal' quality mediated through the metaphor of the dune), is held in tension with the surreal and explicitly 'unnatural' landscape as Woman, skin as sand. In the earlier Dune advert this unreal effect is mediated by the perfume bottle – its suspension disrupts the perspective, making it impossible to gauge whether the bottle and brand name are located in front of, directly above, or behind the figure's face. This maps out the spatial scale of the female figure, or horizon of femininity, as ambiguous. Her boundaries are both defined, yet somehow 'elsewhere', beyond the legibility of her own terms. This femininity is seen both as the epitomized 'naturalness' of language mediated through natural landscape, and as a fabricated, surreal spatial amalgam of signifiers which resist transparency. As discussed in

Chapter 3, the supposed 'literal' nature of this white femininity takes the form of its assumed direct relation of signifier to signified which can be transparently 'expressed' through (visual) language – the sign 'Woman' is as natural and legible as an image of a sand dune. This literal transparency and legibility is simultaneously disrupted by the effect of metaphor, which continually re-states the gap between signifier and signified and 'performs on' that gap (Cornell 1993). So in the Dune advertisement the visible surface of the white skin of the sign 'Woman' is unstable and interchangeable with other signifiers – in this case, sand.

This forms a kind of visual and unintelligible opacity of the ontological and epistemological status of 'Woman' produced in this relation. The closed eyes of the female figure refuse access to the imagined 'inner depths' of female identity and instead emphasise opacity and surface. As in Evans and Thornton's (1989) account of fashion, gender here operates as a recoding of signifiers disconnected from biological sex. Yet gender simultaneously functions here as the epitome of 'naturalness' in an essential relation of gender–sex–nature. It is this surface of femininity and its horizons that the advertisement attempts to brand with the perfume bottle and brand name. The branded product attempts to perform on the gap between the signifier and signified and produce a form of visibility and legibility in its own terms. The brand Dune attempts to intervene in this relation and form the currency of interpretation.

As discussed in Chapter 4, for Virilio (1994) this could be an example of 'phatic' imagery which forces the attention through the visual impact of its precision, colour and high definition. Yet such phatic imagery is now struggling to hold the same eye-catching effect in the face of technological developments in image culture. According to Virilio, advertisements attempt to renew their visual hold on the viewer by engaging a 'third dimension' or 'stereoscopic effect'. This is an explicit temporal connection with the viewer through the time of exposure or visual interpretation. But there is something enduring about the long-running campaigns of repetitive images of (a certain) femininity which belies this idea of an anxious searching by images for a temporal connection with the viewer. I suggest that Virilio's 'time of exposure' in vision operates differently for women. It cannot function for female viewers as a 'moment' which invokes the rights of 'the individual' in a performative enactment of self-constitution. As for male viewers, this contact occurs through forms of temporal movement in what Cornell (1993) has termed 'recollective imagination'. Yet for women these are movements which do not depart from and return to an ideal of self-presence, but rather a partial presence in the elsewhere(s)/elsewhen(s) of discourse. The legibility of these potentially narrativised times of access to femininities has been subsumed under notions of the 'literal' and 'unreflexive' nature of both lived femininities and images in magazines. In the following sections I explore what forms of (self-)knowledge might be enabled through visual contact as a form of tactility and textured experience between and across categories of 'difference'.

The materiality of vision

In this section, I explore the relation between vision, materiality and the 'support surfaces' of images. I examine how the 'intangibility' of seeing can be experienced in 'felt' ways which open up questions of self-consciousness and self-knowledge in new dimensions. I argue that this accessibility, and the terms in which knowledge is experienced, are dependent on multiple positionings within and across boundaries of sexual, 'racial', ethnic, class and age differences.

Lauren Berlant (1993) explores the epistemological movements in 'passing' and privilege through the interrelations of 'race', nationality, class, gender and sexuality. She discusses the habitable bodies and spaces available to black women who aim to 'pass' for white through certain strategies of performing class and sexuality within the frame of 'nationality'. I would like to consider this notion of performance or simulation in relation to available spaces of femininity in terms of visibility and spaces of 'the image'. In a discussion of literary texts, Berlant (1993: 174) suggests how the available positions for (black women passing for white) women in public spaces revolve around the poles of the 'bourgeois norms of good taste, which means submitting the body to a regime of discipline and concealment', and the exotic sexuality of 'the specular erotics of the white female body'. This emphasis on the visual underlines the visible production of forms of femininity tied to the female body as spectacle. In Berlant's framework, visibility, embodiment and performance are crucial in generating habitable spaces. In a discussion of a novel, Berlant suggests that 'one style of femininity tends towards the invisible or the 'abstract', which involves a wish to cast off the visible body, and the other, toward the erotic, the sensational, which emphasizes the visual frame' (1993: 174). In Berlant's discussion, these strategies are aimed at deflecting the racialising gaze of white bourgeois society away from black women who attempt to pass as white in order to gain a greater freedom of movement in public space. The success of these performances relies on the repetition of a formula of white, classed femininity. In this sense, both styles are tactics of the concealment of 'blackness' as 'race' through the hypervisibility of white, middle-class femininity as invisible norm, either as spectacularly (hetero-)erotic or as disciplined and understated. Berlant describes how the two light-skinned black women who aim to pass for white see and recognise each other's performance. In this recognition, they reinvoke blackness not as a foundational 'real' beneath the performance, but as a future-oriented imaginative wish for habitable spaces; 'thus each woman returns the other to her legally "other"' body by seeing her, and seeing through her – not to another "real" body, but to other times and spaces where the "other" identity might be inhabited safely' (Berlant 1993: 174).

The spaces and times of this performance or passing are situated in the physical setting of the performance and its spectators. Yet, simultaneously, they are displaced in the moment of visual recognition to an 'elsewhere'/'elsewhen'. This temporality can be seen to invoke 'the image' in which a printed image, or another's body functioning as a textual support surface displaying a version of femininity, forms the temporally mobile time/space of the interaction of narratives of past/present/future self. This moment of recognition, Berlant argues, is bound up with a desire on the part of both women 'to wear her [the other's] way of wearing her body' (1995: 175). For one of the women aiming to pass, it would be a relief to share the burden of her spectacular white erotics with one who understands the terms of her performance. For the other woman, it would be an escape from the stifling discipline of her classed body. What they want, I suggest, is a flexibility in the wearing or performance of the visibility of the racialised female body that projects the self towards new forms of potential. The theme of imagining and projecting habitable (national) spaces is taken up in Chapter 6 in relation to citizenship. At this point, I want to explore this displacement, visibility and performance in terms of the times/spaces of magazines, the times/spaces of 'the image' generated between print and viewer, and the times/spaces of national and popular cultures.

The generation of the borders of the self and a sense of this self through multiple narrativised accounts, I suggest, occurs in and through a performance on *distance*. This distance is mediated by the spatio-temporality of 'moments', in which the betweenness of moments both separates and links distinct formulations of space/time. I want to consider the contact between moments in terms of the temporalised visual contact and movement of seeing. Michael Taussig (1993: 21) suggests that processes of vision involve a form of contact which is 'a palpable, sensuous, connection between the body of the perceiver and the perceived'. This is a conception of the visual as tactile in which 'the very concept of 'knowing something becomes displaced by a "relating to" in a physical and epistemological sense' (*ibid*.: 26). Roland Barthes discusses the *feel* of senses which are not generally considered in terms of tactility through a notion of 'grain': 'The "grain" is the body in the voice as it sings, the hand as it writes, the limb as it performs' (1977: 188). In the following sections, I want to explore how seeing can be thought of as the grain or texture of the movement, contact and narrative potential of vision.

Yet Butler (1993) argues that conventional notions of the materiality of the sexed, racialised, classed body cannot be taken categorically as the 'support surface' for performances of 'gender' and other intracategorical differences. If this is so, what forms of contact, tactility and referentiality might this involve? From where do the narrativised accounts of retrospective and prospective 'autobiographies' generated in visual contact depart and to where do they return? As I discussed in Chapter 4, Burnett (1995) argues that our only access to 'the image' is through a retrospective engagement with the interaction of vision and knowledge. This, I have argued, articulates narrativised accounts of self and simultaneously constitutes the viewing self through 'recollective imagination' (Cornell 1993). I want to consider these issues in terms of how the performing of certain types of femininity through magazine use enables visual access to forms of a tactile 'wearing' of another's way of wearing femininity. In the context of print advertisements, this is not a performance on the body in the presence of others. Rather, it is a performance on the texture of 'the image', mediated by metaphor and generated in the spatio-temporal 'distance' between the print and the viewer which frames a bodily awareness of self.

The concept of texture can be employed to think about the experience of contact between the following diverse levels; of narrative spaces of magazines, of the times they authorise for explicitly 'female' pleasures and leisure, and of the movement between 'self' and 'print' in 'the image' mediated by metaphor. In this sense, texture articulates the boundaries between the materiality of the lived experience of sex/gender and its representations. Texture can also be thought of as a way of mapping the movements and contradictions between the 'constant intersection and mutual implication' of differences of 'race', sex, class and sexuality (de Lauretis 1990: 133). These positionings, I would argue, engender differing access to 'textures' which may be experienced more as friction than pleasurable tactility.

I will consider these tactile spatio-temporal movements in relation to a Lancôme advert (Plate 5.2) for Trésor perfume,[6] 'Trésor, le parfum des instants précieux' ['Treasure, the perfume of precious moments'] and a Fendi advert (Plate 5.3).[7] These advertisements mobilise visual ambiguity both to fix certain moments and to produce a timeless, enduring quality of white, classed femininity. In the Trésor advert, the sepia tint and neutrality of the clothes situate the image outside changing fashion and in a timeless zone of 'classic' white, middle-class femininity which is difficult to place at a specific moment in time. This mode of femininity corresponds to Berlant's (1993) 'neutral', disciplined and 'abstract' middle-class model of femininity. The aura of timelessness is generated through the invisibility of this white, middle-class norm. Paradoxically, its repetition throughout popular culture as part of an identifiable series of such signs of femininity confirms its atemporal status. Whilst women's magazines are conventionally seen as one of the lowest forms of popular culture, many of the female-targeted advertisements I discuss in this book draw on vocabularies of cultural value from high art/culture conventions and relocate and rearticulate them in the female space of the magazine. The Dune advertisement (Plate 5.1) draws on artistic conventions of surrealism in painting and photography; the Fendi advert (Plate 5.3) draws on the genres of sculpture and painting. In addition, a Sun Moon Stars perfume advert[8] and the Trésor adverts from my study elicit references to film through the use of the actresses Daryl Hannah and Isabella Rossellini respectively. These are cultural genres which have traditionally used 'Woman' as frame of knowledge and currency in the production of certain (white, middle-class) male identities (Betterton 1987,

Plate 5.2 Trésor advertisement, 'The fragrance for treasured moments', late 1990s version of earlier Trésor advertisements found in the sample.

Source: (Courtesy of Lancôme).

Plate 5.3 Fendi advertisement, 'La passione di Roma'.
Source: British *Elle*, April 1988 (courtesy of Fendi).

1996; Nead 1992; Pollock 1988, 1992). This use of high art/culture conventions enables the production of a 'timeless' femininity, and simultaneously targets the lucrative middle-class market. The corollary of the temporal ambiguity of female identity is an uncertainty in the imaginary mapping of past moments or origins. This unanchored quality of the printed image's origins corresponds to female identity's lack of definite origins in the discourses of 'the individual'. She functions as currency which constitutes male identity, and so can never achieve (the fiction) of momentary self-presence available to (certain) men. She remains 'elsewhere(s)', crossing the boundaries of discourses of visibility/invisibility and legibility/illegibility.

It is this lack of conventionally coherent, unitary origins which must be projected on the future/potential self in order to draw out the meaning or identity of the present-tense self. This lack of origins paradoxically facilitates a 'trying on' or momentary inhabitation and performance of different femininities: the spatio-temporal non-fixity of the referentiality of 'Woman' opens up a non-directed, nebulous potential. It draws on ambiguous origins and projects them onto future or potential femininities as ways of imagining other spaces and times in and through which certain women may inhabit femininities in different ways. As in Berlant's (1993) account, this performance does not invoke a certain racialised, embodied femininity as a foundational 'real' behind the performance. Nor does it reference and materialise a bodily ideal of middle-class identity as 'real'. The notion of 'the real' as material support surface in this context is superseded by a racialised and classed idea of 'the authentic' as the hyper-visible (yet, in practice, invisible) norm. This cannot be reduced to 'the real' as the operation of metaphors of ambiguous femininities preclude a definitive 'moment' of presence. Yet the binary of the artificial/the authentic here works as a paradox which authorises 'the authentic' as the timeless, middle-class ideal.

The tactility of this intertemporal visual experience bears witness to the differences which constitute this form of 'femininity'. The *feeling* of already having seen this timeless image, of having already (repetitively) followed the visual and discursive movements between 'here' and 'elsewhere(s), between 'now' and 'elsewhen(s)' are multiply experienced and have differing relations to social privilege. The image generated between print and viewer is not a singular model of self-representation: its multiplicity testifies to friction and incommensurable difference as well as pleasurable tactility and affirming narrativised experiences of selfhood. For instance, positionings in terms visual signifiers of available femininities are severely limited for working-class women. As Carole-Anne Tyler (1991) argues, white, middle-class femininity functions as the norm from which performances depart and return. In relation to the ideal of femininity often invoked in gay male drag, she argues that:

> a real women is a real lady; otherwise she is a female impersonator, a camp or mimic whose 'unnaturally' bad taste – like that of the working-

class, ethnic or racially 'other' woman – marks the impersonation as such. Miming the feminine means impersonating a white, middle class impersonation of an 'other' ideal of femininity.

(Tyler 1991: 57)

Evans and Thornton (1989) stress the paradoxical position of women caught between epitomising both 'the natural/authentic' and 'the artificial'. Tyler shows how this is fundamentally a classed paradox, as working-class women cannot occupy a position which is both 'authentic' and valorised. It is only middle-class women and men who occupy the position of necessary distance from 'artificiality' from which a play on artificiality and bad taste confirms their own status and taste: 'it is only from a middle class point of view that Dolly Parton looks like a female impersonator' (Tyler 1991: 57). So artificiality for working-class women in the performance of femininities does not attest to a distance between self and representation which they can pleasurably negotiate. Rather, it is a de-legitimising paradox which distances them from class privilege (Skeggs 1997).

This paradox operates multiply, although not symmetrically, with other differences which cross-cut sexual and gender difference. For the two black women passing as white, as described by Berlant (1993), this norm of middle-class, white femininity can offer them camouflage in their attempts at greater access to public spaces and privilege. Yet 'race' as 'blackness' is always waiting in the wings, threatening them with delegitimisation. So, for groups of women beyond the demarcations of white middle-class identities, the distance between images and metaphors of femininities presented in advertisements and self-images may not offer a pleasurable opportunity for performance. The image produced between print and viewer may not invoke retrospective and prospective imaginative movements which articulate new forms of potential. Many women have never had access to these spaces/times in order to return to them.

Branding the elsewhere(s)/elsewhen(s)

It is the ambiguity of the retrospective and prospective temporalities of vision that the female-targeted advertisements in my study attempt to brand. This 'time/space' for women is less a 'moment' of self-constitution than a paradoxical movement. It is a movement between impossible times (of time-less, authentic femininity), which even middle-class white women cannot inhabit consistently, to imagined potential narrativised experiences of femi-ninities. It is also a movement between impossible spaces of performing these paradoxical femininities and potential zones of living femininities differently. The invocation by the Trésor advertisement of the 'precious moments' of femininity aims to isolate spatio-temporal zones of this iden-tity in order to articulate them in terms of a branded commodity. But this branding in the Trésor advertisement can only ever be partially successful as the ambiguous and shifting referentiality of its terms refuse closure, particularly at the level of metaphor. The multiform operation of metaphor in the Trésor advertisement is more evident in its reference to 'other spaces' than in the Dune advert. Like the Dune advert, Trésor draws a relation of 'like and not like' between 'Woman' and 'treasure'. This allows movement, contradiction and possibilities for certain groups of women of 'trying on' femininities. However, the Trésor advert makes more explicit what is present, yet implicit, in Dune; the metaphoric movement encompasses the 'precious moments' of a female space and time of self-oriented pleasure, magazine-reading and play at 'dressing up' or performing certain identities. The frame of both the advert and the magazine becomes a metaphorical female time/space through 'the image' which is generated between print and female viewer. Within, and projecting beyond, this time/space there is made available to (certain) women what Radner (1995: xiv) terms 'the pleasure in the movement itself, of returning and departing, only to return again'. This is articulated through the knowledge and the repetition of a range of formulae; of the ambiguous origins of female identity, of the metaphors of 'Woman' and of the female time/space of magazines and adverts, of the non-linear narratives of the magazine format, and of the narratives of self in the moment of exposure performing femininities and re-producing/reprojecting times/spaces of how women can inhabit those femininities.

Yet, I suggest, the attempted branding and the imaginative movements are only available through a particular heritage of exclusive identities. For instance, the metaphors available to imagine female subjectivity are coded primarily as heterosexual. In an Estée Lauder Beautiful perfume advertisement from 1990 (which I was unable to secure copyright permission to reproduce), a female figure in a wedding gown gazes out at the viewer. Here the temporality of female identity is presented very much as a narrative with the conclusion, and high point, as heterosexual marriage – as the tagline promises, 'this is your moment to be beautiful'. There is not much scope for narrative flexibility in this advertisement: the 'ends' of female identity are quite clearly identified. Exclusivity also operates on the level of 'race' and ethnicity in which European political, social and cultural structures frame possible meanings and access to their rearticulation. 'Race' may be waiting in the wings for its reappearance, but it may now operate in conjunction with shifting meanings of the visibility and significance of 'Europeanness'. In the Fendi advertisement (Plate 5.3), the ontological status of the female figure is tied to that of the ancient Greek sculpture by presenting a matrix of visual parallels; their pallor, their finely etched features especially around the nose and lips, and the blank eyes of the statue and the closed eyes of the female figure. She has no controlling presence within the print and is, in fact, as much an object of art as the statue. Her status could be seen as artist's model/muse,[9] a pure icon of classed, racialised femininity. Within the Western tradition, representations of women have conventionally been used to signify the nation or homeland (McClintock 1995; Yuval-Davis and

Anthias 1989). In this advertisement the narratives of nation, culture and civilisation produce a specifically 'European' model of selfhood through the 'visibility' of 'Woman' as metaphor. The female figure represents what is presented as a uniquely 'European', classed history of civilisation and high art, which is discursively tied to the emergence of European democracy and Christianity. In contrast, the Marlboro advertisement (Plate 4.1) discussed in the previous chapter presents narratives of the production of 'the European individual' through the displacement of (male) European colonisers to 'frontier' America. There they 'found themselves' or defined themselves through adventure and contact with wild landscape and 'uncivilised savages'. As I have argued, these narratives and particular forms of address offer certain British and French viewers (ironic) modes of re-imagining 'Europeanness' in relation to colonial history.

In the Fendi advertisement, 'Woman' as metaphorical sign is produced to delimit the borders of European culture and civilisation: 'Woman' forms the frame of knowledge within which the visible articulates with the legible. To adapt Bhabha's phrase (1993: 149), the sign 'Woman' is a discursive map through which Territory is turned into a Tradition of European heritage. The Italian phrase 'la passione di Roma', placed in a British magazine for a perfume which is available Europe-wide, does not make a claim for a European identity based on linguistic homogeneity. Rather, it places emphasis on a tradition of a 'European' culture of high art through the sign 'Woman'. The visible borders of the female self as metaphor are temporalised to frame and bind together spatially distinct European nations in the form of a sign of a distinct 'European' cultural tradition of art and civilisation. The figure's visibility does not have its referents in a representation of 'the true nature' of women. Her visibility is a territorial signpost in a tradition in which women have been mobilised as the currency, or system of equivalence, transparency and exchange in the discursive production of the category of the (white, male, middle-class) 'individual' (Diprose 1994). The territory is marked through a movement between and across discursive frames, and, as de Lauretis (1989) argues, the possibilities of representation are dependent upon the impossibility of the full presence of women and racialised others who remain 'elsewhere'. Yet, any access certain women have is mediated through an exclusionary discourse of white 'Europeanness'.

At this point I want to draw explicit links between Stolcke's (1995) formulation of 'cultural fundamentalism', as introduced in Chapter 1, and the ambiguous discursive positioning of women as the condition of representation (de Lauretis 1989) and signifiers of difference. Stolcke (1995: 4) argues that the contemporary concept of a national 'culture' is defined as 'a compact, bounded, localized, and historically rooted set of traditions and values transmitted through the generations'. Cultures, she continues, are seen as distinct, unique and incommensurable, and yet are universally identifiable as situated within the discursive parameters of the concept of 'culture'. Paradoxically, the very fact that they have differences and particularities is what they have in common. Their mutual difference is the system of equivalence in the concept of 'culture'. This discursive sliding is visible in the Fendi advertisement in which there is an attempt to mobilise the sign 'Woman' as metaphor to generate the necessary distance and difference to produce unitary, unique selfhood (for certain people). At the same time, it functions as the icon whose borders represent the 'sameness' or self-presence of European cultural identity. The 'emptiness' of the concept 'culture' is filled by the re-production of sexual, class and racial difference in terms of visibility. The whiteness of the female figure is 'invisible' due to the universal Lockean ideal of white European selfhood, and can only be 'known' or recognised as racialised through oblique reference to upper-/middle-class, white European traditions of classical high art.

Crucially, the 'colour' of race as signifier in the Fendi advert of national and cultural difference is displaced by the concept of 'ethnicity' as 'cultural tradition' or heritage. This ethnicity, Stolcke (1995) argues, is seen as historically rooted, unique to each national cultural grouping, and fundamentally incommensurable with any other. 'Contemporary cultural fundamentalism unequivocally roots nationality and citizenship in a shared cultural heritage' (Stolcke 1995: 12). However, as I have argued, historical narratives of origin and belonging can be rearticulated and a 'European' (white) ethnicity based on contemporary middle-class narratives of civilisation, art, democracy can be generated. This oscillates between the cultural difference between European nations (and regions) and cultural similarity based on cultural tradition. I develop these ideas more fully in the next chapter, but want for the moment to focus on the boundaries of female subjectivity which are inscribed in relation to popular culture in general.

Boundaries of the feminine

As I indicated in earlier sections, certain forms of popular culture have a history of being gendered, and specifically mass or popular culture is often seen as a feminised domain (Huyssen 1986). The forms of knowledge and self-knowledge available through popular culture tend to be denigrated, for example, women may be seen as being 'duped' by advertising which 'misrepresents' and manipulates them. Yet, for certain groups of women, it enables a 'trying on' of different femininities and of different modes of performing/interpreting which access self-consciousness and reflexivity in a way which runs counter to the notion of 'literal' advertisements as unreflexive. This literal, unreflexive quality is set against the 'ironic' not only in my study of advertisements but also in Fredric Jameson's (1983) influential discussion of pastiche and parody in the context of 'post-modern culture'. For the aims of my analysis, Jameson's use of 'parody' might be usefully seen as 'irony performed'. Jameson (1983: 113) argues that both parody and pastiche imitate other styles but that parody produces 'an imitation which mocks the original'. It calls on a norm or original which it challenges through satirical imitation. For Jameson, parody is politically incisive, due to its impulse towards satire. He argues that pastiche, in contrast, is a kind of 'blank irony' which imitates styles without making reference to the normative status of an original and without the humorous or satirical edge. Jameson goes on to argue that contemporary post-modern culture is characterised by the omnipresence of pastiche and the impossibility of parody. Indeed, 'in a world in which stylistic innovation is no longer possible, all that is left is to imitate dead styles, to speak through the masks and with the voices of the styles in the imaginary museum' (Jameson 1983: 115). Pastiche as an intertextual collaging or juxtaposition of different styles could indeed be said to be characteristic of much advertising. As I have discussed in previous chapters, advertising images draw on diverse codes from different historical periods, geographical settings and cultural and artistic forms and styles. Yet certain (white, male, middle-class) viewers are offered privileged discursive positions for the interpretation of this collaging. In contrast to Jameson's account of the contemporary impossibility of parody, such privileged positionings reinvoke an ironic stance to narratives of self and others. As I discussed in Chapter 4 in relation to Bhabha (1990), the privileged can 'speak through the masks' of racial and cultural others in new ways.

In Jameson's terms, women's 'literal' relation to femininities is a humourless and politically passive pastiche or 'blank parody'. It does not make reference to origins or norms, and therefore forecloses the question of agency. From my discussion of the different terms in which we might imagine 'self-reflexivity', it is clear that the invocation of (ambiguous) origins and norms of femininity operates in a more complex fashion. The 'imitation' occurs as forms of performance which do not invoke an original or foundational 'reality' (of 'race' or femininities) which it parodies. Yet, crucially, such creative interpretative responses are still bound to the specific contexts of their performance in adverts and magazines.

The tactics of repetition and experience of textured relationality in these narrativised movements are *responses* to discourses which women are unable to rearticulate actively, unlike some groups of men. Like the tactics of the subversion of established meanings, repetition as a mode of self-reflexivity is constrained by the discursive context of the representations. Reina Lewis (1997) discusses how subversion, or reading against the grain (or texture), is mobilised by lesbian readers of mainstream glossy women's magazines to draw pleasure from representations. She argues that it is the deliberate activity of reading against the grain of heterosexualised imagery and imagining the existence of other lesbian readers doing the same, that constitutes the pleasure of reading mainstream magazines. In contrast, she suggests that reading lesbian-produced magazines with evident 'lesbian' content and imagery does not produce the same frisson of pleasure which ultimately derives from the process of subversion. This, I would argue, forms part of the pleasure of textured visuality, of experiencing the movements between levels of response, yet also indicates the degree to which both possible and pleasurable responses are context-dependent. This is what Umberto Eco, cited in Evans and Thornton (1989), calls 'semiotic guerrilla warfare', in which specific instances of meaning-production may be subverted, but the broader scale of power relations remains intact.

In conclusion, whilst the branding by advertising of specific movements in the potential production of feminine identities may be fraught with ambiguity, the general terms in which female readers have access to representation remains bound to certain contexts. Certain groups of men have a flexible, non-context-specific access to negotiation of meaning. In contrast, female engagement in narrativised accounts of selfhood is circumscribed by the terms of specific cultural forms and is excluded from access to the supposedly 'neutral' terms of 'the individual'. In relation to my discussion, this context is women's magazines and advertising's forms of address and, more generally, popular culture. In both the female and male-targeted adverts I have discussed, 'the image' becomes disconnected from the material support surface of the print, and draws on a temporal visual connection with the viewer. This contact invokes a temporal mobility of narrativised recollective imagination. For male viewers this is authorised by – and takes as its point of departure and return – the historical constitution of the rights of 'the individual'. This is a flexible interpretative and self-constitutional movement, only *elastically* connected to the specific material context of the advertisement and mediated by 'the image' between print and viewer.

Yet women have never had access to these originary rights. The temporal movement of recollective imagination relies on a reconnection with the printed image in its connections of meaning through metaphors. The departure and return of these constitutional narrativised moves re-engage the printed image within the magazine as material support surface. This is not an invoking of a 'real' femininity, although as I have argued, certain femininities hold more authorisation and potential for movement than others. As in Butler's (1993) argument, each movement and return demarcates the boundaries of sexed, gendered, racialised, classed identities. It demarcates the boundaries of the material and the discursive anew. This movement is a visual, narrativised account of the paradoxical relation between female representation and self-representation. Experienced as textured movements, they shift between here and elsewhere(s), and now and elsewhen(s), between impossible spaces/times and, in Berlant's terms, a wish for inhabitable spaces. In this sense, female potential articulated through consumerist discourses is tied to specific paradoxical contexts in which culture (and specifically the relation between popular and high culture) functions as the support surface for possible identities. To adapt Ricoeur's (1981) argument in relation to narrative conclusions, narrativised female identities cannot be predictable, as they have no firm originary status from which to depart. Yet, contrary to Ricoeur's account, a female narrativised identity can never be 'acceptable', in that there cannot be an imagined sequential logic to 'her' development. It is not possible to look back from an imagined conclusion, or achievement of potential, and concede that the end required those particular narrativised 'events' or moments. In the next chapter, I develop these issues of origins and ends/aims in relation to rights, obligations and citizenship in the context of shifting definition of 'Europe'.

6 Visual epistemologies and new consumer rights

The preceding chapters have discussed the relation between consumerism, identity and belonging through a focus on the visual in advertising. By outlining the way in which knowledge of the consumer circulates within the advertising industry and within the advertising campaigns it produces, I have argued that visuality and knowledge articulate in powerful and complex ways. Colin Campbell (1997, 1999) has argued that studies of advertising and consumerism should not restrict themselves to a simplistic tracking of meanings in 'messages' about identity. Campbell wants to get away from the idea that consumer acts do not so much *do* something as *say* something or communicate something. As I have demonstrated in previous chapters, theories of performativity can be useful for exploring how 'saying something can be doing something'. This 'doing' does not necessarily centre on sending messages, but rather is the very action of constituting the self. Performativity looks at how speech acts produce the subject and aims to show how something as apparently 'immaterial' as speech can form the very materiality of the bodily self. I have adapted this framework to consider the visual and have explored how the origins of meanings and their relation to the awareness of the self produce complex forms of intent and responsibility.

A central theme of my analysis has been the significance and the signification of 'differences', and particularly sexual, 'racial' and cultural differences. As Donna Haraway (1991: 249) notes, 'some differences are playful; some are poles of world historical systems of domination. "Epistemology" is about knowing the difference'. Drawing from this insight, I have explored *visual* epistemologies in advertising and how processes of vision are about *seeing the difference*. Seeing the difference combines processes of visual perception with frames of knowledge. This fusion creates the social legibility of signs – it produces social meanings linked to images. But seeing the difference also involves seeing *through* difference: the seeing subject draws on epistemological status in order to authorise itself. In this way, the self becomes authorised as seeing subject. I have argued that the neutral epistemological status of this subject is in fact an enduring myth which hides the sexed, racialised, classed nature of the subject. Focusing on the 'playful' differences in reflexive advertising targeted at men, I have explored how discursive structures of privilege are consumed and reproduced. 'Knowing the difference' is a powerful visual and epistemological tool and grants certain subjects a flexible relationship to that knowledge; meanings can be decoded and recoded in multiple ways which in turn reconsolidate epistemological privilege.

Throughout the discussion so far, I have examined the relations between knowledge and the visual in terms of performativity. In this chapter I continue my emphasis on performativity and extend my analysis of the terms of 'culture' which I introduced in Chapter 1. I argue that culture and advertising form a key site through which the terms of belonging and rights are articulated. As I have argued, an analysis of the content of images is insufficient. In addition, we must explore the modes of interpreting or engaging with culture which are made available to viewers unevenly through the discursive framework of 'the individual'. In previous chapters, this emphasis has developed into a discussion of intent and time in what I have called 'retroactive intentionality'. This chapter re-engages with this focus and explores the notions of time, intent and responsibility articulated through constructions of 'culture'. I explore this in relation to contemporary debates about the nature and boundaries of Europe and the distribution of citizenship and other rights within these borders. This is an example of the processes involved in creating the 'imagined communities' that Benedict Anderson (1991) has famously discussed. I examine how the imagination, and particularly the visual imagination, can be said to be a social practice (Appadurai 1997) and can actively create 'reimagined responsibilities' through reworking the relation between intent and meaning.

Performativity and the origins of the self

In the previous two chapters I have shown how the visual can operate as a site of the performative constitution of the self and relation to 'others'. In this framework, the 'origin' or epistemological status of the self is ambiguous. Paradoxically, the self is produced in the moments of engagement with discourses of rights, and yet it requires the status of selfhood in order to begin the processes of engagement with those rights. The rights of the self and a notion of self as identity occur simultaneously in a performative (visual) enactment. Following Foucault, Butler (1993) argues that the self is simultaneously *subjected to* regulation and produced *as a subject* through that very regulatory framework. As I have argued, this is a hierarchical production of self. It generates political and cultural privilege by invoking a notion of historical and epistemological origin through a Western democratic tradition of 'the individual'. Yet the fluidity of meanings in contemporary image-spaces allows for multiple and/or ironic approaches to a notion of the origin of meaning and the origin of self. For female viewers, this temporal ambiguity echoes the discursive construction of women's status as 'non-present' – it reiterates women's delegitimisation whilst allowing for certain imaginative spaces. The transformative potential of these imaginative spaces is circumscribed by the dominance of certain male positions which allow for a translation of discursive flexibility to social privilege. For male viewers, the ambiguity of the originary status of (always already white, male, classed) 'self', citizen and nation opens up new ways of accessing privilege. In the following section, I explore what is involved in that accessing of privilege in the movement between subject and status. But what happens when a notion of origin is radically disrupted?

Butler (1997) argues that performativity operates through concealing its origins and force,

> If a performative provisionally succeeds ... then it is not because an intention successfully governs the action of speech, but only because that action echoes prior actions, and *accumulates the force of authority through the repetition or citation of a prior and authoritative set of practices*. It is not simply that the speech act takes place *within* a practice, but that the act is itself a ritualized practice. What this means, then, is that a performative 'works' to the extent that *it draws on and covers over* the constitutive conventions by which it is mobilized.
>
> (Butler 1997: 51, emphasis in original)

In order to dislodge a notion of agency residing in the subject and expressed through intent, Butler points to the authoritative status of *prior* practices. The 'doing' of the speech act originates not in the imagined agency of the speaking (or seeing) self. That agency is only produced in the citing or repeating of authoritative practices. The force of these speech practices is congealed in their repetition, but in that very repetition their actual existence is also concealed. This consolidates the myth of an autonomous self that exists prior to an engagement with social practices – or a self-contained seeing self that exists prior to an engagement with the visual. This is a myth in which the self is its own origins of agency.

In a discussion of the problematics of prosecuting sexual or racial 'hate speech', Butler develops her notion of priority and origins in relation to historical responsibility and the self. Speech acts actively construct the subject, rather than merely express the subject's agency and intent (which are imagined to exist prior to that speech act). The self is momentarily generated as agentic by the very utterances which name it as originator. Yet, paradoxically, the self requires that very agency in order to produce the capacity to utter. The result is that in an act of 'hate speech', the speaking self is conventionally imagined to be the origin of the meanings that are produced,

> The subject who utters the socially injurious words is mobilized by that long string of injurious interpellations: the subject achieves a temporary

status in the citing of that utterance, in performing itself as the origin of that utterance. That subject-effect, however, is the consequence of that very citation; it is derivative, the effect of a belated metalepsis by which that invoked legacy of interpellations is dissimulated as the subject as 'origin' of its utterance.

(Butler 1997: 49–50)

The corollary, Butler argues, is that the question of where the prosecution of that utterance of hate speech would begin and end becomes blurred. How can historical processes be held accountable? History itself cannot be prosecuted, as 'history, by its very temporality, cannot be called to trial', and so 'the subject is ... installed in order to assume the burden of responsibility for the very history that subject dissimulates' (Butler 1997: 50). The conventional approach to 'hate speech' assumes that the significance of its meanings resides in the fact that they originate from the action and, hence, intent of the subject. In effect, the subject is considered wholly responsible for historically embedded structures of racism or sexism, and thus liable to prosecution. It is these historically embedded structures which lend force to the acts of sexual and racial 'hate speech' and make their meanings resonate with power. So in line with Campbell's (1997, 1999) critique, Butler is emphasising that the acts and intent of the self do not operate in a transparently causal manner. The self is authorised through pre-existent practices or norms. It is not the origin of its own agency and intent: it 'performs' itself as origin and agent. The performance conceals the operation of the normative structures which are, in fact, the origins of the force of the acts. So, in the context of consumption (of goods, of images), consumer acts should not be seen as discrete acts which express the agency of the subject. Their action should not be seen as unproblematically meaningful or communication-oriented, as it does not link seamlessly with the actor's intent.

I would like to place Butler's argument in the context of my discussion of narratives of self. What I find useful is the way in which she maps out the trajectories of the self from imagined origin/agency of the self to the production of ends or aims of the self. As Campbell (1999) argues, many accounts of consumerism assume that the end or aim of the self is the reflexive self-construction of meaningful identity and the communication of these meanings of self to others. Indeed, meaning is often associated with intent or 'such cognate terms as goal-directedness or purposiveness' (*ibid.*: 49). But how should we consider the origins, agency and acts of the self when they have a non-symmetrical relation to meaning and intent? In what follows I consider these questions in terms of performativity and origins.

Gayatri C. Spivak (1992) suggests that questions of what it is *to stage* or *to be staged* must be seen as prior to the questions of what it is to perform or be performed. This can be considered in relation to the issues of framing and being framed which I discussed in previous chapters. Spivak here invokes the significance of origin, which stubbornly remains at issue in continual questionings of identity or essence,

> One of the most tenacious names as well as strongest accounts of the agency or mechanics of staging is 'origin'. I perform my life this way because my origin stages me so: national origin, ethnic origin ... . The notion of origin is as broad and robust and full of affect as it is imprecise. History lurks in it somewhere. And, even when we have gone around the claim to identity or essence, the question of origin does not disappear, as witness ideas of class origin, where class is clearly seen as a social inscription rather than a human essence.
>
> (Spivak 1992: 9)

Origin is, then, a complex and tenacious theme in people's self-understandings. Yet Spivak cautions, 'the question of origin can dis-able as much as it can en-able' (1992: 12). In Spivak's account, origin is not a fixed notion of beginnings which functions essentially as either transformative or conservative. Also, I would argue that origin can operate in the construction of selfhood in ways contrary to the inexorable citational concealment of the mechanisms of its own generation outlined in Butler's (1993, 1997) account. In Chapter 4, my analysis of the Marlboro advertisement (Plate 4.1) expands the horizon of these questions. The ironic suspension of temporalities of the self and historical origins of 'the individual's' rights points to a range of complexities. The existence of ironic temporal disruption may signal a more multi-dimensional approach to conceptualising selfhood, intentionality and agency. In the Marlboro advertisement, an ironic address makes visible and explicit the mechanisms of multiple narratives of self-constitution. These mobilise different citations of epistemological 'origin': origins in explicitly fictionalised popular culture genres are held in tension with political origins of the Western 'individual' in capitalist and democratic traditions. Origins of the nationness of North America and of 'Europe' are suspended together with the self's 'origin' of interpretative flexibility. The operation of normative narratives of origin are not concealed, but are self-consciously *displayed* as cultural resources and made available (to some) for re-articulation. Mediated through the 'present-tense' moment of visual exposure, the retrospective and prospective narratives of self-constitution play on the conventional formulation of the distinct boundedness of 'moments' and sense of temporal origin. This should not be seen in terms of the privilege of *not knowing* or not having to address issues of the subordination of 'others' (Sedgwick 1991). Rather, this is the privilege of suspending and moving between a knowledge of historical 'origin', knowledge of self and knowledge of others. These are suspended in frames of visibility which continually shift temporal relations of (origins of) knowledge and legible identities. As Haraway (1991) argues, 'knowing the difference' is a powerful epistemological tool.

These narratives, I suggest, produce the self in a different relation to 'origin', and the self's originality or creativity. In effect, these narratives initiate an ambiguity of 'ends'. As in Butler's (1997) formulation, the self is granted the temporary status of origin in the citing of the utterance. In my discussion, this occurs in the performative 'act' of seeing/interpreting, whose histories are implicated in forms of sexual, colonial and classed subordination. Yet this 'origin' can have a new ironic status which holds incommensurable narratives of origin together in tension. This, in turn, transforms the terms of the intent of the self attributed in that performance of origin. Meanings, acts of vision and the origins of intent are disrupted and can be reworked into new forms. The (white, male, middle-class) self is produced as an open-ended potentiality in which both the temporal positionality of origin and future-oriented 'ends' of the self are ambiguous. As I argued in Chapter 5 in relation to Ricoeur's (1981) theory of narrative conclusivity, certain male positions are offered flexibility in relation to constructions of selfhood and intent. In one sense, the ends or aims of the (white, male, classed) self are a 'foregone conclusion' – the temporal performative always retroactively confers self-authoring/authorising status. In a simultaneously retrospective and prospective 'moment' the self's potential will inscribe the self *as potential.* This is always, in Ricoeur's terms, an 'acceptable conclusion', as it is fundamentally self-authored/authoring.

So the self performs on and rearticulates the rights of the individual (its potential) by the authorisation of those very rights which it has historically accrued in encounters with 'others': the flexibility and controlled de-control of the performance becomes the sign of the self which calls it into being. Yet at the same time, the privileged self is offered a flexible position on intent, and, as I will discuss in later sections, on responsibility and obligation in relation to citizenship. The performative manoeuvre which both reflects and calls into being the rights of the self to self-presence and self-possession *simultaneously* constitutes a notion of intent. This radically disrupts a conventional notion of intent as preceding action. In the ironic suspension of meaning offered to certain individuals, knowledge of self and relations to other (in moments of constitution) can be self-conscious, explicit and can actively display and rearticulate different narratives of 'origin'. Yet, in another sense which is simultaneously available to some, the projected and enabling rights of the self 'know' that self's rights and intent before *he* can have self-conscious access to them. This can function to disrupt a conventional notion of intent, retroactively attributing intent in a flexible manner. This allows for a suspension of different levels of meaning and also a deferral of responsibility for actions, including the performative constitution of the self through the visual.

So, the suspension of intent that I have outlined operates in a different manner from the discursive move discussed by Butler (1997). In her account, the subject is installed as origin of intent in order to take on the burden of responsibility (and be prosecuted) for subordinations which cannot be attributed to a reified notion of 'history'. Instead, the discursive enactment I am discussing allows that (exclusive) subject an active rearticulation of diverse 'histories' of self-constitution and difference. In this way the subject is authorised to *suspend* intent and responsibility, and can avoid taking on that burden of historical responsibility and legal liability. Spivak (1992: 9) acutely points out that in discourses of origin 'history lurks in there somewhere'. I suggest that there is a shift occurring in understandings of history, such that 'history' may be available not (only) as a fixed notion of 'origin' but as a fluid *resource* for some at the expense of others. In later sections I explore how this idea of history as resource is related to consumer 'rights' of ownership. For the moment, I want to examine how the temporal dislocation of origins and narratives of self functions to relocate the agency or intent of the self and the terms in which duty, rights, citizenship, choice and potential are articulated. What and where is the referent for these rights and duties if a sense of historical origin is disrupted?

Identifying duty: agency, choice and rights

In contemporary Western culture, an explicit temporal engagement with narratives of the self (through 'the image' in the moment of exposure) can be produced as 'an identity'. In the same movement that Foucault (1990) identifies as consolidating a particular set of acts to form 'the identity' of the (male) homosexual, the (performative) 'act' of seeing/interpreting and the rights which authorise this 'acting' becomes the basis of an identity. Yet identity is here manifested in terms which disrupt standard notions of internality and externality and the spatio-temporal boundedness, or origins and ends, of the self which is 'identified'. The referent, or origin, of this 'identity' is not a preconstituted, spatially and temporally bounded voluntaristic self. Instead, it is the explicit performance of the 'rights' of 'the individual' in their engagement in interpretative 'moments'. In other words, it is the self's access to, and the *flexibility* of the self's engagement with, the rights of the (white, male, middle-class, heterosexual) 'individual' that actively *produces* the individual and the legal, political and cultural 'status' this entails. So there exists an oscillating movement from subject/self to status, and from status to subject, which is neither symmetrical nor circular. Moreover, this shift displaces and reformulates a notion of voluntaristic agency. If the notion of 'origin' is put into question through an explicit and visible display, conceptions of the duties and rights of identity and belonging shift. They become unanchored from the conventional terms of affiliation to the 'free will', or agency, of a temporally bounded self.

The concept of 'free will' has a long pedigree which includes the Hobbesian ideal of the 'naturally' self-interested individual. This individual, seen as free to create his/her world anew, was overlaid by the Kantian emphasis on reason and the morally autonomous modern individual (Somers and Gibson 1994). This stress on freedom and agency was then compounded by the French Enlightenment in which, 'Voltaire's, Diderot's, and Rousseau's free self was naturally driven to repel the force of political authority, tradition, custom, and institutional bonds – all in the name of freedom from domination' (*ibid.*: 48). As I initially discussed in Chapter 1, these ideals of the innately reasonable self (as male and Western) defined freedom as independence from external control, thus generating a conception of agency as free self-expression (James 1992; Yeatman 1994). The development of modern conceptions of citizenship was intimately bound up with these ideals in which the citizens' duties to the state were traded against the state's obligation to maximise individual freedom (James 1992). This freedom takes the form of the enjoyment of conditions which enable 'undistorted political self-expression' which defines a contemporary notion of political agency (*ibid.*: 50).

This ideal of political self-expression is materialised in the form of political, economic and social rights of national, and now European, citizenship. But the flexible ways in which the legal terms of citizenship are interpreted and implemented indicate that the supposedly 'inalienable' rights and obligations of citizens within European nations are more permeable than they may appear. Definitions of the legal terms of access to citizenship occur on the terrain of more diffuse notions of 'cultural belonging'. These can be invoked legally to override technical access to citizenship status and rights. For instance, Ann Dummett and Andrew Nichol (1990) cite the well-known fact that Britain does not have a single-document constitution which outlines legal rights and obligations of citizenship. This translates in practical terms as a provision of considerable discretionary powers which can be exercised by the Home Secretary, the immigration services and entry clearance officers following guidelines issued by the Home Office which are not published (Nichol 1990).[1]

This flexibility in the terms of belonging is not confined to British national citizenship laws. Brubaker (1992) argues that French citizenship is based on a civic or political tradition of the acquisition of rights through birthplace (*jus soli*), whereas German citizenship is founded on 'ethnic' principles of rights through blood relations (*jus sanguinis*). This rigid categorisation has been criticised by Yasemin Nuhoglu Soysal (1996), who argues that ideas of 'ethnic' and 'civil/political' access to rights have co-articulated in different historical moments of the extension or denial of citizenship rights to 'others' and the attribution of 'ethnicity' as shared values, language or culture. The rigidly drawn conceptual boundary between 'citizen' and 'alien' based on 'shared ethnicity' runs counter to the reality of residence and political status of large groups of immigrants in Europe. An estimated 15 million immigrants in Europe are technically 'foreigners' in their country of residence, in that they do not hold formal citizenship status (and many do not want it), but the majority have permanent resident status (Soysal 1996). This means that they have full access to civil and social rights (welfare, public health provision, etc.), but do not have the right to vote (*ibid.*). In this way, the terms of belonging and political affiliation do not always operate in a symmetrical manner, and complicate the conceptual boundaries between ethnicity, national residence and 'shared culture'.

The flexibility of citizenship laws in European member states, together with the mutually constitutive relation of 'ethnicity' and civil/political rights, indicate that the terms of belonging, culture, rights and obligations are highly fluid and contestable. My concern in these debates is to address how the formulation of concepts of 'art-culture', 'national culture' and 'European culture' are central to debates on national and European belonging and rights – they have been implicated historically in the constitution of the exclusive white, European, male, classed, heterosexual 'individual'.

Dislocating agency – re-locating cultural heritage in a European future

The temporalised national narratives of 'culture' involve an emphasis on origins linked to a notion of authenticity. This in turn is implicated in specific 'art-culture' concepts of authorship, value and 'civilisation'. Shifts in discourses of citizenship articulate different histories of the constitution of the categories of 'national culture' and the 'art-culture' system, both in terms of 'high culture' and 'popular culture'. Understandings of national 'culture', Strathern (1996) argues, have evolved in part as an anthropological tool for spatial mapping which has a tendency to *subsume* an incommensurability of certain factors (for example, gender and ethnicity) within a certain production of the boundaries of 'the culture', and *emphasize* incommensurability with other 'cultures'. In this way, the concept of 'culture' can become a self-referential framework for mapping, and thus producing, a diversity of human 'cultures' and ascribing 'difference' (*ibid.*). This notion of national culture should, however, be seen in relation to spatialised formulations of 'art', 'authenticity' and historical origin.

James Clifford (1988) argues that constructions of 'the art-culture system' have been produced historically in relation to specific formulations of national cultures. Clifford argues that in Europe after 1800, art and culture emerged as 'mutually reinforcing domains of human *value*' (1988: 234). Here, the term 'culture' refers to a process which 'orders phenomena in ways that privilege the coherent, balanced, "authentic" aspects of shared life' (*ibid.*: 232). It operates in relation to the art-culture system, drawing certain 'creative products' together in a historical and geographical unit which 'seem to give continuity and depth to collective existence' (*ibid.*). This art-culture system, which Clifford calls 'a machine for making authenticity' (*ibid.*: 224), operates through a fluid system of relative values of art/culture, masterpiece/artefact and authentic/inauthentic. The perceived 'authenticity' of traditional (national/'tribal') cultures and their 'artefacts' functions as a currency to re-produce the boundaries and status of Western 'art' masterpieces as opposed to fakes or popular culture forms. Moreover, they function to create a sense of depth and historical continuity of national and European communities. During the nineteenth century, art-culture came to signify the most highly valued creative 'genius' quality of a culture, which, I would argue, can be seen in terms of the culture's potential and uniqueness. This occurred through the shift in status of exotic objects from that of 'curiosities' to a means of comprehending a historicised notion of the development of distinct bounded 'cultures' and Western 'civilisation' (*ibid.*). 'The value of exotic objects was their ability to testify to the concrete reality of an earlier stage of human Culture, a common past confirming Europe's triumphant present' (*ibid.*: 228). The objects were used to generate a sense of relative historical origin and a progressive temporal development of 'Western civilisation'. In a dual move, Western commodities came to represent the forward march of European capitalist societies and their export was seen to reflect the bringing of 'civilisation' to colonised lands (McClintock 1995). But the value of the 'exotic' objects, in their testimony to the authenticity of the context they represented, relies on their having been removed from that historical moment to be placed in a collection or display (Clifford 1988). This forms a 'present-becoming-future' (*ibid.*: 228), and as such articulates the 'authentic' temporalities of non-Western peoples with Western concepts of the advanced, 'civilised' nature of Europe, epitomised by 'art-culture'.

In the context of my discussion of origin, the force of Clifford's argument lies in his demonstration of how ideas of a geographically bounded European 'cultural heritage' of 'art' and civilisation were historically constituted through a relation of temporality and 'authenticity' with non-Western peoples. Clifford goes on to suggest that these hierarchical structures of artistic/cultural values came to be displaced in the twentieth century by a democratising impulse from the West to extend its notion of 'art-culture' to all the world's populations. 'Culture', in the dual senses of art-culture and an idea of geographically bounded national/tribal culture, came to be a relative value of both what all peoples had in common and also what made each people distinct. As Strathern (1996) ironically states in the title of her essay, 'the nice thing about culture is that everyone has it'. Yet, 'culture' here operates through Western terms of reference, which were produced using non-Western peoples as a system of currency or value to produce a formulation of Western culture as the pinnacle of 'civilisation'. As I indicated in Chapter 4, Homi Bhabha (1990) argues that this notion of 'culture', which is ostensibly based on equal value, is in fact implicated in Western ideals of a hierarchical notion of 'civilisation' based on knowledge and connoisseurship:

> the sign of the 'cultured' or 'civilised' attitude is the ability to appreciate cultures in a kind of *musée imaginaire*; as though one should be able to collect and appreciate them. Western connoisseurship is the capacity to

understand and locate cultures in a universal time-frame that acknowledges their various historical and social contexts only eventually to transcend then and render them transparent.

(Bhabha 1990: 208)

In Clifford's (1988) terms, Bhabha's 'universal time-frame' within which the Western connoisseur locates diverse cultures is generated from a Eurocentric imagined point of reference – Western 'advanced' art-culture/civilisation were constituted through non-Western peoples' 'non-civilised' culture of artefacts.

Concepts of 'art-culture' and national and European 'culture' can be clearly tracked in their mutual interaction in certain contemporary rhetorics of European identity. In EU policy circles, cultural difference and identity are seen both as obstacles to economic rationalisation *and* as resources in the same processes (Schlesinger 1997). For the European Commission, cultural difference and diversity are often seen as assets and positive characteristics to be fostered (*ibid.*). Official European Commission publications aim to generate an idea of a common European bond between (certain) nations in Europe in terms of an essential 'Europeanness' of shared cultural heritage. This ideal of European identity is limited primarily to Western European nations, marginalising others – such as Turkey, whose traditions of Islam are considered to distance it from the dominant Christian heritage of Western Europe (Morley and Robins 1995). David Morley and Kevin Robins (1995) examine documents produced by the Commission of the European Communities between 1983 and 1987[2] in the run up to forms of European union, identifying the key theme of 'unity in diversity'. They cite a Commission document from 1987 which aims to evoke an image of unity between individual European nations through historical ideas of *culture* founded on 'a common cultural heritage characterised by dialogues and exchanges between peoples and men [sic] of culture based on democracy, justice and liberty' (Commission of European Communities, cited in Morley and Robins 1995: 77). This is a call to recognise 'the heritage of Western civilisation' which is presented as a specifically European identity to be celebrated and preserved (*ibid.*). In an official European Commission document written by Pascale Fontaine (1993), called *A Citizen's Europe*, 'culture' is explicitly identified as a key site for the formation of national and 'European' identity:[3]

Everyone knows what an important part the transmission of culture through images plays in Europeans' everyday lives. .... Tragically, Europe, the cradle of critical reasoning, cultural creativity and technological innovation in the media, is allowing itself to be overtaken by its main Western partners, the Americans and the Japanese, in the production and distribution of this type of image-based culture. If a European counterattack is not launched soon, 340 million Europeans will be doomed to a diet of American programmes on Japanese television sets.

(Fontaine 1993: 45)

The definitions of culture in the different forms of rhetoric described above exhibit implicit (and yet constitutive) contradictions. For instance, in the last quotation 'culture' is presented as a quality rooted in and exclusive to *European* nations and defined in terms of a history of creativity and artistic value, opposed to the implied 'mass' or 'popular' American media culture.[4] However, at the same time 'culture' is presented not as an intrinsic characteristic common to all European nations, but is explicitly defined as a *resource* from which to *produce* a common identity. Within this paradoxical discourse, European nations are seen to hold in common a European cultural heritage of democracy and 'civilisation'. Simultaneously, 'access to culture' as consumers (Fontaine 1993: 26) is presented as a precondition for the *generation* of a unified European identity.

The concept of 'culture' here, as in Strathern's (1996) account, functions as a device for mapping and simultaneously generating ideas of difference and identity. As I discussed in Chapter 1, this mapping has a historical precedent in colonial eras in which European nations 'mapped' the terms of their national identity in articulation with an emerging formulation of 'the individual'. Mary Louise Pratt (1992) charts how the production of classificatory systems of 'natural history' and the associated development of taxonomies generated a sense of early capitalist 'Europe' as distinct from the colonies:

> In the sphere of culture the many forms of collection that were practised during this period developed in part as the image of that accumulation, and as its legitimation. The systematizing of nature carries this image of accumulation to a totalized extreme, and at the same time models the extractive, transformative character of industrial capitalism, and the ordering mechanisms that were beginning to shape urban mass society in Europe under bourgeois hegemony. As an ideological construct, it makes a picture of the planet appropriated and redeployed from a unified, European perspective.
>
> (Pratt 1992: 36)

Europe came to be imagined as 'centre' through this mapping of the 'contact zones' between cultures in these processes of capitalist expansion and accumulation. Its centrality was constructed not merely in geographical terms but also in terms of the civilised advancement and, hence, the value of 'culture'. The framing of nature as 'natural history' articulated this hierarchisation through the cultured, civilised capacities of European travellers to map 'the natural' or biological. 'Biological racial categories' were developed which produced taxonomic hierarchies installing white Europeans as the most developmentally 'advanced' and 'civilised' (Pratt 1992). European 'culture' rendered nature transparent to the scientific rationality of the emerging 'individual' and confirmed *his* status as master.

This historical development of discourses of the European 'individual' and nation forms what Butler (1997) has called the 'legacy of interpella-tions'. This is invoked, yet dissimulated, in the contemporary expression (and constitution) of self through performative enactments, such as speech acts or the attempted accessing and implementation of certain rights. Yet there have been contemporary shifts from a 'natural history' of the develop-ment of the European 'individual' and nation to what Pierre-André Taguieff (1992) calls a 'culturisation' of nature. This is a taxonomy of national differ-ences through a mapping of 'cultural history' or 'cultural heritage'. Now European discourses of 'culture' draw their referents not only from a biolog-ical notion of 'race' (expressed through colour) but also from an essentialised notion of 'culture', as in Stolcke's (1995) formulation of 'cultural fundamentalism' which I initially discussed in Chapter 1. This discourse locates the responsibility for expressing (and simultaneously gener-ating) cultural heritage as a specific narrative of origin, protecting the 'uniqueness' of both the nation and Europe.

'Culture' can then function to 'naturalise' differences (Appadurai 1997), so that inequality can come to be framed as difference (Malik 1998). Such a conflation of difference and inequality has material consequences, such as a tightening of immigration controls of both national and European bound-aries. Yet these moves are defended in political rhetoric through distancing the legislation from 'racism', based on supposed biological 'origins', and instead mobilising a vocabulary of cultural belonging and difference (Stolcke 1995). Taguieff argues that this is a new form of racism in which 'le nouveau racisme doctrinal se fonde sur le *principe d'incommensurabilité radi-cale* des formes culturelles différentes' ['the new doctrine of racism is based on *the principle of a radical incommensurability* of different cultural forms'] (1992: 33–4, emphasis in original). In contrast, Stolcke (1995) argues that this new form should be seen not as a neo-racism but as a radically different form of 'cultural fundamentalism' which introduces a notion of *natural* antagonism between different cultures. Paradoxically, this is a *natural* 'cultural' difference based on the idea that cultures are intrinsically different and therefore 'naturally' hostile to one another (Stolcke 1995). This posi-tions 'human nature' as naturally ethnocentric and enforces an ideal that the rigid maintenance of national borders expresses this natural, inevitable ethnocentrism (*ibid.*). In a similar argument, Etienne Balibar (1991: 22) argues that 'culture can function like a nature' and can inscribe antagonism mechanisms for the defence of its boundaries. This antagonism is framed as natural, and the natural result of the abolition of difference would be the rise of 'defensive reactions, 'interethnic' conflict and a general rise in aggres-siveness' (Balibar 1991: 22). This notion of incommensurability derives from the articulation of two specific rhetorics of identity and difference;

elles dérivent d'un bricolage idéologique portant sur deux schèmes fondamentaux: la défense des *identités culturelles,* et l'éloge de la différence, tant interindividuelle qu'intercommunautaire, retraduit en *droit à la différence.*

[they derive from an ideological bricolage drawing on two fundamental schema: the defence of *cultural identities,* and the valorisation of difference whether between individuals or communities, rearticulated as *the right to difference.*]

(Taguieff 1992: 33)

In this formulation, the mutual operation of identity and difference is what different individuals and different 'cultures' have in common – yet it is also that which marks them as distinct, unique and valuable. They are equivalent in their difference, yet remain incommensurable; equally different and differently equal. This is a paradoxical discursive move in which the 'authentic' origins of different national cultural heritages are held in tension with a notion of 'difference' which has become detached from specific definitions of the 'authenticity' of historical, ethnic, geographical rootedness; all differences are equivalently different. To illustrate, Penelope Harvey (1996) describes how 'Expo '92', the recent universal exhibition, provided the site for a transnational 'dialogue' over difference and identity. Some national exhibits drew on the idea that the contemporary nation-state no longer required cultural homogeneity or strict territorial boundedness for its identity. This imagined transnational shared *experience* of deterritorialisation was translated into an imagined shared *response* to deterritorialisation, in which individuals are no longer tied to a nation-state (Harvey 1996). This notion of collective yet individualised response could be seen as a form of unity in individuals' engagement with a notion of 'culture' disembedded from specific contexts. Cultural difference becomes a fluid resource, rather than a fixed notion of authentic origin.

The incommensurability of cultures described by Balibar (1991), Stolcke (1995) and Taguieff (1992), does not draw on 'race' as a biological given, but on 'culture' as an essentialised form, 'les "cultures" étant transformées en "natures" secondes' ['cultures' being transformed into 'second natures'] (Taguieff 1992: 35). Celia Lury (1997) calls this a 'cultural essentialism' which produces a framework within which is possible a fluid play on 'race' and 'gender' as mix-and-match categories. They are not completely untethered from their 'natural' referents but operate in an elasticised relation to them which enables shifts in the terms of referentiality. 'Nature still works as a foundational resource, but in an inverted way, that is, through its artifice' (Lury 1997: 8). Indeed, Stuart Hall (1992: 23) has argued that there has been a displacement of European models of high culture and a decentring of old hierarchies, resulting in a flux of signifiers of difference and a 'deep and ambivalent fascination with difference'. In this context of disrupted cultural signs, the concept of 'culture' does not function merely as an imagined fixed and homogeneous *context* of ethnic, 'racial', geographical, historical and linguistic identity. Now the very *interpretation* of 'culture' can become a 'hermeneutic exercise' in which culture is 'something to be mastered cognitively, as a meaning' (Bauman 1992: 23).

These hermeneutic exercises occur not solely on an individual level, but also on a national level. The rhetorics of European unity *and* diversity in the European Commission's publications discussed earlier invoke an image of European identity through notions of the authenticity of historical origins of democracy, civilisation and creativity. These articulate with contemporary discourses of equivalent difference, culturised 'natural' difference, contingency and irony in the context of a dereferentiality of signs of difference. The notion of a European 'cultural heritage' is projected through present-tense moments of interpretation (authorised by histories of the constitution of 'the individual'), 'appreciation' and connoisseurship onto a European future as an ever-advancing ideal of civilisation, art and creative innovation. Simultaneously, ironic positions can actively refigure notions of 'culture', origin and hierarchy. The ironic address of the Marlboro advertisement (Plate 4.1) opens up intertextual possibilities (of Western films, etc.) at the same time as making possible an explicit form of 'inter-temporality' of narratives of origin and authenticity. This inter-temporality draws on the 'origins' of the historical constitution of the rights of the individual, yet, contrary to Butler's (1993, 1997) formulation, does not conceal their operation. The explicitness of the ironic address blatantly *displays* the mechanisms of its operation. Yet this visibility is in terms which simultaneously affirm and deny specific originary narratives. This is a self-conscious play on the authenticity and *origin*-ality of the viewing (white, male, middle-class) self. In the moments of visual exposure, the inherent elasticity of the moment of constitution that occurs between the rights and the 'individual' is played on through an ironic tension. This realigns different narratives of origin and generates an open-ended potential in a diffusion of temporality, drawing on past, present and future. This transgresses the frame of contemporary knowledge and engages the (white, middle-class male) self in imaginative, narrative exercises which rearticulate potential selfhood.

Active citizenship and the enterprising self

In Taylor's (1994) account, the articulation of authenticity and potential of the self is framed as a duty to the self. It occurs in an inner-directed search which is authorised by the very inner characteristics which are the aim or ends of the search. In the shifts I have outlined, the boundaries of the 'inner self' are not self-evident – they have been elasticised in ironic temporalised narrative movements which self-consciously play on 'origins' of the self. In this sense, Clifford's (1988: 224) formulation of 'the art-culture system' as 'a machine for making authenticity' now operates concurrently with a culture system which could be seen as *a machine for making irony*. In this formulation, the individual's active response or engagement with a notion of 'culture' becomes a key site for the performative constitution of that very self.

The notion of the 'active' self has gained considerable weight through its implementation in discourses of 'active citizenship'. Paul Heelas and Paul Morris (1992) outline how the development of 'enterprise culture' in Britain has installed an individualistic culture promoting 'the autonomous self' in a welter of rhetoric around self-reliance, self-respect, ambition and competitiveness. In relation to his discussion of French cultural politics, Balibar (1991) notes the rise of an 'individualistic' culture based on individual enterprise. As individuals, we must take an active responsibility for our educational, health, housing needs, etc., rather than being part of a passive 'dependency culture' (Heelas and Morris 1992). We should become 'enterprising consumers', actively engaging in such consumption practices as buying our council house, buying shares, investing in private pensions, health insurance, etc. In this framework, individual 'freedom of choice' is paramount (*ibid.*).

Kieron Walsh (1994) situates this notion of choice in the context of 1980s Britain, in which the state engaged in a devolution of financial control, contracting out public services on a market basis. The state shifted from a monolithic controlling role and took on an 'enabling' role as 'protector of citizen rights in the market for public services' (Walsh 1994: 190). A series of service charters developed in the 1980s and early 1990s, initially for refuse collection and street-cleaning, then for social care, education and policing, and culminating in the *Citizen's Charter* in 1991. As I discuss in the following sections, the subsequent British Government has developed the 'Third Way', with a focus on individual self-reliance and 'no rights without responsibilities'. As I initially discussed in Chapter 1, the key themes of the *Citizen's Charter* were 'quality, choice, standards and value', which were to be implemented through the mechanisms of privatisation, contracting out for services, performance-related pay and published performance targets (Gabriel and Lang 1995; Walsh 1994). These shifts defined the rights of the citizen as those of the consumer and tax-payer (Miller 1993), and, in effect, 'under the rhetoric of a share-owning democracy, the concept of the citizen was itself being privatized' (Gabriel and Lang 1995: 179).

This focus on the individual's responsibilities for autonomy occurs in a context of a shift from external state regulation to 'internal self-control' or self-management (Foucault 1988; Rose 1992; Strathern 1992). The inner search for our 'true self', as Taylor (1994) describes, also involves the self's duty for the independent identification and provision for our individual needs. As I discussed in Chapter 2, the 'politics of needs interpretation' (Fraser 1989) in welfare provision reinscribes the autonomy of white, male, middle-class groups (as rights-bearers and consumers) at the expense of others who are defined as 'dependent' or non-active – beneficiaries or clients of welfare to which they have no automatic right (Fraser 1989). In effect, consumer status and choice becomes the key tropes through which individual rights are expressed, yet free choice is a right which is unevenly conferred across social groups. In the following section, I explore how a specific discourse of choice comes to inhabit the disrupted space between 'intent' and action in relation to active citizenship.

Strathern (1992) argues that, in this context, choice becomes the very essence of individuality. It requires no external control, yet is in itself a form of 'prescriptive individualism' (1992: 152) in that we have no choice but to choose if we are to express ourselves as individuals. This is what Taylor (1994: 92) calls 'self-expressive choice', in which the expression and enactment of choice (and the capacity to choose) is framed as a duty to the self. In this sense, I suggest that choice forms a 'compulsory individuality' in which choice does not merely *represent* a preformed self – it is a performative enactment of self, invoking the category of selfhood in the 'moment' of expression. Indeed, in Western societies, we have no choice but to consume, as there is no other access to many of the goods and services we require. Yet Strathern's account overlays this predetermination by stressing that we have no choice but to *choose* to consume: every action (or lack of action) is defined as 'choice' in a compulsory attribution of choice as 'free will'. 'Not choosing' (as distinct from 'choosing not to') becomes a logical impossibility, a discursive blank space or kind of non-being.

In the terms of the *Citizen's Charter*, the use of public services automatically becomes an implicit consumer choice, rather than a citizen's right. In effect, it has no opt-out clause. This framework also operates in relation to images, both on the level of a individual viewer's relation to 'the image' and on the level of institutional provision for audiences/readers. With regard to television audiences, Ien Ang sees this emphasis on choice as a 'compulsion to activeness' in which 'the 'active audience' represents a state of being *condemned* to freedom of choice' (1996: 13).[5] In terms of Butler's (1997) discussion of a legacy of interpellations, the enactment of choice can be seen to install the subject as an entity capable of choice. Choice comes to form the definition of what it is to be an individual and etches out the arc of the individual's potential. Choice is here the origin, the potential and discursive drive of the individual – it is simultaneously defined as its aims or ends, also as its potential. As in Pateman's (1988) account of the contractual basis of the modern 'individual' discussed in Chapter 1, each 'moment' of contract or choice is a compulsory part of self-constitution. In these terms, choice becomes the framework through which the individual engages with a notion of 'culture', as with the definition of 'active citizenship' discussed in the previous section. This engagement with a notion of culture becomes the site for the performative constitution of self, authorised by histories of subordination in its exclusionary constitution.

This model of choice produces the self as 'an entrepreneur of itself' (Rose

1992: 150) in which the exercise of choice in its own enterprise is an ethical responsibility to itself and to society in general.

> The enterprising self is thus a calculating self, a self that calculates *about* itself and works *upon* itself in order to better itself. Enterprise, that is, designates a form of rule that is intrinsically 'ethical': good government is to be grounded in the ways in which persons govern themselves.
>
> (Rose 1992: 146)

Yet there is no pre-constituted self to work upon: the ethical duty to work upon the self calls into being the very notion of selfhood. Precisely what does the self have a responsibility towards? This is ambiguous and disrupts the relations between responsibilities and their related rights. As I have argued, the disruption and suspension of the originary status of these discursive movements in the visual opens up the possibility (for some) of a rearticulation of intent and also duty or responsibility.

The spaces of voluntarism

The intersection of the 'non-space' of media images and 'the image' gener- ated between print and viewer mobilises a politics of time and origins which relocates and redefines agency. This fluid non-space as a form of contact zone between fluid definitions of self and other becomes a mobile site of will/agency. Eve K. Sedgwick (1994) traces how 'free will' and ethics have historically emerged in relation to one another, articulated in one form through the tension between voluntarity and compulsion:

> So long as an entity known as 'free will' has been hypostatized and charged with ethical value ... for just so long has an equally hyposta- tized 'compulsion' had to be available as a counterstructure always internal to it, always requiring to be ejected from it.
>
> (Sedgwick 1994: 133–4)

Free will or agency is produced through citizenship as 'rights', whereas compulsion forms the necessary counterpart of 'duties' or 'obligations' of citizenship. These are constitutive one of the other, for, as Pateman (1988) argues, it is imperative that the rights of the individual be continually expressed and enacted (as a duty) in order for that very constitution of the ideal and rights of the agentic individual. The shift that Strathern (1992) identifies, which locates 'choice' as a primary expression of individuality and individual rights, can be usefully seen in relation to Sedgwick's (1994) interest in free will. Sedgwick argues that contemporary rhetoric around compulsion posits the possibility of addiction to anything, including exer- cise, shopping, relationships, even self-help groups for 'addicts'. This addiction attribution is driven 'by its own compulsion to isolate some new, receding but absolutized space of *pure* voluntarity' (Sedgwick 1994: 134). This voluntarity, I would argue, can be mobilised through a vocabulary of 'cultural essentialism' (Lury 1997) which allows (certain people) a mobile play on taxonomies of difference.

Sedgwick (1994:140) argues that this space of pure voluntarity is contra-dictorily positioned as 'Just Do It' in antagonism with 'Just Say No' (as in anti-drugs campaigns). This antagonism, I would argue, could be seen as a *compulsory individuality*, expressed through the exercise of will, in which there is no choice but to choose. The well-known series of Nike advertise-ments can function as a useful example. These engage with this imperative for producing a space or site of 'pure voluntarity' and potential. They attempt to brand the non-demarcated 'ends' of this potential in terms of Nike sportswear, with the imperative 'Just Buy It'. The non-defined impera-tive to 'Just Do It' is a performative hailing of the self in order to express and perform the rights of the self and so produce that self. The invocation of voluntarity takes as its reference-point discourses of the interiority of the self as inner-directed contact with the 'authentic' self (Taylor 1994): nobody but that individual may know their own true depths, and so only that person will know what it is they must do in the imperative to 'Just Do It'. This is a form of the 'transparent self' which I introduced in Chapters 1 and 4. Yet the terms of this self have been transformed from an epistemological trans-parency to others in moments of 'dialogue', to a self-reflexive transparency to itself. The temporal moment in which certain privileged viewers are invited to '*Just* Do It' is the interpretative moment of self-constitution. Yet at the same time, the context of disrupted origins and a 'culturised' nature alters the terms of reference of 'the authentic inner self'. In this shift, the *art of artifice* becomes another route to the pure expression of the rights of the self and its capacities for self-actualisation. Now, contact with the self through the transparency of (the knowledge of) others does not only occur in terms of authenticity. It can also occur in terms of the flexible capacities for rearticulating the terms of authenticity through a transparency of self or self-knowledge. In this sense, some contemporary forms of reflexive adver-tising do not operate through an explicit intent to manipulate 'natural' human will, as in some of the accounts of advertising that I discussed in Chapters 2 and 3. Rather, the address of such adverts explicitly rearticulates and displays the terms of will, intent and self-expression, such that the 'act' of interpretation calls into being that self and allows for a suspension of intent. In the following section, I address the implications of this self-referential movement for the constitution of rights of citizenship in the shifting definitions of 'Europe'.

'Europe': history, responsibility, rights

Boaventura de Sousa Santos (1999) suggests the tensions in human-rights politics function as a form of litmus test, signalling better than anything else the problems facing contemporary Western modernity. These tensions exist between social regulation and social emancipation, the state and civil society, and the nation-state and globalisation. For de Sousa Santos, the way through the maze of competing, cross-cultural claims to identity, difference and rights is through 'diatopical hermeneutics' (1999: 222). Designed to challenge false universalisms and resist cultural cannibalism, diatopical hermeneutics is a context-specific, context-sensitive framework for generating cross-cultural dialogue. The assumption is that the ethics and rights of each culture are valuable but incomplete, and would be ameliorated through dialogue with other cultures. The aim is to 'raise the consciousness of reciprocal incompleteness to its possible maximum by engaging in the dialogue, as it were, with one foot in one culture and the other in another. Herein lies its *dia-topical* character' (*ibid.*).

What can this mean in the context of my focus on consumerism and rights? In Britain, discourses of choice, responsibilities, rights and will have come to crystalise in 'consumer-citizenship'. As exemplified in the *Citizen's Charter*, the notion of choice comes to be framed as both a duty (to the self and nation) and as a *right* (expressing the self's potential). This merging of duties and rights disrupts the conventional terms of intent and agency which presuppose the deliberate identification of an aim, and the implementation of instrumental rational actions to achieve this aim. Yet this projected narrative of aims may not operate as a form of knowledgeable intent. Strathern argues that, as the self is seen in Western culture as the source of inner-generated knowledge of duty which is inextricably bound to 'correct' choice, 'it will follow that whatever the sense of duty is attached to will be the right thing; one may perform one's duty *without knowing what the ends are*' (1992: 153, emphasis added). This solipsistic dynamic encompasses a knowledge of self (and other), potential and duty, together with an unknown and unknowable future-oriented end.

This merging of agency/rights and duty/responsibility in discourses of citizenship, selfhood and consumerism disrupts the terms of intent and relocates historical responsibility. Butler (1997) discusses the prosecution of 'hate speech' through the establishment of responsibility and origins of the self. My discussion of dislocated origins and ambiguous future-oriented intent, suggest that the dislocation radically opens up the mechanisms for (temporarily) producing the self as origin of the utterance. So whilst the (white, middle-class, heterosexual) self can evade responsibility for (economically, socially and politically) benefiting from a history of racial and sexual oppression, he may still enjoy the discursive status accrued through this history. He is discursively positioned so as to display this status and negotiate cultural and political power through the suspension of different levels of meaning and temporal narratives. In doing so, he engages what Cornell (1993) calls 'the natality' of the self: that is, the need to re-produce a unitary self over time, by regenerating his self and his rights in a performative enactment. His historical responsibility is displaced onto a duty to his *own* potential – as Strathern (1992) argues, he becomes his own point of ethical reference. Yet for this self-reflexivity, he requires 'others' as currency and guarantee in the production of these meanings. In effect, the shifting reference-point for this privileged self becomes the flexible, sometimes ironic, capacities for engagement in these forms of 'dialogue' through the image. This dialogue is in fact a self-reflexive monologue about the rights and duties of 'the individual' which guarantee these capacities. So, whilst de Sousa Santos (1999) suggests that the contemporary tensions in the production of human rights may be approached through dialogue, my analysis suggests that such a dialogue may in fact be a self-reflexive monologue which subsumes difference. In the following paragraphs, I explore how Jacques Derrida (1992) has examined the themes of incompleteness and dialogue in relation to discourses of Europe.

In *The Other Heading: Reflections on today's Europe*, Jacques Derrida (1992) approaches the concept 'Europe' in terms of the solipsistic discursive production of the nature of 'civilisation' and 'culture' as the pinnacle of human endeavour (or potential):

> Europe is not only a geographical headland or heading that has always given itself the representation or figure of a spiritual heading, at once as project, task, or infinite – that is to say universal – idea, as the memory of the memory of itself that gathers and accumulates itself, capitalizes upon itself, in and for itself. Europe has confused its image, its face, its figure and its very place, with that of an advanced point, ... and thus, once again, with a heading for world civilisation or human culture in general.
>
> (Derrida 1992: 24)

Derrida argues that, in the contemporary crisis in European cultural identity, we must take responsibility for this privileged 'heritage' (1992: 28–30). As Europeans, it is our duty 'to respond to the call of European memory, to recall what has been promised under the name of Europe, to re-identify Europe' (*ibid.*: 76). This duty must take the form of critiquing the assumption of a uniquely European heritage of the idea of democracy and demands 'respect' of 'differences, idioms, minorities, singularities' (*ibid.*: 78). This is a duty to the past and a duty to a rethinking of the future of democracy, in which our understanding of the present cannot be thought without a critical return to the past and European responsibilities for histories of subordination. For Derrida, this calls for a politics of undecidability and a demand to exercise responsibility through thinking the impossible:

The condition of possibility of this thing called responsibility is a certain *experience and experiment of the possibility of the impossible: the testing of the aporia* from which one may invent the only *possible intervention, the impossible intervention.*

(Derrida 1992: 41, emphasis in original)

Yet, as I have argued, this notion of duty or responsibility can be disrupted through a fluid and retroactive self-attribution of intentionality. As Strathern argues (1992), one may perform one's duty without knowing what the ends are, and, I would argue, the ambiguity of these non-demarcated ends/aims (or non-teleological movement) offers spaces for a reworking of identity. This openness may become inhabited by the solipsistic dynamic of the reinscription of the (white, male, classed) self through the self-fulfilling prophecy of its narratives of self. As in the example of the Nike campaign, the duty of the self is to know and articulate its potential (or non-demarcated aims/ends) in the imperative to 'Just Do It'. This is an inner-directed, self-reflexive, self-constitutive dynamic which is nonetheless reliant on the historical legacies of the exclusion of the 'others' from the category of 'the individual'. The duty or responsibility to the past and the rethinking of the future which Derrida proposes is translated as a rearticulation of the terms of the past/present/future self in 'recollective imagination', as discussed in Chapter 5. Cornell (1993) offers this formulation of recollective imagination as a means of insisting on the openness of interpretation and, hence, the possibilities of re-imagining subjectivity, difference and justice. Yet, this very openness can offer those with privileged access to the category of individual selfhood, and (tenuous) self-presence, the possibilities for rearticulating the very terms of responsibility and rights.

In this rearticulation, the 'respect for difference' which Derrida calls for in thinking of the possibilities of the impossible becomes imbricated in a reformulation of the liberal call for *'le droit à la différence'* ['the right to difference'] as discussed by Taguieff (1992). Despite the intention of openness, such a move may be foreclosed by the cultural politics of difference. In the context of French liberal thought on 'cultural difference', and more generally in 'identity politics', 'the right to difference' (as 'the right to be different') represents what is seen as an intrinsic human need and right to a cultural identity which should be protected from homogenisation.[6] I am arguing that this liberal discourse is operating concurrently with a reformulated notion of the right (for some) *to difference as a cultural resource*, particularly through images in the production of identity. Difference is simultaneously denied as an available self-present identity, and affirmed as a necessary resource in the identity-production of privileged selfhood.

I am suggesting that this visual display of difference becomes an explicit site of the enactment of the terms of 'active citizenship' in which definitions of 'cultural belonging' are constituted and contested. For example, Brubaker (1992) cites the debates in France in the 1980s around the possible restriction of the terms of the attribution of French citizenship. In the 1986 French legislative campaign, there was a nationalist critique of automatic citizenship attribution based on place of birth. The Centre Right and Far Right questioned the idea that 'French identity' was merely related to birth place, and Jean-Marie Le Pen, of Le Front National, famously proclaimed 'être français, cela se mérite' ['to be French, you have to deserve it'], which set the tone of the critique (Brubaker 1992). There was an emphasis on the need to be 'français de coeur' ['French at heart'], not merely 'français de papier' ['technically/legally French'] (*ibid.*). This shifted the terms of 'natural' belonging firmly onto the 'cultural terrain' in which certain groups were seen as more assimilable than others. For instance, the focus of much of the French Right's attack on immigration was on North African Muslims, despite the fact that the largest group of foreign citizens in France was in fact Portuguese (*ibid.*). Islam was seen as a 'fundamental' cultural difference, not merely as an 'assimilable' difference as represented by other European nations such as Portugal (*ibid.*). In effect, this unassimilable difference was seen as a naturalised or essentialised cultural difference, as in Stolcke's (1995) formulation of 'naturally' antagonistic, incommensurable cultural difference. This is the legacy of European formulations of selfhood described by Stolcke (1995) and Taylor (1994) which function to reinscribe Europe as epistemological centre. In this context, 'the right to difference' also translates as the right to retain firm national (and European) boundaries to protect the essential uniqueness of national cultures (and European cultural heritage of Christian democracy) from unassimilable threats. Here, 'respect' for difference involves respecting the European right to discursive centrality and 'protecting' other cultures' inherently valuable uniqueness by denying them access to what Robins and Morley (1995) call 'Fortress Europe'.

The right to difference – drawing on this European epistemological heritage – simultaneously operates on the level of 'the individual'. In this context, the right to difference as a resource conceptually merges with the duty to the self. In the Nike advertisements, the imperative 'Just Do It' refers to 'the right to be individual', which is defined as an inner-directed contact with the potential of the self. The right to be individual is based on the right to be different. This is in turn reliant on the discourses of identity and self-presence which mobilise women, racialised groups, and classed groups as discursive currency. The 'duties' or responsibilities for this exclusionary constitution which Derrida (1992) invokes, I would argue, can be avoided by some through their rearticulation in 'retroactive intentionality'. This is certainly a destabilisation of identities and their associated rights, but one which is not necessarily emancipatory. European democracy may be in the process of being redefined, as Derrida hopes, but may come to be refigured as a 'duty-free capitalism' (O'Neill 1997).

Concluding remarks

The density of affect attached to the ideals of consumer sovereignty, rights and self-expressive choice in the West attests to the ways in which culture has become an explicit site for contesting identities and rights. I have argued that this is an intensely visual culture in which images play a central role in constituting subjects. Yet I have not taken an 'images-of-women' approach to studying gender in advertising – I have placed less stress on the representation of gender roles in images, gendered stereotypes, or the commodified of ideals of feminism such as self-expression or equality in advertising (see Goldman 1992). Many feminist analyses have outlined the centrality of women and tropes of femininity to the construction of Western consumerism (Bowlby 1985, 1993; Felski 1995; Nava 1997; Radner 1995). Such accounts demonstrate that gendered images in advertising only tell part of the story of women, advertising and consumerism – they extend the scope of analysis by pointing to the structurally gendered nature of consumerism and the ways in which gender underwrites discourses of (consumer) rights.

In my analysis of advertising I have attempted to develop this insight to consider how gender and processes of vision constitute the seeing subject and how advertising 'mediates' this constitution. I have explored these issues through the theoretical framework of performativity which shifts the focus of how we should consider the role of advertising images. Advertising does not so much provide a resource or image-pool from which the subject chooses and rearticulates meanings to express forms of selfhood. This is not a communicative paradigm of consumer acts in which the consumer orients the meanings of goods and images towards communicating their identity to others (see Campbell 1997, 1999). Rather, the subject is produced performatively in those very modes of engaging with culture. The visual process of interpretation which advertising attempts to engage does not reflect the agency of a preconstituted subject – these interpretative processes act to form that very subject performatively. This performative process draws on the rights of 'the individual' which have been accrued through histories of sexual and 'racial' subordination. The historically sedimented discursive weight of 'the individual' and *his* rights authorises the forms of visual interpretation that the contemporary subject enacts. This is a form of visual performativity which highlights the importance of temporality in both the performative constitution of the self and the time of vision. I have argued that the reflexive modes of address offered by some forms of advertising resonate with this, offering new relationships between intent, time and responsibility. Through generating ideal target markets, the structure and practices of the advertising industries reflexively re-produce a masculinist, 'creative', 'innovative' framework in the way they promote themselves and also in the way they produce specific advertising campaigns. The knowledge of markets which circulates between agencies, clients and magazines is an imagined 'dialogue'. Yet in fact this is a solipsistic monologue which re-produces certain forms of gendered, classed and racialised hierarchy. The textual strategies of adverts are produced through this ethos and delimit the available viewing positions through which viewers are offered narrativised accounts of selfhood. Certain middle-class, white, Western male viewers are offered the possibility of flexible rearticulations of images of difference. Through what I have called 'retroactive intentionality', they are then authorised to have a flexible relation to rights and obligations of citizenship in new discourses of 'consumer citizenship'. In effect, privileged subjects are performatively produced as *flexible* subjects.

I have also argued that this re-production of selfhood does not only operate through concealing its generative mechanisms, as in Butler's (1993, 1997) account. It also operates through explicitly and reflexively displaying its discursive manoeuvres in visual terms. The explicit foregrounding of temporality and vision allows for a reworking of intent and responsibility. Certain subjects enjoy the social, cultural and economic privileges accorded by historically embedded discourses of entitlement. At the same time, their reworking of temporality and intent distances those privileged subjects from the responsibilities that they should bear for enjoying those benefits. I have argued that intent and agency can be displaced to the time of vision which is also the time of the constitution of the subject in visual performativity. It is this time of vision that advertising attempts to brand. In the reflexive advertising campaigns I have discussed, the aim of advertising is not a blatant 'manipulation' of the viewer. Rather, advertising aims to intervene in the very constitution of the self in acts of vision and make the self function through its own branded terms. I have also argued that intent and responsibility come to be suspended in the time of vision. For privileged subjects, this allows an ironic, controlled swing between involvement and distance, rights and responsibilities. Women and other subordinated groups are offered a different form of dislocation. As de Lauretis (1989) has argued, such groups are always already in a discursive 'elsewhere(s)'/'elsewhen(s)' whose dislocation functions through subordination rather than privilege.

These shifting forms of responsibility and rights operate on transnational as well as individual levels. The 'imagined communities' of Benedict Anderson (1991) articulate with the reimagined responsibilities and rights enacted in visual performativity. This is a kind of epistemological 'having your cake and eating it' which draws on discursive privilege but uncouples that privilege from responsibility. One corollary of this is the rearticulation of respect for difference as 'difference as a consumer resource' or discursive currency in the production of selfhood. The emphasis on difference and 'identity politics' that I have outlined is not new, yet has enjoyed an intensified significance in shifts in 'the grammar of political claims-making' (Fraser 1997: 2). This is a 'culturisation' of discourses of rights in which 'identity politics' has gained considerable influence.

In previous chapters, I have outlined Nancy Fraser's (1989) argument around 'needs interpretation'. Within structures of welfare provision (as an unevenly allocated 'right' of citizenship), the politics of needs interpretation has long been a cornerstone of the unequally structured system of access to welfare (Fraser 1989). Fraser argues that women's 'needs' are generally defined in relation to men, for example as a mother in a family in which the male is framed as the 'breadwinner'. In the light of my analysis of culturally mediated rights, I think that future research could productively examine how a politics of explicitly 'culturised' *rights interpretation* may function concurrently with needs interpretation in mechanisms of exclusion and subordination. This area is of particular contemporary significance as shifts in the legal, political and economic structure of European Union membership has meant that a multiplicity of rights now exist at both national and transnational levels (Soysal 1994, 1996). On this transnational level, organisations such as the UN and UNESCO have codified the collective rights of nations as a right to 'culture', in which all nations have the right to express their differences (Soysal 1994). This parallels Stolcke's (1995) formulation of 'cultural fundamentalism' which I discussed in Chapters 1 and 6. Significantly, these ideas of cultural essentialism are now legally protected through established organisations at transnational level (Soysal 1994). On an individual level, the Maastricht Treaty of 1993 forged a direct link between the individual and Europe through according an individual a *right to a nationality*, codified in Article 15 of the Universal Declaration of Human Rights (Guild 1996). This formulation defines nationality both as a right and simultaneously a mandatory status – everyone within the EU must have at least one nationality. Indeed, this paradoxically mandatory right parallels my analysis of 'compulsory individuality' and 'compulsory choice' in relation to consumerism and performative self-constitution.

In effect, this politics of 'rights interpretation' is occurring in explicit ways around contested definitions and rights of national and European citizenship. As I have argued, this contestation is articulated through the terms of consumerism, cultural difference and cultural belonging. Yet the politics of rights interpretation is also occurring through the discourses of individual 'potential'. In Britain, Tony Giddens' (1998) *The Third Way* has proved to be a touchstone for Tony Blair's Labour government. For Giddens, the main concern of Third Way politics is a redefinition of rights and social responsibilities, the motto of which can be seen as 'no rights without responsibilities'

(1998: 65). This is very much a *culturised* form of rights interpretation which emphasises not social justice, entitlement and a redistribution of wealth, but rather a 'redistribution of human potential' (Giddens 1998: 101). 'Human potential' becomes the trope through which 'the individual' is actualised. The state's responsibility is framed as enabling individual potential rather than reworking the social structures within which that 'potential' is contained; 'The cultivation of human potential should as far as possible replace "after the event" redistribution' (Giddens 1998: 101). At a Labour Party conference speech in Bournemouth on 28 September 1999,[1] Tony Blair explicitly drew on these ideas by arguing for 'the liberation of human potential not just as workers but as citizens'. In his speech, Blair argued that 'true equality' should not be seen as 'equal incomes' or 'uniform lifestyles or taste or culture'. True equality' is 'equal worth, an equal chance of fulfilment'. This highlights what might be called 'a culture of potential' which places emphasis on identifying and expressing individual potential. It is a form of cultural essentialism and identity politics which flattens understanding of social hierarchy and dissimulates social privilege. It emphasises both universalism and particularism and uses such a structure to explain and condone injustices of outcome. As I have discussed, discourses of individual potential frame subjects as equally different and differently equal – each individual's potential will be different (unique, individual) and this difference will account for unequal incomes and social privilege (cf. Taylor 1994). Yet individual potential is also a universalising discourse; what we have in common, paradoxically, is the fact that we are individual, that we are different. We are equivalently different. In the political rhetoric of Blair's speech, this emphasis on equivalence is designed to resonate with equality, individual rights and social responsibility; 'equal rights. Equal responsibilities'. This is not a state responsibility to the individual but rather an individual responsibility to actualise their own potential. Yet as I have argued in my discussion of the category of 'the individual', identity and difference are not transparent. 'The individual' is not a neutral, universal, equivalent category, and differential access to the category of 'the individual' structures contemporary forms of inequality and subordination. What questions may these inequalities and forms of rights-interpretation raise?

Future visions

My discussion of intent and visuality suggests that many academic analyses of advertising should be reformulated so as to readdress concepts of agency. My analysis proposes that the relations between intent, agency and vision are flexible and connect and disconnect in multiple ways. Expressed through intent, agency can be flexibly and retroactively self-attributed. This disrupts the conventional formulation of intent as preceding and motivating action. In effect, the visual interpretation of advertising displaces intent and meaning and generates agency in the very acts of vision. Therefore, advertising cannot be seen to 'distort' ostensibly authentic agency through lack of 'accurate' information or through manipulative forms of address such as subconscious 'depth manipulation' (Packard 1981/1956).

Indeed, the very terms of depth, surface, individual interiority and the exteriority of 'others' may be put into question. In one account, the extension or displacement of the site of subjectivity has been seen in terms of memory and the use of prosthetic devices such as video (Lury 1997). In my analysis, the 'spaces' of the formation of subjectivity are less a material locus or technological mediated event, but rather a zone of temporality in the 'moment' of interpretation. This could be seen in terms of Sedgwick's (1994) analysis of the search for the 'space of pure voluntarity' which, I have argued, is paradoxically articulated as *compulsory individuality*. In another account, the space of the body is seen to operate in a way which actively and continually reformulates its interconnections in a flexibly integrated bodily system. Emily Martin (1994) argues that medical and popular discourses of the interactions of the body's organs have shifted through various definitions, ranging from that of the body as a 'complex system' to that of the body as a 'flexible system'. A flexible system is seen to operate through 'loose coupling', or flexible connections and incorporations of shifts to maximise the body's integrated efficiency and defences, particularly in the face of rapidly mutating viruses (Martin 1994). It would be interesting to relate my analysis of flexible interpretative practices (and retroactive intentionality) to Martin's emphasis on the significance of flexibility in 'human survival', particularly in the context of much of the advertising literature's emphasis on authentic or 'natural' human needs. What does flexible subjectivity 'naturally' need? To what might it have a 'natural right'? Rights discourses have recently gained a renewed prominence in 'universal human rights' discourses (Soysal 1994, 1996). Crucially, these discourses emphasise the right of access to interpreting rights and effectively reformulate the terms of the human subject and human potentiality. Soysal (1994) argues that women's rights are currently being reformulated at an international level as 'women's human rights'. Yet, if processes of (restricted access to) flexible interpretation and retroactive intentionality can reformulate the way in which human subjectivity is discursively framed, the very terms of 'human' may be in a flexible process of redefinition.

Indeed, interventions into the arena the human rights debate are already occurring in commercial terms – the Human Rights Awards are distributed by *The Reebok Corporation* (Soysal 1994). In corporate terms and in more general consumerist terms, certain groups may be authorised to 'own' access to rights. They can defer responsibility for 'the individual's' (and corporate) exclusionary constitution whilst benefiting from, and reformulating, economic and political privileges accrued in histories of colonial, class and sexual subordination. In this politics of temporality, the terms of what counts as 'our' 'European cultural heritage' and associated democratic rights may be accessed only by the few who are authorised to configure what will count as 'our' 'European democratic future'.

Appendix
Research findings

Table 1 Total sample

	reject	reflexive	unreflexive
British	50	12 (5 ironic)	73
French	43	26 (10 ironic)	66
Total	93	38	139

Table 2 Non-reflexive adverts: placement magazine

GB *Economist*	GB *Elle*	GB *Q*	France *L'Expansion*	France *Elle*	France *Première*
13	3	8	4	6	16

Table 3 Reflexive advertisements: target market

	youth	women	men
GB	0 (1 'non-sexed')	3	9
France	13	6	7

Table 4 Non-reflexive adverts: placement magazine

GB *Economist*	GB *Elle*	GB *Q*	France *L'Expansion*	France *Elle*	France *Première*
26	36	8	15	32	19

Table 5 Non-reflexive advertisements: target market

	youth	women	men
GB	0	36	36
France	3	34	28

Notes

Introduction

1 In fact, the flow of knowledges between academia and the advertising industry is complex and multidirectional (see Lury and Warde 1997).

1 The individual, the citizen and the consumer

1 Cited in Finzi (1992: 126).
2 My own translation. All following unattributed translations are my own.
3 In later chapters, I explore these exclusions in terms of 'race', cultural difference and 'Europeanness'.
4 Stolcke uses the term 'fundamentalism' in an ironic way to highlight the extension of this discourse to secular rhetorics and to stress that this should be seen as an extension of Western stereotypical views of Muslim fundamentalism (Stolcke, personal correspondence). I sympathise with Stolcke's intention to disrupt conventional Western views of fundamentalism and with her aim to emphasise that neo-liberal economics are similarly fundamentalist. However, my own analysis points to the complex relation between irony and the re-production of privilege (see Chapters 4 and 6). For this reason, I suggest the term 'cultural essentialism' in the place of Stolcke's concept of 'cultural fundamentalism'. In later chapters I discuss issues of the supposed incommensurability of Islam with Europe.
5 In Britain the 'Rushdie Affair' has highlighted notions of incommensurable 'cultural difference' between Islam and European democratic traditions (Brah 1996).
6 In her later work Fraser (1997) has developed this conceptual structure, yet the principal thrust of her argument remains the same.

2 Advertising knowledges

1 Issues of materiality have been discussed in the context of debates about the direction of cultural studies, in which 'textualising' approaches are often set against 'empirical' work. See Morley (1998) for an overview of these debates.
2 The expression 'visual persuasion' is taken from the title of Messaris (1997). I am not suggesting that his arguments mirror those described above.
3 The terms of meaning, intent and action discussed by Campbell raise some problematic issues around the role of language and the assumed inertia or passivity of the body (see Kirby 1997).
4 Focus groups are small sample groups of consumers who are interviewed in some depth by market researchers in order to gauge opinions and shifts in taste.

164   *Notes*

5 I will discuss this in relation to Bauman's (1990) concept of the 'consumer attitude' in later sections.
6 This is the title of an article in Campaign (12 February 1988: 67–74).
7 For debates on risk and authority, see Beck (1992), Bauman (1992), Featherstone
   (1991). For a discussion of the media literacy of the young, see Nava (1992).
8 Bauman (1992) proposes a similar development of this class segment and
   describes them in terms of 'interpreters' who frame cultural ideas for the public.
9 I discuss the method and rationale of my study in Chapter 3.
10 In support of this notion being shared by advertisers, Campaign magazine (13
   May 1988: 26), reported that the 'over-25 Q magazine generation' were the target
   of Channel Four's music show Wired. Interestingly, the target market is
   presented here as 'over 25' (which, as a group, is seen as having a high disposable
   income) despite the fact that 46 per cent of its actual readership is aged 15–20 (Q
   media pack).

3 Advertising, texts and textual strategies

1 I was prompted to explore this area by the suggestion of Leiss *et al.* (1990) that
   visuals are becoming increasingly significant in relation to written text in print
   advertising.
2 I discuss the findings of this analysis in Chapters 4 and 5.
3 I do not include a chart of all the product types and their relation to other variables, as the range is very broad. Instead, I identify what I consider to be the key
   relational sites of analysis.
4 As argued in Chapter 1, the individual is structured as exclusively male.
5 This Becks advertisement is taken from the April 1990 edition of Q magazine.
6 The Q media pack states that its readership is primarily young (78 per cent is
   between 15 and 34) and male (72 per cent).
7 In Chapter 4 I analyse a Marlboro cigarette advertisement (Plate 4.1) and discuss
   its use of a reflexive address in the context of restrictions on tobacco advertising.
8 The British Codes of Advertising and Sales Promotion (1995–), Specific rules:
   alcoholic drinks, rule 46.7. <http://www.asa.org.uk/codes/spec_page_41.htm>
   (accessed 10 February 2000).
9 Ibid., rule 46.9.
10 See McClintock (1995) for an analysis of commodity fetishism in colonial
   contexts.
11 This analysis uses the British version, taken from the April 1995 edition of Elle.

4 Branding vision: advertising, time and privilege

1 John Donne, cited in Nowotny (1994: 45).
2 This advert was taken from the April 1995 edition of *Q* magazine.
3 *The British Codes of Advertising and Sales Promotion* (1995–), Cigarette code,
   rule 66.16, <http://www.asa.org.uk/codes/cig_page_52.htm> (accessed 10
   February 2000).
4 *Ibid.*, rule 66.19.
5 *Ibid.* This rule is very similar to the rules governing alcohol advertising. See
   Chapter 3.
6 Henning does not discuss the specific advertisement analysed here.
7 The production of privileged discursive positions has material consequences for
   those excluded from them in terms of citizenship rights, access to welfare, etc.
   (see Fraser 1989, discussed in Chapter 1).

8 For Virilio, the kinematic is 'energy resulting from the effect of movement, and its varying speed, on ocular, optical or optoelectronic perception' (1994: 61).

5 Female visions: advertising, women and narrative

1 Butler's position on the relation between language and the materiality of the body has been criticised for privileging the linguistic over the 'substance' of the body (Kirby 1997). This raises important issues around materiality that are beyond the scope of my present study.
2 Hermes (1995) indicates that women's magazines do in fact have a male readership, often the partners of the female readers. The targeted readership is, however, female, and the content, including the advertisements, is aimed at the imagined tastes of women.
3 *Elle*'s media pack states that its average monthly circulation in 1995 was 205,511, and its readership 1,097,000.
4 The first Dune advert in my study appeared in French *Elle* 1993.
5 Plate 5.1 is a late 1990s version of an earlier Dune advert found in my sample of adverts. Unfortunately, Parfums Christian Dior no longer holds the copyright for the original advert, and I have substituted this more contemporary version. It uses metaphor in the same way and has the same imagery and structure.
6 The original Trésor advert from my study is taken from the April 1990 French edition of *Elle*. Unfortunately, Lancôme could not grant me permission to reproduce the original advert, due to the prohibitive fees payable to the model used (Isabella Rossellini). I am here using a late 1990s similar version of the advert.
7 This advert is taken from the April 1988 British edition of *Elle*.
8 I was unable to reproduce this advertisement, due to fees payable to the model used (Daryl Hannah).
9 Her pallor, pose and hair are reminiscent of pre-Raphaelite female models.

6 Visual epistemologies and new consumer rights

1 The legal terms of these discretionary powers are currently being challenged by new legislative provisions following the ratification of the Treaty on European Union (the Maastricht Treaty) in 1993. In conferring EU citizenship on all nationals of member states, this has highlighted the grey areas in many member states' citizenship laws (Guild 1996).
2 This period is significant, as it overlaps with the timescale of my sample of advertisements (1985–95).
3 This document is printed in all of the languages of the European Community, and it states its purpose on the back jacket; 'This booklet has been written for you as a European citizen in an attempt to answer some of the questions you may have about the European dimension that is now part of everyday life'.
4 Morley and Robins (1995) discuss how an opposition to America is key to the production of a specifically 'European identity'. Yet I will discuss in later sections how immigration, nationality and citizenship legislation, and the associated debate around belonging, focuses heavily on intra-European difference and opposition to other identities, such as Islam.
5 This compulsory activeness would disrupt Baudrillard's (1988) proposed form of mass resistance by calculated passivity to what he sees as the bombardment of signifiers in the mass media.
6 Brubaker (1992:148) notes that most of rhetoric around le droit à la différence in France in the 1980s came not from the immigrants themselves, but from the French Left, and 'reflected less of a refusal of assimilation on the part of

immigrants than the rejection of the traditional Republican formula of assimilationist civic incorporation on the part of the French left'.

Concluding remarks

1 http://www.labour.org.uk/lp/new/labour/docs/speeches/tonyblair280999.html>
   (accessed 29 September 1999).

Bibliography

Alcoff, Linda and Elizabeth Potter (eds) (1993) *Feminist Epistemologies*, London and New York: Routledge.

Alcoff, Linda (1997) 'The politics of postmodern feminism', *Cultural Critique* Spring: 5–27.

Anderson, Benedict (1991 [1983]) *Imagined Communities: Reflections on the origin and spread of nationalism*, revised edition, London and New York: Verso.

Ang, Ien (1996) *Living Room Wars: Rethinking audiences for a postmodern world*, London and New York: Routledge.

Appadurai, Arjun (1990) 'Disjuncture and difference in the global cultural economy', in M. Featherstone (ed.) *Global Culture: Nationalism, globalization and modernity*, London: Sage.

—— (1997) *Modernity at Large: Cultural dimensions of globalization*, Minneapolis: University if Minnesota Press.

Balibar, Etienne (1991 [1988]) 'Is there a "neo-racism"?', in Etienne Balibar and Immanual Wallerstein *Race, Nation, Class: Ambiguous identities*, first published as *Race, Nation, Classe: Les Identités ambiguës*, Editions La Découverte, trans. Chris Turner, London and New York: Verso.

Barthes, Roland (1977) *Image Music Text*, trans. Stephen Heath, London: Fontana.

Battersby, Christine (1989) *Gender and Genius: Towards a feminist aesthetics*, London: The Women's Press.

Baudrillard, Jean (1988) *Selected Writings*, ed. Mark Poster, Cambridge: Polity Press.

Bauman, Zigmunt (1990) *Thinking Sociologically*, Oxford: Blackwell.

—— (1992) *Intimations of Postmodernity*, London and New York: Routledge.

—— (1997) *Postmodernity and its Discontents*, Cambridge: Polity Press.

—— (1998) *Work, Consumerism and the New Poor*, Buckingham, Philadelphia: Open University Press.

—— (1999) *Culture as Praxis*, London: Sage.

Beck, Ulrich (1992) *Risk Society: Towards a new modernity*, trans. Mark Ritter, London: Sage.

Benjamin, Walter (1982) *Illuminations*, trans. Harry Zohn, London: Fontana/Collins.

Berlant, Lauren (1993) 'National brands/national body: *imitation of life*', in Bruce Robbins (ed.) *The Phantom Public Sphere*, Minneapolis: University of Minnesota Press.

Betterton, Rosemary (ed.) (1987) *Looking On: Images of femininity in the visual arts and media*, London and New York: Pandora.

—— (1996) *An Intimate Distance: Women, artists, and the body*, London and New York: Routledge.

Bhabha, Homi K. (1990) 'The third space: interview with Homi Bhabha', in J. Rutherford (ed.) *Identity: Community, culture, difference*, London: Lawrence & Wishart.

—— (1994) *The Location of Culture*, London and New York: Routledge.

Bowlby, Rachel (1985) *Just Looking: Consumer culture in Dreiser, Gissing and Zola*, London: Methuen.

—— (1993) *Shopping with Freud*, London: Routledge.

Brah, Avtar (1996) *Cartographies of Diaspora: Contesting identities*, London and New York: Routledge.

Bright, Deborah (1989) 'Of Mother Nature and Marlboro Men: an inquiry into the cultural meanings of landscape photography', in Richard Bolton (ed.) *The Contest of Meaning: Critical histories of photography*, London and Cambridge MA: MIT Press.

The British Codes of Advertising and Sales Promotion (1995–), London: Committee of Advertising Practice. Online. Available HTTP: <http://www.asa.org.uk/> (accessed 10 February 2000).

Brubaker, Rogers (1992) *Citizenship and Nationhood in France and Germany*, Cambridge MA and London: Harvard University Press.

Brunsdon, Charlotte (1991) 'Pedagogies of feminist teaching and women's genres', *Screen* 32, 4 (Winter): 364–81.

Bryson, Lois (1992) *Welfare and the State: Who benefits?*, Basingstoke and London: Macmillan Press.

Burnett, Ron (1995) *Cultures of Vision: Images, media and the imaginary*, Bloomington IN and Indianapolis IN: Indiana University Press.

Buscombe, Edward (1995) 'Inventing Monument Valley: nineteenth century landscape photography and the Western film', in P. Petro (ed.) *Fugitive Images: From photography to video*, Bloomington IN and Indianapolis IN: Indiana University Press.

Butler, Judith (1990) 'Contingent foundations: feminism and the question of postmodernism', in Judith Butler and Joan Scott (eds) *Feminists Theorize the Political*, London and New York: Routledge.

—— (1993) *Bodies That Matter: On the discursive limits of 'sex'*, London and New York: Routledge.

—— (1997) *Excitable Speech: A politics of the performative*, London and New York: Routledge.

Campbell, Colin (1987) *The Romantic Ethic and the Spirit of Modern Consumerism*, Oxford and New York: Blackwell.

—— (1997) 'When the meaning is not a message: a critique of the consumption as communication thesis', in M. Nava, A. Blake, I. MacRury, B. Richards (eds) *Buy This Book: Studies in advertising and consumption*, London: Routledge.

—— (1999) 'Action as will-power', *The Sociological Review* 47, 1: 48–61.

Clifford, James (1988) *The Predicament of Culture: Twentieth-Century ethnography, literature, and art*, Cambridge MA and London: Harvard University Press.

Cornell, Drucilla (1991) *Beyond Accommodation: Ethical feminism, deconstruction and the law*, New York and London: Routledge.

—— (1993) *Transformations: Recollective imagination and sexual difference*, New York and London: Routledge.

Crapanzano, Vincent (1991) 'The postmodern crisis: discourse, parody, memory', *Cultural Anthropology* 6, 4: 431–47.

Crary, Jonathan (1993) *Techniques of the Observer: On vision and modernity in the nineteenth century*, Cambridge MA and London: MIT Press.

Derrida, Jacques (1992) *The Other Heading: Reflections on today's Europe*, trans. Pascale-Anne Brault and Michael B. Naas, Bloomington IN and Indianapolis IN: Indiana University Press.

Diprose, Rosalyn (1994) *The Bodies of Women: Ethics, embodiment and sexual difference*, London and New York: Routledge.

Dummett, Ann and Andrew Nichol (1990) *Subjects, Citizens, Aliens and Others: Nationality and immigration law*, London: Weidenfeld & Nicholson.

Dyer, Gillian (1992) *Advertising as Communication*, London and New York: Routledge.

Evans, Caroline and Minna Thornton (1989) *Women and Fashion: A new look*, London and New York: Quartet Books.

Evans, David T. (1993) *Sexual Citizenship: The material construction of sexualities*, London and New York: Routledge.

Featherstone, Mike (1990) 'Global culture: an introduction', in Mike Featherstone (ed.) *Global Culture: Nationalism, globalization and modernity*, London: Sage.

—— (1991) *Consumer Culture and Postmodernism*, London, Newbury Park, New Delhi: Sage.

Felski, R. (1995) *The Gender of Modernity*, Cambridge MA: Harvard University Press.

Finzi, Silvia Vegetti (1992) 'Female identity between sexuality and maternity', in Gisela Bock and Susan James (eds) *Beyond Equality and Difference: Citizenship, feminist politics and female subjectivity*, London and New York: Routledge.

Fontaine, Pascale (1993) *A Citizen's Europe*, Luxembourg: Office for Official Publications of the European Communities.

Foucault, Michel (1988) 'Technologies of the self', in L. H. Martin, H. Gutman and P. H. Hutton (eds) *Technologies of the Self: A seminar with Michel Foucault*, London: Tavistock.

—— (1990) *The History of Sexuality: An introduction*, vol. 1, London, New York, Victoria, Toronto, Auckland: Penguin.

Fraser, Nancy (1989) *Unruly Practices: Power, discourse and gender in contemporary social theory*, Cambridge and Oxford: Polity Press in association with Blackwell.

—— (1997) *Justice Interruptus: Critical reflections on the 'postsocialist' condition*, London: Routledge.

Frith, Simon (1993) 'Youth/music/television', in Simon Frith, Andrew Goodwin and Lawrence Grossberg (eds) *Sound and Vision: The music video reader*, London and New York: Routledge.

Gabriel, Yiannis and Tim Lang (1995) *The Unmanageable Consumer: Contemporary consumption and its fragmentation*, London: Sage.

Giddens, A. (1998) *The Third Way: The renewal of social democracy*, Cambridge: Polity Press.

Goldman, Robert (1992) *Reading Ads Socially*, London and New York: Routledge.

Guild, Elspeth (1996) 'The legal framework of citizenship of the European Union', in David Cesarani and Mary Fulbrook (eds) *Citizenship, Nationality and Migration in Europe*, London and New York: Routledge.

H.M. Government (1991) *The Citizen's Charter: Raising the standard*, White Paper, July 1991, Cmnd 1599, London: HMSO.

Hall, Stuart (1992) 'What is this "black" in black popular culture?', in G. Dent (ed.) *Black Popular Culture*, Seattle: Bay Press.

Haraway, Donna (1991) *Simians, Cyborgs and Women: The reinvention of nature*, London: Free Association Books.

——(1997) *Modest_Witness@Second_Millennium.FemaleMan©_Meets_Onco-Mouse ™ Feminism and technoscience*, London and New York: Routledge.

Harvey, Penelope (1996) *Hybrids of Modernity: Anthropology, the nation state and the universal exhibition*, London and New York: Routledge.

Haug, W.F. (1986) *Critique of Commodity Aesthetics: Appearance, sexuality and advertising in capitalist society*, trans. Robert Bock, Cambridge: Polity Press.

Heelas, Paul and Paul Morris (1992) 'Enterprise culture: its values and value', in P. Heelas and P. Morris (eds) *The Values of Enterprise Culture: The moral debate*, London and New York: Routledge.

Henning, Michelle (1995) 'Digital encounters: mythical pasts and electronic presence', in Martin Lister (ed.) *The Photographic Image in Digital Culture*, London and New York: Routledge.

Hermes, Joke (1995) *Reading Women's Magazines: An analysis of everyday media use*, Cambridge and Oxford: Polity Press in association with Blackwell.

Hindess, Barry (1993) 'Citizenship in the modern West', in Bryan S. Turner (ed.) *Citizenship and Social Theory*, London: Sage.

Hutcheon, Linda (1994) *Irony's Edge: The theory and politics of irony*, London and New York: Routledge.

Huyssen, Andreas (1986) 'Mass culture as woman: modernism's other', in Tania Modleski (ed.) *Studies in Entertainment: Critical approaches to mass culture*, Bloomington IN and Indianapolis IN: Indiana University Press.

James, Susan (1992) 'The good-enough citizen: female citizenship and independence', in Gisela Bock and Susan James (eds) *Beyond Equality and Difference: Citizenship, feminist politics and female subjectivity*, London and New York: Routledge.

Jameson, Frederic (1990) 'Postmodernism and cnsumer society', in Hal Foster (ed.) *Postmodern Culture*, London and Concord MA: Pluto Press.

Jay, Martin (1993) *Downcast Eyes: The denigration of vision in twentieth-century French thought*, Berkeley, Los Angeles CA and London: University of California Press.

Kirby, Kathleen M. (1996) 'Re-mapping subjectivity: cartographies of vision and the limits of politics', in Nancy Duncan (ed.) *BodySpace: Destabilizing geographies of gender and sexuality*, London and New York: Routledge.

Kirby, Vicki (1997) *Telling Flesh: The substance of the corporeal*, London: Routledge.

Lash, Scott and John Urry (1994) *Economies of Signs and Space*, London: Sage.

De Lauretis, Teresa (1989) *Technologies of Gender*, Bloomington IN: Indiana University Press, Basingstoke: Macmillan.

—— (1990) 'Eccentric subjects: feminist theory and historical consciousness', *Feminist Studies* 16, 1 (Spring): 115–50.

Lee, Martyn (1993) *Consumer Culture Reborn: The cultural politics of consumption*, London and New York: Routledge.

Leiss, William, Stephen Kline, Sut Jhally (1990) *Social Communication in Advertising: Persons, products and images of well-being*, London and New York: Routledge.

Lewis, Reina (1997) 'Looking good: the lesbian gaze and fashion imagery', *Feminist Review* 55 (Spring): 92–109.

Lister, R. (1997) *Citizenship: Feminist perspectives*, Basingstoke: Macmillan.

Longhurst, B. and M. Savage (1996) 'Social class, consumption and the influence of Bourdieu: some critical issues', in S. Edgell, K. Hetherington and A. Warde (eds) *Consumption Matters: The production and experience of consumption*, Oxford: Blackwell.

Lury, Celia (1989) 'The advertising industry', unpublished paper presented at the Sociology Dept, Lancaster University.

—— (1996) *Consumer Culture*, Cambridge and Oxford: Polity Press in association with Blackwell.

—— (1997) *Prosthetic Culture: Photography, memory and identity*, London and New York: Routledge.

Lury, Celia and Alan Warde (1997) 'Investments in the imaginary consumer: conjectures regarding power, knowledge and advertising', in Mica Nava, Andrew Blake, Iain MacRury and Barry Richards (eds) *Buy This Book: Studies in advertising and consumption*, London and New York: Routledge.

McClintock, Anne (1995) *Imperial Leather: Race, gender and sexuality in the colonial conquest*, London and New York: Routledge.

McCracken, Ellen (1993) *Decoding Women's Magazines*, Basingstoke: Macmillan.

McNay, Lois (1999) 'Gender, habitus and the field: Pierre Bourdieu and the limits of reflexivity', *Theory, Culture and Society* 16, 1: 95–117.

Maffesoli, Michel (1997) 'The return of Dionysus', in P. Sulkunen, J. Holmwood, H. Radner, G. Schulze (eds) *Constructing the New Consumer Society*, New York: St Martin's Press.

Malik, Kenan (1998) 'Race, pluralism and the meaning of difference', *New Formations* 33: 125–35.

Marshall, T. H. (1992) 'Citizenship and social class', in T. H. Marshall and Tom Bottomore, *Citizenship and Social Class*, London and Concord MA: Pluto Press.

Martin, Emily (1994) *Flexible Bodies: The role of immunity in American culture from the days of polio to the age of AIDS*, Boston MA: Beacon Press.

Mattelart, Armand (1991) *Advertising International: The privatisation of public space*, trans. Michael Chanan, London and New York: Routledge.

Messaris, Paul (1997) *Visual Persuasion: The role of images in advertising*, London: Sage.

Miller, Toby (1993) *The Well-Tempered Self: Citizenship, culture and the postmodern subject*, Baltimore MA and London: Johns Hopkins University Press.

Minh-Ha, Trinh T. (1991) *When the Moon Waxes Red: Representation, gender and cultural politics*, London and New York: Routledge.

Morley, David and Kevin Robins (1995) *Spaces of Identity: Global media, electronic landscapes and cultural boundaries*, London and New York: Routledge.

Morley, David (1998) 'So-called Cultural Studies: dead ends and reinvented wheels', *Cultural Studies* 12, 4: 476–97.

Morse, Margaret (1990) 'An ontology of everyday distraction: the freeway, the mall, and television', in Patricia Mellencamp (ed.) *Logics of Television: Essays in cultural criticism*, Bloomington IN and London: Indiana University Press and the British Film Institute.

Mort, Frank (1996) *Cultures of Consumption: Masculinities and social spaces in late twentieth century Britain*, London and New York: Routledge.

Murdoch, Graham (1992) 'Citizens, consumers and public culture', in M. Skovmand and K. Schrøder (eds) *Reappraising Transnational Media*, London: Routledge.

Myers, Kathy (1986) *Understains: The sense and seduction of advertising*, London: Comedia.

Nava, Mica (1992) *Changing Cultures: Feminism, youth and consumerism*, London: Sage.

—— (1997) 'Framing advertising', in Mica Nava, Andrew Blake, Iain MacRury and Barry Richards (eds) *Buy This Book: Studies in advertising and consumption*, London and New York: Routledge.

Nead, Lynda (1992) *The Female Nude: Art, obscenity and sexuality*, London and New York: Routledge.

Nicholson, L. (1996) 'To be or not to be: Charles Taylor and the politics of recognition', *Constellations* 3, 1: 1–16.

Nixon, Sean (1996) *Hard Looks: Masculinities, spectatorship and contemporary consumption*, London: UCL Press.

Nowotny, Helga (1994) *Time: The modern and postmodern experience*, trans. Neville Plaice, Cambridge: Polity Press.

O'Neill, John (1997) 'What gives (with Derrida)?', unpublished paper presented at the Institute for Cultural Research, Lancaster University.

Packard, Vance (1981 [1956]) *The Hidden Persuaders*, (first published in Britain by Longman), London: Penguin.

Parekh, Bhikhu (1995) 'Liberalism and colonialism: a critique of Locke and Mill', in Jan Nederveen Pieterse and Bhikhu Parekh (eds) *The Decolonization of Imagination: Culture, knowledge and power*, London: Zed Books.

Parker, Andrew and Eve Kosofsky Sedgwick (1995) 'Introduction: performativity and performance', in Parker and Sedgwick (eds) *Performativity and Performance*, London and New York: Routledge.

Pateman, Carole (1988) *The Sexual Contract*, Oxford: Blackwell.

—— (1989) *The Disorder of Women: Democracy, feminism and political theory*, Cambridge and Oxford: Polity Press in association with Blackwell.

—— (1992) 'Equality, difference, subordination: the politics of motherhood and women's citizenship', in Gisela Bock and Susan James (eds) *Beyond Equality and Difference: Citizenship, feminist politics and female subjectivity*, London and New York: Routledge.

Pollock, Griselda (1988) *Vision and Difference: Femininity, feminism, and histories of art*, London and New York: Routledge.

—— (1992) 'Painting, feminism, history', in Michèle Barrett and Anne Phillips (eds) *Destabilizing Theory: Contemporary feminist debates*, Cambridge and Oxford: Polity Press in association with Blackwell.

Pratt, Mary Louise (1992) *Imperial Eyes: Travel writing and transculturation*, London and New York: Routledge.

Probyn, Elspeth (1993) *Sexing the Self: Gendered positions in cultural studies*, London and New York: Routledge.

Radner, Hilary (1995) *Shopping Around: Feminine culture and the pursuit of pleasure*, London and New York: Routledge.

Radway, Janice (1987) *Reading the Romance*, New York and London: Verso.

Ricoeur, Paul (1981) *Paul Ricoeur, Hermeneutics and the Human Sciences: Essays on language, action and interpretation*, ed., trans., and intro. by John B. Thompson, Cambridge: Cambridge University Press.

Riessman, Catherine Kohler (1993) *Narrative Analysis*, London: Sage.

Robins, Kevin (1991) 'Tradition and translation: national culture in its global culture', in J. Corner and S. Harvey (eds) *Enterprise and Heritage: Crosscurrents of national culture*, London and New York: Routledge.

—— (1994) 'Forces of consumption: from the symbolic to the psychotic', *Media, Culture and Society* 16, 3: 449–68.

Rose, Nikolas (1992) 'Governing the enterprising self', in Paul Heelas and Paul Morris (eds) *The Values of Enterprise Culture: The moral debate*, London and New York: Routledge.

Ross, Kristin (1995) *Fast Cars, Clean Bodies: Decolonization and the reordering of French culture*, Cambridge MA and London: MIT Press.

Santos, B. de Sousa (1999) 'Towards a multicultural conception of human rights', in M. Featherstone and S. Lash (eds) *Spaces of Culture: City–nation–world*, London: Sage.

Sassoon, Anne Showstack (1987) 'Women's new social role: contradictions of the welfare state', in Anne S. Sassoon (ed.) *Women and the State: The shifting boundaries of public and private*, London: Hutchinson Education.

Schlesinger, P. (1997) 'From cultural defence to political culture: media, politics and collective identity in the European Union', *Media, Culture and Society* 19: 369–91.

Schudson, Michael (1993) *Advertising, the Uneasy Persuasion: Its dubious impact on American society*, London: Routledge.

Sedgwick, Eve K. (1994) *Tendencies*, London: Routledge.

Shohat, Ella and Robert Stam (1994) *Unthinking Eurocentrism: Multiculturalism and the media*, London and New York: Routledge.

Sinclair, John (1987) *Images Incorporated: Advertising as industry and ideology*, London and New York: Croom Helm.

Skeggs, Beverley (ed.) (1995) *Feminist Cultural Theory: Process and production*, Manchester and New York: Manchester University Press.

—— (1997) *Formations of Class and Gender: Becoming respectable*, London: Sage.

Slater, D. (1997) *Consumer Culture and Modernity*, Cambridge: Polity Press.

Somers, Margaret. R. and Gloria D. Gibson (1994) 'Reclaiming the epistemological "other": narrative and the social construction of identity', in Craig Calhoun (ed.) *Social Theory and the Politics of Identity*, Cambridge MA and Oxford: Blackwell.

Soysal, Yasemin Nuhoglu (1994) *Limits of Citizenship: Migrants and postnational membership in Europe*, Chicago IL and London: University of Chicago Press.

—— (1996) 'Changing citizenship in Europe: remarks on postnational membership and the national state', in David Cesarani and Mary Fulbrook (eds) *Citizenship, Nationality and Migration in Europe*, London and New York: Routledge.

Spivak, Gayatri, C. (1995) 'Asked to talk about myself ... ', *Third Text* 19 (Summer): 9–18.

Stafford, Barbara Maria (1991) *Body Criticism: Imaging the unseen in enlightenment art and medicine*, Cambridge MA and London: MIT Press.

Stolcke, Verena (1995) 'Talking culture: new boundaries, new rhetorics of exclusion in Europe', *Current Anthropology* 36, 1, February: 1–24.

Strathern, Marilyn (1992) *After Nature: English kinship in the late twentieth century*, Cambridge: Cambridge University Press.

—— (1996) 'The nice thing about culture is that everyone has it', in M. Strathern (ed.) *Shifting Contexts: Transformations in anthropological knowledge*, London and New York: Routledge.

Taguieff, Pierre-André (1992) 'Les métamorphoses idéologiques du racisme et la crise de l'anti-racisme', in P.-A. Taguieff (ed.) *Face au racisme. tome 2: Analyses, hypothèses, perspectives*, Paris: Editions la Découverte.

Taussig, Michael (1992) *The Nervous System*, London and New York: Routledge.

—— (1993) *Mimesis and Alterity: A particular history of the senses*, London and New York: Routledge.

Taylor, Charles (1994) 'The politics of recognition', in D.T. Goldberg (ed.) *Multiculturalism: A reader*, Oxford: Blackwell.

Turner, Bryan S. (1993) 'Preface', in Bryan S. Turner (ed.) *Citizenship and Social Theory*, London: Sage.

Tyler, Carole-Anne (1991) 'Boys will be girls: the politics of gay drag', in Diana Fuss (ed.) *Inside/Out: Lesbian theories, gay theories*, London and New York: Routledge.

Van Zoonen, Liesbet (1994) *Feminist Media Studies*, London: Sage.

Virilio, Paul (1994) *The Vision Machine*, London and Bloomington IN: British Film Institute and Indiana University Press.

Walsh, Kieron (1994) 'Citizens, charters and contracts', in R. Keat, N. Whiteley and N. Abercrombie (eds) *The Authority of the Consumer*, London and New York: Routledge.

Warner, Michael (1993) 'The mass public and the mass subject', in Bruce Robbins (ed.) *The Phantom Public Sphere*, Minneapolis MN and London: University of Minnesota Press.

Wernick, Andrew (1991) *Promotional Culture: Advertising, ideology and symbolic expression*, London: Sage.

Williamson, Judith (1978) *Decoding Advertisements: Ideology and meaning in advertising*, London: Marion Boyars.

Winship, Janice (1987) *Inside Women's Magazines*, New York and London: Pandora Press in association with Methuen and Routledge & Kegan Paul.

Yeatman, Anna (1994) *Postmodern Revisionings of the Political*, London and New York: Routledge.

Yuval-Davis, N. and F. Anthias (eds) (1989) *Woman–nation–state*, Basingstoke: Macmillan.

Index

Frith, S. 51

Gabriel, Y. and Lang, T. 4, 5, 148
Giddens, A. 4, 12, 158–9
Goldman, R. 37–8, 54–5, 77, 156
GQ 52
Guerlain advertisement 78, *79*, 80–2, 115
Guild, E. 158, 165

Hall, S. 146
Haraway, D. 66, 88–9, 94, 114, 133, 137
Harvey, P. 146
Haug, W.F. 54
Heelas, P. and Morris, P. 4, 148
Hegel, G.W.F. 18
Henley Centre for Forecasting 47–8
Henning, M. 97, 100
Hermes, J. 109, 110, 165
'Hidden secrets of the insecure client'
  (*Campaign*) 44–6
historical narratives 10, 23–6, 97–104,
  136, 139, 152, 156
Howell Henry Chaldecott Lury agency
  43
Hutcheon, L. 67–8
Huyssen, A. 129

identity 9, 16–20, 139; European 143;
  mapping of 23–4, 25; temporality of
  34–6, 125; through choice 31
image 3, 92–3, 100, 103–4, 106; phatic
  103, 119; repetitive 115, 117–19
imagination 40–1; expanded role of 5–6;
  recollective 112, 115, 119, 122
the individual 58, 91, 100, 105; and
  capacity to act 32; and citizenship 4,
  26–9; construction of 6–7, 36; and
  consumerist choice 30–4; exclusion of
  women from 8–9; feminist critiques
  10, 11–16; historical discourse 10,
  23–6; and honour/dignity 20–1; and
  identity 7; as performative 7, 16–23,
  89; as political category 22;
  political/conjectural nature of 16;
  potential of 20, 21–2; and self-
  presence/identity 16–20, 22; shift
  from status to contract 11–16, 35;
  socio–political aspects 10; status of
  17; and temporality of identity 34–6
intent 9, 138–9, 151
ironic/literal advertising 57, 58, 84–5, 88,
  97, 107, 109, 118, 119, 147; and
  boundaries of the feminine 129–32;

described 66–7; and distraction 71–2;
  dual character of 67–8; and the
  elsewhere(s) 70–1; features of 68; and
  levels of meaning 98, 102–3; locus of
  68–9; shelf–life of 117; and
  simultaneity 73–4, 76–8; textual
  production of 78, 80–2

James, S. 140
Jameson, F. 129–30
Jay, M. 85, 87

Kant, I. 140
Kirby, K.M. 23–4, 34, 70, 163, 165
knowledge 85–9

Lancôme advertisement (Trésor
  perfume) 122, *123*, 126–7
Lauretis, T. de 8, 14–15, 16, 19, 22, 33,
  35, 64, 65–6, 70–2, 78, 84, 87, 92, 108,
  113, 118, 122, 128, 157
Lee, M. 4, 38
Leiss, W. *et al.* 5, 55, 57–8
Lewis, R. 130
L'Expansion 56, 60, 61, 62
Lister, R. 28
the literal *see* ironic/literal advertising
Locke, J. 16–17, 99
Longhurst, B. and Savage, M. 49
Lury, C. 43, 46, 146, 160; and Warde, A.
  43, 163

Maastricht Treaty (1993) 5, 158
McClintock, A. 13, 23, 34, 70, 127, 142
McCracken, E. 110, 114
McNay, L. 3
Maffesoli, M. 3
magazine advertising: elsewhere(s),
  irony, distraction 70–3; findings of
  analysis 60–1; images/social
  difference 61–3; irony/simultaneity
  73–4, 76–8; literal/ironic 66–9;
  methods of analysis 55–60; non-
  space of images 69–70;
  reflexivity/difference 63–6; textual
  production of 'the literal' 78, 80–2;
  see also advertising
Malik, K. 145
mapping 23–4, 25, 42, 144
market research 45
Marlboro advertisement 94, *95*, 96–104,
  117, 128, 137, 147
Marshall, T.H. 27

natality of 104, 153; origins of 134–9;
temporalities of 106–7, 110
self-actualisation 20–2, 91
self-consciousness 114–15
self-expression 11, 140, 149
self/other: ambiguous/contradictory
status 14–15, 16, 19, 33–4; and
citizenship 28–30; construction of 13,
20; and culture 31–2; distance
between 65; exchange relationship
18–19; and gender 13–16, 89;
mobility of 104; origins of 113–14;
reflexivity of 65–6; temporal
concerns 34–6, 65; transparency of
86
self-presence 22, 119, 138, 154; Hegelian
18–19, 89; Lockean 16–18;
spatial/temporal concerns 19–20,
34–6
Shohat, E. and Stam, R. 102
Sinclair, J. 42
Skeggs, B. 126
Slater, D. 1, 2, 3, 12
social status, access to 11–12
Somers, M. and Gibson, G. 111, 139
Soysal, Y.N. 4, 29, 140, 158, 160
speech acts 135–6
Spivak, G.C. 136–7, 139
Stafford, B.M. 85, 87
Stolcke, V. 7, 24–5, 26, 28–9, 31–2, 35,
128, 129, 145, 146, 155, 158
Strathern, M. 141, 142, 148, 149, 150
subjectivity 30, 160

tactility 121–2, 125
Taguieff, P.-A. 28, 29, 146, 154
targeting 41, 48, 53; female 65–6, 105,
109; gendered 57, 60–1; male 94, 109,
131
Taussig, M. 71, 109, 121
Taylor, C. 20–2, 30, 31, 147, 148, 149,
151, 155, 159
The Third Way 33, 158–9
transparency 85–9, 100, 101, 102, 151
Turner, B.S. 26–7
Tyler, C.-A. 125–6

UNESCO 158
United Nations (UN) 158
universalism 22, 98, 159

value 141–2
Van Zoonen, L. 54
Virilio, P. 92–3, 103, 105, 106, 119, 165
vision 8, 9, 57, 83–5, 133, 138, 156;
future 159–60; and imagination 88;
knowledge/transparency 85–9;
materiality of 120–2, 125–6; as
performative 89–91; as tactile 121;
temporal/textual meanings 94,
96–104, 157; time/advertising image
91–4
visual performativity 8, 89–91, 103, 105,
156–7
voluntarism, spaces of 150–1

Walsh, K. 148
J. Walter Thompson 44, 47
Wernick, A. 4
Williamson, J. 37–8, 54, 55
Winship, J. 109
women: in advertising industry 46;
ambiguity/contradiction of 14–15,
17, 33–4, 78, 81, 92, 125;
artificial/authentic paradox 107,
125–6; and contract theory 12–15;
discursive position of 14–16, 86–7;
exclusion of 13–14, 106; paradoxical
positioning of 107–8, 126;
positioning of 12–16, 70; and reading
109–10, 114; and selfhood 104, 134;
stereotype images of 54–5
women's magazines: and branding the
elsewhere(s)/elsewhen(s) 126–9;
female time/space 108–10; lesbian
readings against the grain 130; and
materiality of vision 120–2, 125–6;
metaphor/image in 115, 117–20;
narrative structuring of 110–15

Yeatman, A. 4, 20, 27, 28, 32, 140
youth market 50, 51–3, 61
Yuval-Davis, N. and Anthias, F. 127–8